D1156556

Looking at Modern Painting

GIBSON A. DANES
YALE UNIVERSITY

THERESA ZEZZOS FULTON
POMONA COLLEGE, CLAREMONT, CALIFORNIA

CARL D. SHEPPARD, Jr.
UNIVERSITY OF CALIFORNIA AT LOS ANGELES

FREDERICK S. WIGHT
UNIVERSITY OF CALIFORNIA AT LOS ANGELES

Looking at Modern Painting

LEONARD FREEDMAN, *Editor*
UNIVERSITY EXTENSION
UNIVERSITY OF CALIFORNIA, LOS ANGELES

NEW YORK · W · W · NORTON & COMPANY · INC ·

Library of Congress Catalog Card No. 61-9154

PRINTED IN THE UNITED STATES OF AMERICA
56789

Contents

Illustrations

Preface

THE FIRST edition of *Looking At Modern Painting* was published in 1957. Initiated by the Fund for Adult Education, it was prepared at the University of California at Los Angeles with the financial assistance of the Fund. It was designed for the use of adult study-discussion groups, and it quickly became the basis of one of the largest and most successful discussion programs yet produced in this country. Its use has not been limited to adult education, however, for many colleges have adopted it as a modern art text.

This new and substantially revised edition has been designed for three kinds of audiences: (1) college classes; (2) adult study-discussion groups; (3) the general reader.

Looking At Modern Painting is not intended to be a definitive historical and analytical treatment of the art of our century. Its purpose is to introduce the reader to the main schools of modern painting and to enable him to approach current controversies with increased discernment and sensitivity.

Thus, Chapter One suggests there are different types of judgment appropriate to different kinds of twentieth-century painting. Chapters Two through Seven take up several schools of modern painting in turn: Cubism, Abstract Art, Expressionism, Symbolism, Surrealism, and Abstract Expressionism. The last three chapters deal with problems pertaining to all of these schools: Chapter Eight with the question of whether, in all this diversity, there are common standards of craftsmanship; Chapter Nine with the relationship between the artist and his time; and Chapter Ten with the eternal problems of the freedom and responsibility of the artist.

A good deal of biographical, historical, and technical material is to be found in sections at the back of the book. It was placed there so that the flow of ideas in the text itself would not be interrupted. It is nonetheless an integral part of the book, and should be referred to in connection with each chapter.

The division of responsibility for the writing of the book was as follows: Theresa Zessos Fulton: Chapters One and Two; Carl D. Sheppard, Jr.: Chapters Three, Four, and Seven; Frederick S. Wight: Chapters Five, Six, and Eight; Gibson A. Danes: Chapters Nine and Ten.

The Introduction was written by Leonard Freedman and Carl D. Sheppard, Jr. Many others helped in the preparation of the revised edition. Several people who had used the first edition in discussion programs sent invaluable suggestions to the editor, and many of their ideas have been incorporated in the revision. The diagrammatic analyses and some of the technical definitions at the back of the books are the work of Mrs. Frances Field, assisted by Jo-Anne Schneider. Mr. Henry Hopkins revised biographical and other material. Mrs. Gloria James undertook the skilled secretarial functions so necessary in a major revision of a text.

For class and discussion group purposes a set of forty-five slides, selected by the authors, is available from the Audio-Visual Center, Indiana University. A guide for instructors and discussion leaders, prepared by Mrs. Frances Field, accompanies the slides and is available from the same source. General advice on the formation of adult discussion groups may be obtained from the American Foundation for Continuing Education, 19 South La Salle Street, Chicago 3, Illinois. The Foundation may also be able to direct the reader to a university or college in his vicinity which is sponsoring discussion groups in Modern Painting, using this book as text.

For the second edition, as for the first, the Fund for Adult Education has been the initiating agency; and it is their encouragement and advice on a personal basis, as well as their financial assistance, which has made this book possible.

Introduction

THIS IS A book about the painting of the twentieth century. It is a controversial subject, and this book—designed for individual study or for group discussion—reflects the existence of controversy. On the whole the authors are sympathetic to the general trends in modern art. But they suggest the various areas of disagreement, and pro and con statements on the issues are quoted.

Certain things ought to be said before we can approach the great issues of modern painting:

1. We are dealing not with one controversy, but with many, for there are many different kinds of twentieth-century painting. A glance at some of the paintings in this book will make this abundantly clear. Look at Mondrian's *Composition* (Plate 6); Braque's *Man with a Guitar* (Plate 5); Beckmann's *The Departure* (Plate 9); Ernst's *Woman, Old Man and Flower* (Plate 12); Pollock's *Painting* (Plate 17); Picasso's *Guernica* (Page 113). The diversity of purpose, of mood, of method is tremendous. The authors discuss these differences at length. You may find it interesting at this point to ask yourself what these differences are.

At the same time you might want to consider what they have in common. At this stage we shall suggest only two of these similarities. First, the rapid succession of styles suggests that the twentieth century has been one of innovation and experiment, of the restless search for new ways of looking at the world. Second, faithful duplication of visual "reality" is never the aim. References from our everyday world are either distorted, as in Cubism and Expressionism; or eliminated entirely, as in Abstract painting; or placed in strange and sometimes terrifying juxtapositions to each other, as in Surrealism.

2. The twentieth century is not the first period in which there has been controversy over painting. The struggle between new and old forms has occurred many times in Western civilization. The Greco-Roman devotion to three-dimensional form and specific subject matter began competing with another attitude toward the qualities of art during the third century. A striving for transcendental values had developed during the first centuries of our era, parallel to the growth of the pagan mystery cults and the rise of Christianity. For over two centuries the conflict continued until the ultimate triumph of a relatively abstract style by about the sixth century. The eleventh century also saw a profound shift in the development of art. Again in the fifteenth and sixteenth centuries Europe saw a battle between two styles —the dying Gothic and the Renaissance.

So there has been conflict and change before. Nor are the other characteristics of modern art entirely without precedent. For example, we noted that in recent years the image in painting has been eliminated or distorted almost beyond recognition. But it is also true that artists have never been concerned with photographic representation. There has always been distortion. The mere fact that painting is two-dimensional has always obliged an artist to create an equivalent for visual and tactile reality. Even the ideally beautiful Madonnas of Raphael do not correspond to what we see; nor do the prismatically-colored landscapes of Claude Monet. Even the tendency to abstraction has happened before—as in European art from the sixth to the eleventh century, when man sought eternal values and translated them into highly simplified graphic devices. And long before Surrealism, fantasy and horror were to be found in such works as the *Temptations* of Hieronymus Bosch and Grünewald's *Crucifixions.*

All this serves to remind us that, even though this book arbitrarily dates modern painting from Picasso's *Les Demoiselles d'Avignon,** the art of painting did not begin in 1907. The way had to be prepared by the Fauves, Cézanne, and by the Impressionists; and before the Impressionists there was the entire tradition of painting, which has influenced even those contemporary artists who have rejected the past most vigorously.

Having said this, we should be careful not to draw all the teeth of the contemporary debate. Twentieth-century painting does differ in many important respects from everything that came before. A glance at the reproductions in this book of works of Rembrandt, Rubens, Goya, Grünewald and Ingres should immediately suggest some of the contrasts between past and present. We shall not say more on this here, for the special characteristics of twentieth-century art are precisely the subject of this manual.

3. While there is much controversy in this book, we must emphasize that understanding and appreciation of art cannot come solely by debating ideas. When all is said and done, the important thing is the painting itself. Learning about painting is primarily a matter of looking at painting.

This manual includes a number of reproductions of modern paintings. This is not enough. Small reproductions cannot give you the full impact of originals.

And even to look at modern paintings in galleries and museums and studios is only a fragmentary kind of experience. For an education in art cannot come without exposure to the products of all of the many rich eras of the past. Without prolonged experience ranging over the entire history of painting it is not possible to achieve the end to which we hope to contribute. That end is to enable you to develop your own judgments, your own informed standards of taste.

* Plate 4.

ONE

Types of Judgment

SOME TIME ago a cartoon appeared in the *New Yorker* magazine showing an art critic standing on a chair, anxiously scrutinizing a painting in an art gallery. The caption read: "He knows all about art, but he doesn't know what he likes." If the art critic knew a little less, he might presumably like a little more and partake of the bliss of the Philistine who knows nothing about art, but *does* know what he likes. Alas for this bliss! It is not necessarily true that what one likes is art or that art is what one likes. At most we can say that we are free to like what we like and that the artist shares this freedom. In a sense, when we study art we enjoy the rewards of this artistic freedom. We seek to understand the artist's taste. The difficulty is that paintings, especially of our own time, exhibit a bewildering variety of tastes. There is not one "Style" with a capital "S" that allows for a neat and secure definition of "Art" with a capital "A." As you consider the varieties of modern painting in this book, it is quite likely that the art critic of the cartoon will engage your sympathy. He must scrutinize the painting, and he needs intellectual and emotional perspicacity to see the artist in his own light. Indeed it is not easy to know what one "likes" in the expert's sense.

It is expected that the art expert or critic will not merely "like" a work of art in the sense of finding it enjoyable or pleasurable, but that he will recognize in specific works something of aesthetic value or significance. Furthermore he is expected to "justify" or "explain" this recognition. The explanation is very important to the layman, who can rightly point out that the "likes" of the expert mean no more to him than the "likes" of the Philistine unless he can enter into the expert's experience. So he will ask the inevitable questions: What is good about the painting? What should we see?

We might reflect at this point on how our expert or critic became one: not primarily by *reading*, but by *looking* at paintings. In this field there is no "chicken or egg" problem. Clearly the paintings come first. Without the paintings, the reading and the "liking" come to nothing. This statement may seem all too obvious, but it is nevertheless important. It is not rare to find a person who seeks vainly for a verbal formula, a set of criteria, a yardstick which will conveniently determine whether a work is, or is not, art. Words do help, but it is important not to expect too much from words. It *is* too much to expect that a painting can be exhaustively explained, for language does not afford the same direct sensuous contact with reality. The expert can "name," "indicate," "suggest," but the specific sensuous contact remains elusive. Consider color, for example. Color terminology is deceptively general. We do not have names for all the colors we find in paintings. Think of reds: how many there are! In comparison how few adjectives we possess! But then it may be argued that the red can be defined by a chemical analysis of the pigment and by determining the character of the light waves which the pigment reflects. This would be a laborious process, but it would yield symbols for specific reds. Yet, it would give us very little information about the optical effect of the specific red which is determined not by its character in isolation but by its relationship to adjacent colors. Much less would scientific analysis indicate the emotional impact which this optical effect creates. In fact, when we describe the gamut of feelings which the red in its pictorial context evokes, it seems that our words are even less adequate than they are in the pinning down of the visible red itself. Although the feelings experienced by the critic may be suggested, they cannot be explicitly demonstrated or explained.

On the other hand, this language barrier is not something special that applies only to art and to painting. Difficulties are encountered in the explanation of a pain in the stomach or the description of a ball game as well as in the discussion of a picture. This does not mean, however, that "anything goes." The discussion may be more or less rewarding. It is important, however, to realize that there is an irreducible core of experience around which language, so to speak, vibrates. The art expert may suggest the nature of the experience, and his discussion often leads to the seeing of images where they were not seen before. By breaking down prejudices in the spectator about what the picture *should* present, it is often possible to see what actually *is* there. By associating a painting with concepts or events, or with other works of art which are already familiar, it may be rendered more accessible. Yet even if these associations are pinned down with precision—let us imagine that a painter has stated that when he uses yellow he means happiness; that where he paints a heart shape, he means love—we still do not have the final meaning of the total visual experience. It is the spectator alone who can supply this experience.

Presumably the art critic "likes" a picture on the basis of his "experience" of the picture; and his capacity for experience is related to his conception of art. The Philistine presumably may "like" a picture for any reason. Incidentally, there is nothing "wrong" with this. It is difficult to imagine a *wrong* reason for liking a picture. A person may like a painting because it was left to him by a cherished great-aunt, or because he likes dogs and the painting depicts dogs. A person may like a work of art simply because it was created by a famous artist. This may satisfy a need to admire the "proper" things or it may reflect a tendency toward hero-worship. There is nothing "wrong" with liking pictures for such reasons. Trouble arises only when the reasons are forgotten and when predilections which have nothing to do with artistic merit are made the basis for *judging* works of art.

Let us go back to the art expert and his conception of art. As we have already pointed out, he became an expert by *looking* at paintings. Further, he probably investigated the conditions under which the paintings were produced and learned what he could of the artists who made them; but *looking* at paintings was the indispensable element. It was in this way that he formed his taste, discovered what he "liked," arrived at a working conception of art. To some degree, although not so intensively, the interested layman must follow this procedure. The notion of a "working conception of art" is especially important, and the reason seems very clear in the case of modern painting. Take a look at the pictures which illustrate this book. They present a cross section of the widely different paths which modern artists have chosen. Even a superficial glance reveals extreme contrasts. Observe the difference in technique between a work by Dali or van Gogh. Consider the different taste for "form" in the emphasis on shapes, lines, and colors as exemplified in the Mondrian and the Pollock. Consider the relative importance attached to the representation of objects by Sheeler in his *Classic Landscape* (Page 100) and Miró in his *Catalan Landscape* (Plate 13). We could go on and on with this type of juxtaposition. The point is not simply that artists have varying personalities and that they are individualists, although this is certainly true. The point is that apart from these differences, the artists *set out to do different things and to explore different realities.* This means that the critic must consider three factors in the process of making his judgment: (1) the kind of approach or avenue of statement which the artist has chosen to use; (2) the specific nature of his statement—what the artist has said and how effectively he has said it in terms of his chosen approach; (3) whether the artist's venture is or is not of consequence and why this is so. You will notice that, at least theoretically, real issues or questions of value come up only with the final step.

Let us consider Edward Hopper's *House by the Railroad* * and Piet Mondrian's *Broadway Boogie Woogie.*† It will be useful for our discussion to distinguish the concepts of *form, content,* and *subject matter.* Form has to do with the organization of, or the relationships among, lines, colors (and light and shade), volumes, and spaces, as found in the paintings. Content has to do with the expressive meaning of the form, with the emotional and ideational connotations of the visual image. It is difficult to talk about content without suggesting that emotion and idea can be

* Plate 1. † Plate 2.

abstracted from form. Actually the dividing or abstracting of emotion and intellect or of form and content does not seem to jibe with our experience of works of art. The image has its own concrete urgency, emotional *and* intellectual *and* formal all at once. Nevertheless "form" and "content" are useful to us as *concepts*. As concepts they function in the discussion or analysis of the paintings. But we must remember that discussion and analysis are not identical with aesthetic experience. Rather, they may be considered as intellectual devices which serve, as it were, to bring the paintings into focus, to encourage aesthetic experience. But the experience itself is not a divisible thing. What is involved is an identity of form and content both from the point of view of the artist who creates the synthesis and from the point of view of the spectator who must experience the synthesis. There is, as the philosopher Croce neatly put it, "*no double bottom to art*."

Form and content do not necessarily imply subject matter. Subject matter has to do simply with the topic of representation. To elucidate, the subject matter in the Hopper is a house by a railroad track. Imagine that a photographer takes a snapshot of the house or that another painter paints it. The subject matter would be the same. The form and content would be different. Again it is important to recognize that "subject matter" is a convenient *concept* but that the image is concrete and "inseparable." In experiencing a picture we do not divide or abstract subject matter from content and form.

To go back to the paintings, it is useful to jot down a list of what each presents at first glance. The list might run as follows:

HOPPER	MONDRIAN
blue house	squares
railroad track	rectangles
sky	blue, red, yellow
spaciousness	blinking effect
bright light	staccato rhythm
shadow	brightness
chimney	

It is easier to talk about the Hopper because it has a recognizable subject and we have words to name what is described. To indicate that the red chimney, for example, is a nice accent, which enhances the contrast of the house against the sky and which establishes a connection with the red color of the railroad track, is fairly simple because there are words which clearly indicate the parts of the painting to which we refer. It is not easy to describe what happens in any one of the constellations of rectangles in the Mondrian or even to identify them. Yet you will certainly *feel* that the large red rectangle at the bottom of *Broadway Boogie Woogie* relates to the other rectangles spread along the yellow band, and that it has a relationship to red rectangles of similar size throughout the canvas. (See pp. 134–135.)

Certainly these artists have followed widely, if not wildly, different paths. On an elementary level we may easily classify the Hopper as a "representational" painting and the Mondrian as a "non-representational" or "non-objective" painting. It should be noted that they both have "form" and "content." To see what is involved in the "form" of the Hopper, imagine that you have never seen a house, much less a picture of a house. The Hopper, as far as you are now concerned, is just as "non-representational" as the Mondrian. If you jot down another list it might read somewhat as follows:

HOPPER

large cubic mass
cubic mass broken with rectangles
strong red and brownish red band
strong contrasts of light and dark
grayed blue
intense red-orange

These formal elements carry the burden of expression. For example, the sharp contrast between the horizontal band of the track and the looming verticals of the house or cubic mass makes for a feeling of dramatic isolation. The windows or "rectangles" that break the mass enliven the surface and provide a certain quality of animation and tension. Similarly, the dark cornices silhouetted against the sky make dark triangular accents which feel sharp by virtue of their very distinctness and their marked contrast with the verticals of the house. Actually, apart from the recognition of a house, the formal qualities alone convey feelings of isolation, monumentality, and dignity. Remember for a moment our discussion of the language problem. The words "isolation," "monumentality," and "dignity" in themselves only suggest what is found in the painting. To each individual they have different connotations. The point here is to experience the isolation, monumentality, and dignity which the form of this specific painting embodies.

In Hopper's painting it is possible to recognize the subject matter and to enjoy the subject matter for its own sake. A picturesque old Victorian house is represented. In this case the value is actually attached to the thing portrayed. No art expert denies that this does happen. Some, however, maintain that what happens is aesthetically relevant and some do not. For instance, Clive Bell, an English critic, has written:

"*The representative* [*subject matter*] *element in a work of art may or may not be harmful; always it is irrelevant. For to appreciate a work of art we need to bring with us nothing from life, no knowledge of its ideas or affairs, no familiarity with its emotions.*" [1]

At another point Bell says: "*That there is an irrelevant representative or descriptive element in many great works of art is not in the least surprising . . . Representation is not of necessity baneful, and highly realistic forms may be extremely significant. Very often, however, representation is a sign of weakness in an artist. A painter too feeble to create forms that provoke more than a little emotion will try to eke that out by suggesting the emotions of life. To evoke the emotions of life he must use representation.*" [2] Clive Bell takes the stand that *only* form in the sense of colors, lines, shapes, and their relationships, and what this form expresses *directly*, really matter. Even ideas or feelings that are associated with the form are not relevant. To take an example, the spectator might feel nostalgia on looking at Hopper's painting. But "nostalgia" really cannot be related to the form in the way that "isolation" can be. The nostalgic element would not, therefore, be of interest to this critic.

Another writer, Walter Abell, has written a book which expounds a radically different point of view. For him subject matter is important, and feelings "associated" with form have supreme aesthetic relevance. Here is one of Abell's statements:

"*Were we to limit painting and sculpture to elements provided in complete form by vision, then color, line, shape, and size would be the only elements available to them . . .* [*Subject matter*] *cannot be legitimately excluded unless we wish to limit ourselves to visual stimuli uninterrupted by any of their meanings, in which case we should have to restrict art to the sphere of geometrical patterns.*" [3]

It would be possible to cite a host of other writers whose ideas exemplify a gamut of the permutations possible between these extremes. For our purposes, suffice it to note that the Clive Bell extreme allows a more sympathetic approach to Mondrian's painting and that the Walter Abell extreme sees a wider range of aesthetic values in the painting by Hopper.

Hopper has stated, "*My aim in painting has always been the most exact transcription possible of my most intimate impression of nature.*" [4] To judge from his work, of which *House by the Railroad* is typical, he has delighted in *visual* impressions of nature. His point of departure is the world as it presents itself to the eye. Mondrian spent a lifetime constructing paintings based on relationships among straight lines, rectangles, the primary colors (red, yellow, and blue), and black and gray. His was a truly heroic dedication to a very special search. He too may be said to have painted his "most intimate impression of nature," but this impression was an intuition of the reality of the ideal, the unchanging, the universal. In a sense he dedicated himself to the feeling that "a thing of beauty is a joy forever." The "foreverness" to him precluded all suggestions of transitory things, including not merely representation, but also any factors, whether stylistic or technical, that would stamp his personality on the work. Thus the perfectly straight lines, the perfectly pure colors, became inevitably linked with his search for an objective *ideal*. (See also Plate 6.)

Actually, in our selection of Mondrian's *Broadway Boogie Woogie* we have already revealed the complexities beneath our form-content-subject matter analysis. For it may be argued that *Broadway Boogie Woogie* has subject matter. Its topic of representation is a jazz rhythm, boogie woogie. In fact Mondrian was criticized by admirers of his earlier work when he painted *Boogie Woogie* precisely because they felt he was returning to subject matter and its limitations. The issue is perhaps less one of semantics than one of degree of specificity of representation. How specific is Mondrian's reference to boogie woogie jazz? Is it as specific as Hopper's reference to a house? It is certainly possible to interpret the concept of subject matter in a sense so broad that any expression of experience becomes a "topic" of representation. But in most discussion this broad notion may be subsumed by the concepts of form and content.

Nothing could be further from Mondrian's ideal of art than the painting of Vincent van Gogh. Where Mondrian sought forms that would be perfectly impersonal and free of all imitative suggestion, van Gogh created an intensely personal style and always found inspiration in nature. Where Mondrian searched for the calm of disinvolvement, van Gogh was passionately involved not only with the realities of nature but with his emotions about these realities. In a letter to another painter he wrote:

"I can't work without a model. I am not saying I don't disregard nature completely when I am working up a sketch into a picture, arranging the colors, enlarging, or simplifying, but as far as the forms are concerned I am terrified of getting away from the possible, of not being accurate. . . . I devour nature ceaselessly. I exaggerate, sometimes I make changes in the subject, but still I don't invent the whole picture, on the contrary I find it already there; it's a question of picking out what one wants from nature." [5]

It is hard to imagine Hopper "devouring nature." The idea simply does not fit his art. It *does* express admirably the quality of van Gogh's art. He has "devoured" nature and stamped it with emotions so powerful that the *emotions themselves*, rather than the natural forms, are the stuff of which the paintings are made.

Look at van Gogh's painting, *The Starry Night.** You can easily recognize village, trees, moon, stars; but clearly this is not the point. Rather you are at once impressed by a grand, almost hypnotic rhythm which binds all the representational elements together into a kind of cosmic unity. Notice that the brush stroke itself functions as an element of the design and thus the brushwork enters the field of form. It dominates the representational elements in the painting. It "devours" them.

We can point to certain qualities of the brushwork and relate them to the impact of the total work. The individual strokes are "rough," they vary, although they hold to a definite scale or size. These individual elements have a nervous energy, and the energy builds up in broader patterns of convolutions and swirls. These patterns are in themselves dynamic and they are insistently repeated. Consider for example how the tree is composed of flame-like brush strokes. The very nakedness of the brush stroke gives an effect of directness and immediacy, a directness analogous to that of a sketch. Seemingly no technical complication has come between the artist and his painting. Van Gogh lays bare his very act of painting and it is partly through the suggestion of his physical activity that we share his emotion. Thus the painting seems to "happen," to say what it has to say with powerful spontaneous impulse.

* Plate 3.

Let us go back to the art expert in the *New Yorker* cartoon and imagine that in his art gallery he is faced with the three paintings by Hopper, Mondrian, and van Gogh which we have discussed. Obviously if he establishes criteria for "liking" or "disliking" on the basis of any one of these three works, he is likely to find the other two sadly deficient. But, Hopper has been concerned *primarily* to express a visual reality, Mondrian, an "absolute" or "ideal" reality, and van Gogh, an emotional reality. Given these essentially different aims, differences in "style," in the sense of "feeling for form," and differences in "technique," in the sense of manner of applying the paint to canvas, inevitably follow. In other words, the paintings are successful in three different ways. In each the painter has realized a specific effect in a specific way. If we ask, *"How do we or the critic know that the paintings are successful?"* we are, in a sense, forced back to the indivisible nature of aesthetic experience and to the notion that description and discussion may encourage this experience, but not supply it. The painting alone defines its success. Since we have not found inconsistencies in these three works we may grant that the paintings satisfy a kind of artistic law of parsimony—the painters have achieved their effects with a minimum of means. However, it is only in terms of each specific painting that we can come to this conclusion. What constitutes effective or economic brushwork for van Gogh in *The Starry Night* might constitute empty rhetoric for another painter. It is the painter himself who must in each creation define the optimum state of tension between his means and his ends.

We have made the point that the critic was faced with three artists pursuing extremely divergent paths. In the following chapters we will consider many other artists pursuing the different ends which their temperaments and inclinations define. It will be useful to remember the categories of a "visual," "ideal," and "emotional" reality, and to ask to what extent each of the paintings you will be studying falls into one or another of these categories.

1. Clive Bell, *Art*, New York, Frederick A. Stokes Company, 1913, p. 25.
2. *Ibid.*, p. 28.
3. Walter Abell, *Representation and Form*, New York, Charles Scribner's Sons, 1936, p. 111.
4. Alfred H. Barr, Jr., Ed., *Masters of Modern Art*, New York, The Museum of Modern Art, 1954, p. 111.
5. John Rewald, *Post-Impressionism from Van Gogh to Gauguin*, New York, The Museum of Modern Art, 1956, p. 218.

TWO

The Independence of Form

TOWARD THE end of the nineteenth and the beginning of the twentieth century there was, at least in intellectual and avant-garde circles, a keen awareness that the work of art, whether in painting, or literature, or music, was an independent and concrete entity. Somehow the work of art was a *thing*, an essential factor in existence, with its own reality. All of this sounds vague and theoretical, yet the concept expressed was of great significance. It underlies all the abstract movements that have developed in this century. The French symbolist poet, Mallarmé (1842–1898), was one of the most important exponents of this point of view. Daniel-Henry Kahnweiler, a famous dealer, collector, and early spokesman for the Cubist painters, reports the following anecdote about Mallarmé and Degas:

"Degas tried to write sonnets and complained to Mallarmé that he was unsuccessful, despite all the ideas he had. 'You don't write sonnets with ideas, Degas,' said Mallarmé, 'but with words.'" [1]

If we understand from this anecdote that the artist must acknowledge, respect, and affirm a certain "matter-of-fact" or "given" nature in his art, we shall have grasped one of the intuitions fundamental to the Cubist and abstract movements: a poem is made of words and sounds; a painting is made of colors, lines, and shapes and has physical entity—it is a thing of paint and canvas. To understand this notion as referring merely to material and technique is to miss the essential point: the "word" or the "color" has an independent reality, and it is the artist's obligation to create independent forms.

This may sound to you like an elaborate circumlocution for a picture is a picture is a picture—to paraphrase Gertrude Stein's "Rose is a rose is a rose is a rose." But this simplicity is deceptive. Compare for a moment Gérôme's *Roman Slave Market* with Picasso's *Les Demoiselles d'Avignon.** "A picture is a picture" obviously does not apply with equal meaningfulness to both. To say that both are made of paint, canvas, colors, lines, and shapes is simply not true in Mallarmé's sense or in that of almost any Cubist or abstract painter. Perhaps the difference will be obvious simply from your study of the reproductions. If it is not, an idea which was emphasized by Mallarmé may help you to see the difference. Mallarmé suggested that a word which is simply useful "dies" as soon as it is used. Thus "Please close the door" dies as soon as the door is closed. The poet must find words and relationships between words which have a life independent of their usefulness. Now, the paint, canvas, colors, lines, and shapes in Gérôme's painting are all utilitarian. They die as they describe. One cannot paint a picture, according to Mallarmé's view, out of beautiful young ladies. One paints with paint, canvas, lines, colors, and shapes!

The octogenarian Gérôme died in 1904, three years before Picasso painted *Les Demoiselles d'Avignon*. Gérôme's was an outstandingly successful academic career. But by 1911 he was already dismissed by the critic Caffin in his *Story of French Painting:*

"Gérôme indifferently played to all the foibles of those who see nothing in a picture but the subject. The three [Gérôme, Cabanel, and Bouguereau] *became painters-in-ordinary to rich Americans and enjoyed every honor that French offi-*

* Plate 4.

Jean Léon Gérôme (1824–1904), ROMAN SLAVE MARKET
The Walters Art Gallery, Baltimore.

cialdom bestows on its successful, as opposed to its great, painters." [2]

It was a fact that Gérôme hated the Impressionists (*"Gérôme regards us as pimps,"* wrote Pissarro in one of his letters) and simply did not understand what they were doing; Picasso's *Demoiselles* would have struck him as madness. Indeed, to juxtapose the two paintings is to dramatize the creative wrench that must have been required to break with nineteenth-century naturalism. That Gérôme's work is naturalistic does not mean that it is either bad or good. The trouble is that the subject matter is *all* that is offered. This limitation is concealed by the painting's scrupulous completeness, which suggests that nothing more could be provided. Actually very little has been provided even on the simple level of defining the spatial and dimensional characteristics of the scene. Consider the auctioneer, for example. His clumsy over-elaborated drapery neither gives clues to his solidity or anatomy nor to his gesture. We are confused by a jumble of folds all contained within a parabolic curve that suggests flatness where a dimensional effect is clearly wanted. His left hand seems to float in an unrelated space at some unknown point with respect to the heads of the spectators. There is analagous confusion in the rendering and placement of the nude. The carefully rendered wooden platform helps us to supply some of the missing spatial relationships. We can supply them because we can associate with subject matter—the platform.

For a complete contrast both in execution and intention, turn to Picasso's *Demoiselles.* This painting is often spoken of as the first major Cubist picture. There are several studies for the painting which reveal the artist's tendency to become increasingly "abstract," and we know a good deal about the influences to which the young Picasso was exposed in this period. Most important was his enthusiasm for the work of Cézanne and his interest in African Negro sculpture.

Alfred Barr fills in this background on the influence of Cézanne:

"Cézanne influenced the pioneers of Cubism both through his art and his theory. But so complex and subtle was his style that they were able only gradually to assimilate its meaning. They developed more literally and much further than his perception of the geometrical forms underlying the confusion of nature. They admired, too, Cézanne's frequent choice of angular forms in his subject matter . . . , but above all they studied Cézanne's late work in which he abandons the perspective of deep space and the emphatic modeling of solid forms for a compact composition in which the planes of foreground and background are fused into an angular active curtain of color." [3]

The connection between Cézanne's ideas and Cubism is far from clear, yet the *visual* connection seems plain enough: Cézanne, especially in his later works, painted not only solids but the spaces between solids. It is a case of "spaces" rather than "space" because Cézanne seemed to feel distances between objects almost as a plastic element welded to the solids. He arrived at this through a kind of empirical approach that had its origins in Impressionism. Cézanne exhibited his work in the first Impressionist shows, and even though he developed in his own independent way, his faith in his "sensations" and in his experience is certainly to be related to the empiricism of the Impressionist movement. We could say that Cézanne applied the Impressionist idea of direct response to effects of light to the sensations of dimensionality and space. In translating these perceptions he formed a new visual language. As we have noted he felt a *multiplicity* of spatial relationships and he had to express this without falling back on preconceived perspectival formulas. From an impression of coherent overall space he moved to an effect of facets of space, each suggestive of depth but at the same time tending to flatten. Thus a special tension at the surface was created. Solid objects for Cézanne became cores, or nuclei, of units of his space, a relativistic space. Paradoxical though it may sound, this relativistic space was made up of flattened planes. It was this relativistic space, the flattened planes with multiple spatial implications, the tension of the surface planes that the Cubists took over from Cézanne. Something of these qualities may be felt in Picasso's *Demoiselles.* But it should be noted that the Cubists learned from Cézanne's *language.* They were not concerned with sensation or experience as he was. This meant that from the beginning there was a greater feeling of independence from visual experience in handling the flattening and geometrizing of forms and in the creating of shifting planes. Very soon as the Cubism of Braque and Picasso developed, the painter became more and more interested in space between forms and less and less interested in solids, until the image in such a work as Braque's *Man with a Guitar* of 1911 (discussed later in this chapter) was "dematerialized"—constructed of space or of spatial planes rather than of solids.

The second source of Cubism was found in the African mask. These masks were beginning to be seen around Paris at this time. They were first thought of as curios, and it was the new painters of the period who began to value them as significant works of art from another culture, offering another form of expression.

In the *Demoiselles*, the influence of this African "primitive" sculpture is clear, especially in the bold expressionistic masks of the two figures on the right. Gyorgy Kepes writes of this influence in *The Language of Vision:*

"An individual confronted with a new complex task seeks at once for some form of precedent to aid him. He makes an inventory of his past experience and that of others. Likewise, in critical times when a group is facing new, complex social or cultural problems, the solution of which is beyond habitual pattern, the first instinctive step is to look back for solutions and borrow wisdom from distant cultures.

"In their search for a new structural order . . . contemporary painters, confused and cornered in this turmoil of the new visual environment, also rediscovered solutions from previous cultures.

"Negro sculpture from Africa gave, on a small scale, one answer to their problem. In these simple forms each enveloping plane does not submerge in an illusory whole but acts as an individual dynamic direction leading to another plane which in turn leads to the understanding of the whole. Each plane, in its simplicity unhindered by details, has a clear dynamic structural function." [4]

Writers who are hostile to the development of Cubism and abstract art take a less sympathetic view of this play of influences. The following quotation from Maurice Grosser suggests that the old subject matter was simply replaced by "style" and that a painter such as Picasso painted "about" Cézanne's style and "about" the style of African sculpture.

"Picasso has developed this idea [of painting about styles] elaborately, and taking as his subject a number of styles, each in turn, he has produced

Paul Cézanne (1839–1906), HOUSE AMONG TREES, 1890–1900
The Museum of Modern Art, New York. Lillie P. Bliss Collection.

both pictures and a career of unparalleled brilliance. His early still lifes and Cubist pictures evoke the essential forms and multiple points of view and shifting perspectives of the mature Cézanne. The famous portrait of Gertrude Stein is a transition piece. It imposes on a Cézannesque body a head derived from Negro sculpture (Picasso, after a number of sittings, was not satisfied with the head and took the picture to the country with him. There he finished it without the model. During that summer he began his next period, the one centered on the Ladies of Avignon, *all about the Negro sculpture of the African West coast. As a result, the head of the portrait came out in the later style and quite different from the body) . . . Very little uncertainty remains any more [as to] what his pictures are about. The objects depicted are for the most part plainly visible and what the titles say they are . . . But his actual subject has never been, since the jugglers and mountebanks of his blue period, the objects on his canvas. His subject is rather how some particular school or race or time would have envisaged those objects."* [5]

Such a passage raises all kinds of questions. What does it mean to "paint about a style"? How many "influences" are required to produce a purely derivative or interpretive painting? The most serious question Grosser raises, stated in general terms, is whether modern painters and their epoch are presiding over a cultural debacle, clutching at any and every vital form from every culture, or whether these men are essentially original, creating an art of many references, for the widely-educated twentieth-century man—just as the Renaissance artists created an art that referred to all the interests of the man of the Renaissance.

As Cubism developed, it became an increasingly impersonal, structural, and formal art. The image which was faceted with Cézanne's planes in *Les Demoiselles d'Avignon* became more fragmented, more "geometrized," more diagrammatic and less solid. This development reached a peak of refinement and complexity in Braque's and Picasso's so-called Analytical Cubism of about 1910–1912. Braque's *Man with a Guitar* * of 1911 is typical of this phase. After this Analytical phase, the impulse toward abstraction and formalization was even stronger. Analytical Cubism (such as *Man with a Guitar*), was followed by Synthetic Cubism (Gris' *Breakfast* for example, page 25), and simpler and more solid images returned. But these images, although they refer to objects, or can be recognized as standing for objects rather than rep-

* Plate 5.

FUNERARY FIGURE, Bakota Tribe, French Equatorial Africa
Collection: Mr. and Mrs. Sam Jaffe, Beverly Hills, Calif.

The symbolic or distorted image is typical of primitive art the world over. In its beginnings art was an attribute or the image of an attribute before it became a representation. The European tradition re-learned this truth from the Near East, the Far East and Polynesia, and then from Africa. The influence of African sculpture came at a crucial time, when modern art was ready to renounce its approximations to nature.

Pablo Picasso (1881–), GRANDE DANSEUSE D'AVIGNON, 1907
Collection: Mr. Walter P. Chrysler, Jr., New York.

The influence of African sculpture, with its highly-stylized forms, helped to free painting from representation, and the African fetish became a modern symbol. In this early example, Picasso is at once bold in his departure from naturalism and cautious in following an African prototype. The arbitrary forms soon led him to the geometric patterns of Cubism.

resenting them, are very clearly constructions which the artist has built from flat "geometrized" elements, from arbitrary textures and shapes. The emphasis on construction and the play between symbol and reality is often forced home by actually pasting bits of reality onto the canvas, whether pieces of newspaper, a ticket, a playing card, or bits of string. Often the paradox of representation is underlined by using commercial textured papers, for example, paper with imitation woodgrain texture. Which is more real, we may ask, a bit of string, imitation paper, or a plane which the artist has defined in charcoal? The technique of pasting material to the canvas is called "collage" or gluing. The technique, as a technique, seems to emphasize the two-dimensionality of the picture image and to force a recognition of the symbolic transformation that allows the spectator to imagine planes, however shallow. It also constituted something of a technical revolution: the artist no longer relied entirely on the brush.

Volumes have been written about Cubist theory and the characteristics of Cubism. A very useful ten-point definition was given by Moholy-Nagy, himself a pioneer artist in the movement toward abstraction. Here is his so-called "dictionary of Cubism":

1. *Distortion.*
2. *Twisting of objects: the profile is simultaneously turned full face (the pipe, table leg, and glass look like pressed flowers).*
3. *Sections: using parts instead of the whole.*
4. *Shifting: dislocation of parts. Refraction of lines, and breaking continuous lines.*
5. *Superimpositions of different views of the objects.*
6. *Introduction of geometrically exact lines, straight and curved.*
7. *Change of positive-negative planes or lines.*
8. *Many forms in one. Pluralism. A contour refers to several forms.*
9. *Objects: Letter types, envelopes, table, table leg, guitar, violin, fruit, fruit bowl, glass, bottle, face, dead bird, fish panel, playing card, pipe, tobacco wrapper. (The atmosphere generated by these objects is that of the Paris café.)*
10. *Materials and technique for surface treatment: Corrugated cardboard, wallpaper, marble, grainywood, sand, newspaper print, marble dust, wire-mesh, combing, sanding, scratching of the pigment.*[6]

These are the devices which Cubism employed. Numbers four to eight are particularly important. (Point seven—change of positive-negative planes or lines—is very easy to understand in terms of the figures standardized by modern experimental psychology which illustrate how the image is differently interpreted as the spectator shifts his attention from an effect of black on white to white on black, or reads a silhouette as convex and then concave. In order to make the shift easy, the image must have a kind of built-in ambiguity or "neutrality" about which of the alternative interpretations is to be preferred. Obviously this kind of effect has always been available or possible, but the Cubists were the first to emphasize and exploit it as an expressive device.) As an experiment, it is illuminating to check Moholy-Nagy's definition against Braque's *Man with a Guitar* and Juan Gris' *Breakfast.*

Merely to "read," that is, to scrutinize carefully and take notice of all the elements in a Cubist painting, takes considerable time. Braque's *Man with a Guitar*, for example, not only gives a first impression of flickering complexity, it *is* complex. The figure is composed of elaborately overlapping and interpenetrating shapes. Actually a wider range of colors is used than is at first apparent, since the color is grayed so that effects of light and dark may be fully exploited. You will notice that the flickering lights break up shapes and planes which are already complex. The lights and dark do not model the form. If anything, they desolidify, and enhance a certain effect of transparency. The paint is applied with a light "feathery" horizontal stroke. The brush stroke, as such, enters the composition, providing a sense of scale, or size, and a horizontality which establishes movement in contrast to the predominantly vertical structure of the figure. The brushwork not only frankly acknowledges the material and technique of which the painting is made, but in functioning as an element in the design, it is assimilated into the artistic reality of the work.

In Braque's painting, the figure and the instrument can be made out, and a head is suggested at the top of the canvas. The apex of the largest triangle marks an elbow. From here it is easy to see the forearm and hand marked by a scroll, suggesting the strumming of the instrument. To the right of the center is the other hand, holding the neck of the fragmentized guitar. As the forms emerge, the play of geometric shapes seems enriched. The strong diagonals at the top, for example, serve to give an effect of turning to the "head." Although the pictorial space seems shallow, the sense of interpenetration and twisting of the planes is very complex, so complex that it is difficult to determine which planes are nearest, which furthest away. The planes have a tendency to vibrate and shift, as was suggested by points seven and eight in Moholy-Nagy's "dictionary of Cubism." It seems obvious that Braque did nothing to make the identification of the guitarist easy. Indeed, as if to underline the extent to which he has created a painting, he painted a "realistic" bit of rope and a nail in the upper left corner.

Now you recall the idea emphasized at the beginning of this chapter: that a painting is made of colors, lines, and shapes, and has its own entity. This may help to make plain some of the qualities in Braque's painting. Really to *see* the painting means to become involved in a visual world which the artist has created and which minimizes the references to anything other than the direct visual experience which his picture affords. If there is any meaning to the rope, it is precisely to remind the spectator that the picture *is* a picture, and that being a picture, it has a special reality detached from the reality of subject matter, anecdote, and even emotion—except in a purely pictorial sense.

At this point you may wonder that the artist suggested a guitar player at all. Why this reference to an "outside" reality? If what the artist creates *is* purely formal, if we are to delight *directly* in such factors as the intersection and twisting of spatial planes and the flicker of darks and lights, does the presence of the guitarist—or of any object—simply confuse the issue?

Such artists as Mondrian have felt strongly that it does confuse the issue, and they developed abstraction to an ultimate of pure formal relationship. Braque and Picasso, however, neither in their Cubist phase nor in their later careers ever gave up references to objective reality. Perhaps they were avoiding a logical conclusion when they both insisted that they were painters, not theoreticians. Here are typical comments by two founders of Cubism:

Braque: *"Cubism, or rather my cubism, is a means which I created for my use, for the purpose, primarily, of giving scope to the expression of my talent. Beyond this cubism does not interest me: it is painting I love above all."* [7]

Picasso: *"Cubist painting is no different from the painting of the other usual schools. The same principles and the same elements are common to all."* [8]

In the light of these statements, one way to understand the presence of the guitarist in Braque's painting is as a "motif." It is useful again to return to the idea brought out at the beginning of this chapter, that color, line, and shape have no life in Gérôme's canvas because they are *used*—used up in this case—to describe a Roman scene with the literal zest of a de Mille. In the notion of "motif" (as developed in the painting of Cézanne) we have the reverse: a "motif" is a subject that has no life of its own. Instead it is *used* as a vehicle of expression for living color, line, shape—in short it is a means or "excuse" for a painting.

By no means do all critics stop at this relatively simple interpretation of the presence of the guitarist that is suggested above. Daniel-Henry Kahnweiler, a man who knew Braque and Gris and

Juan Gris (1887–1927), BREAKFAST, 1914
The Museum of Modern Art, New York. Acquired through the Lillie P. Bliss Bequest.

Picasso well, was writing in 1915:

"Naturally, with this [Cubism] as with any new mode of expression in painting, the assimilation which leads to seeing the represented things objectively does not immediately take place when the spectator is unfamiliar with the new language. But for lyric painting to fulfill its purpose completely, it must be more than just a pleasure to the eye of the spectator. To be sure, assimilation always takes place finally, but in order to facilitate it, and impress its urgency upon the spectator, cubist pictures should always be provided with descriptive titles, such as Bottle and Glass, Playing Cards and Dice *and so on. In this way, the condition will arise which H. G. Lewes referred to as 'preperception' and memory images connected with the title will then focus much more easily on the stimuli in the painting."* [9]

By "assimilation" Kahnweiler seems to mean recognition of what is represented. Indeed he says explicitly at one point: *"The visual conception desired by the painter by no means resides in geometric forms, but rather in the representation of the reproduced objects."* [10] For Kahnweiler, apparently, Cubism "constructed" objects "truer," more real than anything possible with previous illusionistic methods of painting.

As we have already noted, after the analytical phase of Cubism, which we represented by Braque's *Man with a Guitar*, the impulse toward abstraction and formalization became even stronger. The idea that the artist "constructs" his image was given a new kind of expression through the use of *collage*. Juan Gris' *Breakfast* of 1914 is such an example. The table is "made" of imitation woodgrain paper pasted to the canvas; the

Paul Cézanne (1839–1906), GRANDES BAIGNEUSES, 1898–1905
W. P. Wilstach Collection,
Philadelphia Museum of Art.

Cézanne painted deliberate still lifes and landscapes as controlled as formal gardens. By preference he would have filled his scenes with pagan, romantic figures and from time to time with his "bathers" he dared to emulate the sensual freedom of the Venetians. The style of his "bathers" is agitated and tumultuous; and Cézanne draws back from these brief forays to the more sober study of unprovocative apples and peaches, bottles and bowls.

Edouard Manet (1832–1883), THE GUITARIST, 1860
The Metropolitan Museum of Art, New York. Gift of William Church Osborn, 1949.

The guitar is the popular Spanish instrument; Braque and Picasso made the guitar a symbol of Cubism, where it is ever on view, whole or in fragments. Here the instrument is seen at the beginning of the "modern" revolution nearly a century ago. The French Manet was greatly influenced by Velásquez and Goya. He took over their brushwork and dramatic lighting, and here he shows us a typical Spanish subject—sufficient in his poverty and consoling himself with the guitar.

wallpaper *is* wallpaper, and the newspaper *is* newspaper; the folds and strings of the orange tobacco packet are crayon, but the stamp is real. Alfred Barr makes this comment on the result which Gris achieves in this particular painting.

"*Thus does Gris, the metaphysician, juggle density and opacity, texture and color, genuine and counterfeit, flatness and relief, integrity and analysis, space and time, truth and fact. What is the nature of experience, he asks, what is reality—yet he does not press these questions. For Gris, the artist, their resolution lies in his picture, its paradoxical wit, its poetry, its harmony.*" [11]

Barr, in effect, applauds the artist for harmonizing the object and the form in a higher synthesis. Others reproach him for trying to "have it both ways," a purist point of view which will be followed to its conclusion when we come again to

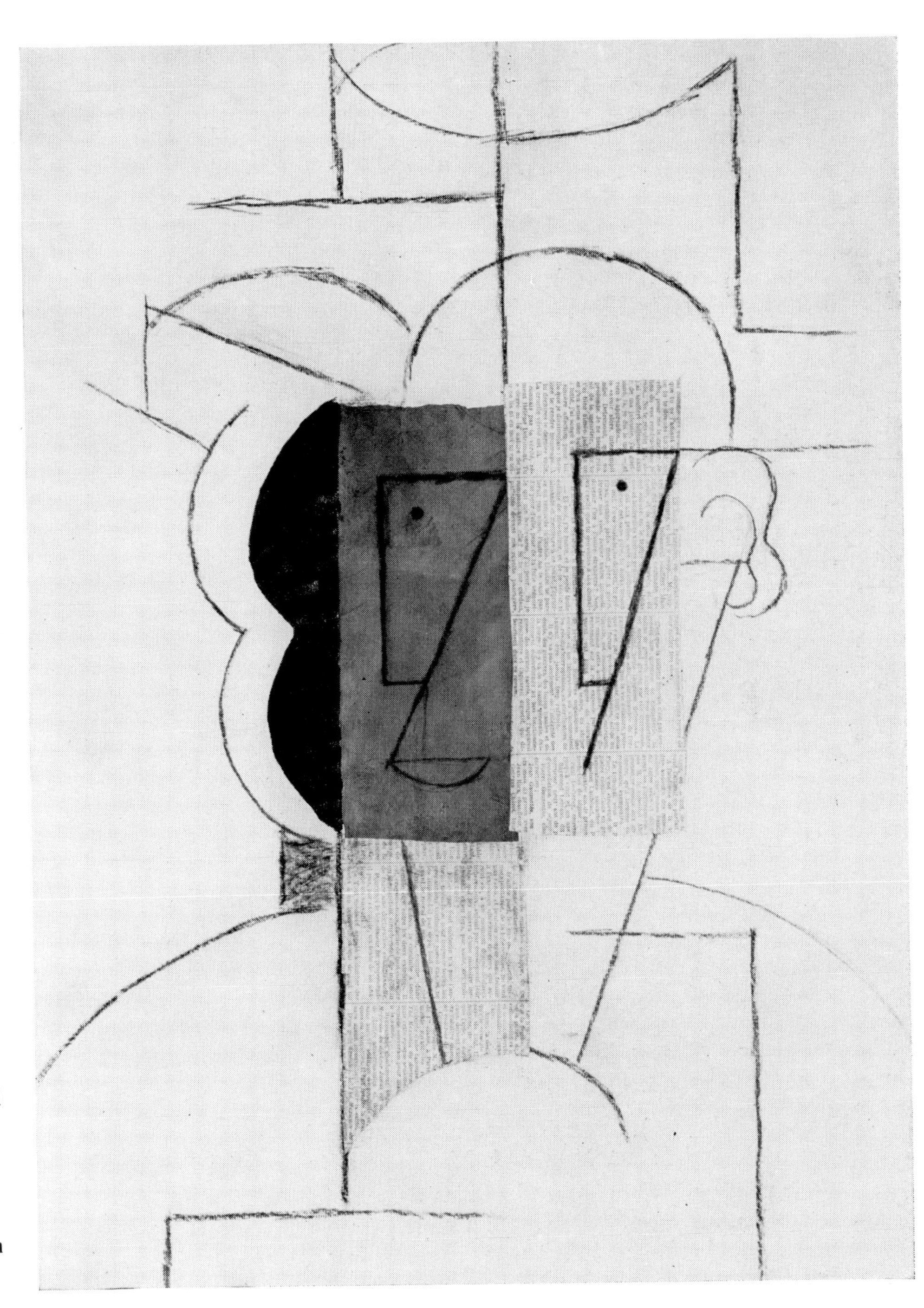

Pablo Picasso (1881–)
MAN WITH A HAT, 1913
The Museum of Modern Art, New York. Purchase.

Until the time of this painting the Cubist movement had been a revolt from the realist tradition, but Picasso and Braque had fought with traditional weapons: brush and palette. Now their patterns were produced by new means: they made paper cut-outs or assembled objects and attached them to a surface. Atmospheric rendering died under this treatment, and the painting came to life as an independent symbol.

the work of Piet Mondrian. But we will find then that Mondrian is faced with opposites, almost antagonisms, in pure color and dimension which it becomes his task to organize or harmonize. Perhaps the artist must always face the task of harmonizing incompatibles in order to make life philosophically tolerable. The Cubist found himself harmonizing concept and object, an achievement which has provided the philosophical basis, and the architectural structure, of much of the art of this century.

1. Marcel Raymond, *From Baudelaire to Surrealism*, Documents of Modern Art Vol. 10, New York, Wittenborn, Schultz, Inc., 1950, Appendix, p. 360.
2. Charles H. Caffin, *The Story of French Painting*, New York, The Century Co., 1915, p. 123.
3. Alfred H. Barr, Jr., *Cubism and Abstract Art*, New York, The Museum of Modern Art, 1936, p. 26.
4. Gyorgy Kepes, *The Language of Vision*, Chicago, Paul Theobald, 1944, p. 94.
5. Maurice Grosser, *Painting in Public*, New York, Alfred A. Knopf, Inc., 1948, pp. 164–165.
6. László Moholy-Nagy, *The New Vision 1928* (fourth revised edition 1947), Documents of Modern Art Vol. 3, New York, Wittenborn, Schultz, Inc., 1949, p. 37.
7. Guillaume Janneau, *L'Art Cubiste*, Paris, C. Moreau, 1929, p. 57.
8. *Ibid.*, p. 61.
9. Daniel-Henry Kahnweiler, *The Rise of Cubism* (trans. by Henry Aronson), Documents of Modern Art Vol. 9, New York, Wittenborn, Schultz, Inc., 1949, pp. 12–13.
10. *Ibid.*, p. 13.
11. Alfred H. Barr, Jr., Ed., *Masters of Modern Art*, New York, The Museum of Modern Art, 1954, p. 76.

Pablo Picasso (1881–), NIGHT FISHING AT ANTIBES, 1939
The Museum of Modern Art, New York. Mrs. Simon Guggenheim Fund.

In this late painting Picasso has used all his resources, in particular the dislocation of features, to convey not only a sense of motion, but a concentration on a most primitive impulse. The fisher and the fish take part in the game of survival, eater and eaten, and the painter seems to fuse two worlds of vision that have all evolution between them: that of the man peering down at his prey, and the fish glimpsing his hunter.

Jacques Lipchitz (1891–   ), SAILOR WITH GUITAR, 1914
Philadelphia Museum of Art.

Cubism, a conceptual manipulation of space, lent itself to sculpture as well as to paint. Lipchitz is one of the foremost sculptors of our period. Of the same generation as Picasso, he played an important part in the Cubist experimentation, as we see in this sculpture which is thoroughly Cubist in spirit, even to the introduction of the guitar.

THREE

The Search for the Absolute

OUR DISCUSSION of Cubism included two points of view, both very much alive: one holds that form has little meaning unless some remnant of subject matter is disclosed, while the other presents form as an absolute, revealed only when stripped of surface appearances. This divergence of views cuts deep. It divided Aristotle, with his scientific outlook, from Plato, for whom "reality" was but the shadow of a world of absolutes. Men have chosen sides on a basis of temperament from that day to this. One man wants to save from the evidence of experience some glimpse of Braque's guitar—or he feels that he has lost his sanity; another feels that reality has no meaning unless it is the reality of faith. For the latter, an image vulgarizes the purity of prayer.

The search for the "absolute" pursued by artists has always been directed by a deeply-held faith. The two modern artists whose dedication to this endeavor has resulted in work of overwhelming influence are Piet Mondrian and Wassily Kandinsky. Although they are very different, they have points in common: each rejected traditional modes of representation, and each created principles of reality or articles of faith for which new symbols were formulated.

Piet Mondrian visited Paris in 1910, when he was thirty-eight, at the precise moment when Cubism fully emerged as a style. He remained there for four years, returning to Holland, his native land, at the outbreak of World War I. He had arrived in Paris as a naturalistic painter; he came home as an abstractionist, a member of the extreme avant-garde. Yet it was not until 1923 that Mondrian achieved his mature style, well illustrated in our color reproduction. During these years of development he had clarified his ideas and perfected the means of expressing them. In his own words he traces dispassionately the struggle of this period:

"*The first thing to change in my painting was the color. I forsook natural color for pure color. I had come to feel that the colors of nature cannot be reproduced on canvas. Instinctively, I felt that painting had to find a new way to express the beauty of nature . . .*

"*Gradually I became aware that Cubism did not accept the logical consequences of its own discoveries; it was not developing abstraction toward its ultimate goal, the expression of pure reality. I felt that this reality can only be established through* pure plastics. *In its essential expression, pure plastics is unconditioned by subjective feeling and conception. It took me a long time to discover that particularities of form and natural color evoke subjective states of feeling, which obscure* pure reality. *The appearance of natural forms changes but reality remains constant. To create pure reality plastically, it is necessary to reduce natural forms to the* constant elements *of form and natural color to* primary color. *The aim is not to create other particular forms and colors with all their limitations, but to work toward abolishing them in the interest of a larger unity.*" [1]

Mondrian's explanation of his philosophy is clear enough; he equates pure reality or the essence of reality with *pure* form, not *representational* form. His problem was to work out this equation, which he did by reducing his artistic vocabulary to what he believed to be its essence. He ultimately retained only the primary colors: red, blue, and yellow, and combined them only through the use of the straight line and the 90-degree or right angle. Mondrian saw these elements as the basic, irreducible minimum of the means of painting; and they combined most dynamically to convey the structure and forces of the world of man and the cosmos. No other means, for instance, could portray the violent impact of two opposing forces more literally than two straight lines meeting at right angles. The right angle became a symbol, all the more appropriate to Mondrian's thought since it represented two forces in opposition, forces which, mystically, could be identified with each other.

"At this point," Mondrian says, *"I became conscious that reality is form* and *space. Nature reveals forms in space.* Actually all *is space, form as well as what we see as empty space. To create unity, art has to follow not nature's aspect but what nature really is. Appearing in oppositions, nature is unity: form is limited space concrete only through its determination. Art has to* determine space as well as form *and to create* the equivalence of these two factors." [2]

Mondrian's *Composition,* 1935–42,* illustrates in a deceptively simple way the ideas just expressed. The unity of the painting could hardly have been achieved with fewer means. Visually, for instance, note how much impact would have been lost if the yellow rectangle at the top had been merely white and if the blue and red rectangles had been white, too. For that matter even the balance of the structure would no longer exist. To verify this, block out the yellow rectangle for a moment and your eye will move inexorably to the left of the picture and then down to the bottom of the frame where it will slip away from the picture altogether.

Another important aspect of the picture is the proportion of the rectangles and lines. The latter are uninterrupted and relatively broad; the shapes are repetitive, but few in number. Contrast these with the lines and shapes in *Broadway Boogie Woogie,* 1942–43. The predominance of small squares imparts a very different quality of meaning to the latter picture. The strength, boldness —in a word, the monumentality of the former are replaced by a different content. The steel-like frame of the *Composition* holds the fewer rectangles and the more positive colors in a stability which is a synthesis of opposing forces, at once quiet and extraordinarily tense.

Unlike Mondrian, Wassily Kandinsky only turned to painting after thorough training in another field: political economy and law. He was born in Moscow, in 1866, and at the age of thirty went to Munich to study painting. Painstakingly and seriously he went about learning his new profession and finally emerged in 1912 as one of a group of extremists called *Der Blaue Reiter* or The Blue Rider. The members of The Blue Rider held more theory in common than their work suggests. Each was in his own way a mystic, seeking to express a universal content in his painting. Two years before, in 1910, Kandinsky had already established the direction of his development when he painted his first *Improvisation,* defined in his own words as *"a largely unconscious, spontaneous expression of inner character, [of] non-material nature."* [3] The contemporary term for this amorphous type of painting is "non-objective" since it repeats nothing of the external world which is reported by the senses.

Kandinsky returned to Moscow in 1914, and after the Revolution he became a power in Russian art politics. It was not long, however, before the members of the Supreme Soviet decided that revolutionary art was not effective socialist propaganda, and by edict they re-established the style popular in their childhood during the waning days of Imperial society. For this reason, Kandinsky was obliged to leave Moscow in 1922. He accepted a post at the Bauhaus, where he taught until the Nazis suppressed the school in 1933. Then he went to Paris, where he remained until his death in 1944, the same year as Mondrian's.

Kandinsky has the credit for the discovery or creation of "non-objective" painting. He expounded his theories at length in his book, *The Art of Spiritual Harmony,* which he wrote as early as 1910:

"As . . . man develops, the circle of [his] experiences caused by different beings and objects grows ever wider. They acquire an inner meaning and eventually a spiritual harmony. It is the same with color, which makes only a momentary and superficial impression on a soul but slightly developed in sensitiveness. But even this superficial impression varies in quality. The eye is strongly attracted by light, clear colors, and still more strongly attracted by those colors which are warm as well as clear; vermilion has the charm of flame, which has always attracted human beings. Keen lemon-yellow hurts the eye in time as a prolonged and shrill trumpet-note the ear, and the gazer turns away to seek relief in blue or green.

"But to a more sensitive soul the effect of colors is deeper and intensely moving. And so we come to the second main result of looking

* Plate 6.

at colors: their psychic effect. They produce a corresponding spiritual vibration, and it is only as a step towards this spiritual vibration that the elementary physical impression is of importance.[4]

"Generally speaking, color is a power which directly influences the soul. Color is the key-board, the eyes are the hammers, the soul is the piano with many strings. The artist is the hand which plays, touching one key or another, to cause vibrations in the soul." [5]

These quotations give clues essential to an analysis of Kandinsky's paintings as he intended them to be felt or understood. He further set up two parallel categories. The first concerns the qualities of color alone, and includes four antitheses: yellow-blue, green-red, orange-violet, and black-white, as well as the antitheses: warm-cold, light-dark, and forwards-backwards, excentric-concentric movement. All of these qualities interact, intensifying or neutralizing one another. Movement is the factor which controls these categories; and Kandinsky equates it to a spiritual essence which underlies all life.

The second category of qualities consists of the emotional particularities of color and their interactions. For example, yellow is energetic, aggressive, restless, whereas blue is recessive, inward, profound; and black is disharmonious, the silence of death, in contrast to white which is pregnant silence and harmony beyond the mundane.

Not all artists, of course, agree with Kandinsky's statements about colors—either their visual dynamic or their emotional meaning. To Kandinsky, however, each color has its specific, incontrovertible significance on both the spiritual and aesthetic levels.

Kandinsky's paintings are as rhythmically flowing as Mondrian's are angular, as amorphous as Mondrian's are precise. The two artists reached their mystic goal, their explanation of the forces of existence, in ways diametrically opposed. Mondrian excluded the particular and the emotional; Kandinsky exploited them. This is one explanation of the difference between Mondrian's *Composition*, 1935–42, and the *Two Compositions*, 1914,* by Kandinsky. The contrast between these works is so clear as not to warrant a detailed analysis, but the more subtle differences between Kandinsky's two paintings deserve further study.

In the Kandinsky on the right of the plate there is a general rising movement of warm to cool color, from a complex centrifugal area to one of dispersion and no cohesion. The area in the lower section of the picture revolves around a curve of red mixed with vermilion and partially covered by deep blue blotches. This movement is limited on the right by a sweep of white which in turn is paralleled by an area of deep blue shading to violet, supported in a field of white streaked with orange, blue, and yellow. At the upper left of the red curve a swath of orange emerges and reaches upwards until it is crossed by fragments of blue turning to green and pink, loses its character, and continues as yellow which reaches a point and stops. To its left are two intermingled red and blue strips, then a blankness of scattered bits of deep colors on fields of washed-out blue and yellow-green, until at the upper left the green intensifies around a blue center lined with red. Movement is then directed downward along the pale blue path bordering the frame until it is caught in the centrifugal area below and again rises.

The picture on the left is full of conflict as compared to the more confident surge of its companion. Although there are many colors, the dominant antithesis is between white and black, the silence of life opposed to the silence of death. This conflict is illuminated and intensified by the bursts of intense red and yellow and other colors scattered over the surface. There are two definite areas of pale blue which rise like fingers across the general drift of colors along a diagonal from lower left to upper right. The dispersion, the disharmony, the wrenching apart of elements is forced by two major areas of menacingly deep tonality, one at the lower right and the other, less concentrated, in the upper middle and left of the picture.

These descriptions should by no means be taken as exhaustive; they are meant to suggest the two characteristics of Kandinsky's art: the highly emotional transcript of personality (which perhaps only a psychologist could interpret), and the fluid movement needed to project these emotions.

Resistance to the claims of non-objective art, whether in the manner of Kandinsky or of Mondrian, has been intense and continuous ever since these artists were first active. As Katherine Dreier, long one of the foremost patrons and exponents of modern art, remarked in 1949, *"When I think of the anger which still continues towards us I am amazed. There are always people who wish to kill us off and so, from time to time, learned or amusing books have been written as to why we are degenerates and why we should be annihilated."* [6] The texts referred to by Miss Dreier deny the validity of abstraction as a style

* Plate 7.

of art. To be valid, they suggest, any art form must have content, i.e., convey meaning, which abstraction is unable to provide.

Among those whose writings oppose Miss Dreier is art patron Huntington Hartford, who wrote: "*There is a swiftness and excitement in the painter's manner of telling a story by depicting real objects on canvas which the writer himself has often envied. Is there any more sense in the painter giving up the very reason for his use of lines and colors in the first place—the realism of subject matter—than there is for the author to write abracadabra such as James Joyce attempted? Why throw unnecessary obstacles in a path which predecessors for so many centuries have been trying to clear? . . .*

"*The reason is evident. In each case the method of communication so carefully developed over the years has been partially destroyed, and whatever the artist may have had in mind when he created the work, only a portion of it reached the audience.*" [7]

Selden Rodman has expressed a similar point of view: "*But does it not just as basically follow that without serious* content—*a projection through tangible symbols of the artist's attachment to values outside art itself—all the formal virtues in the world add up to no more than decorative play? To say so is to commit, in the eyes of those dedicated to a 'non-objective' art, a cardinal heresy.*" [8]

Another vigorous indictment of modern abstract art was contained in an article by Francis Henry Taylor, then (1948) Director of The Metropolitan Museum of Art, New York.

"*The issue for our generation is not so much one of principle as it is one of the degree of communicability versus incommunicability. And, while no sensible person would wish to turn back the clock, there are many who might wish to read its face without having to take its works apart.*

"*If we accept the definition of art as the rendering of truth in sensible form, and truth as the interpretation of human experience, it is obvious that a work of art is essentially communicative. It must mean something to someone other than the person who created it—in fact, and more important still, it can mean the same thing or several different things to a number of persons. But meaning it must have. Not until the second quarter of the twentieth century was the essential communicability of art ever denied. Communication has been common to all the great racial traditions and, once established, can take any variety of expression. It is unlimited in content or subject matter, free to adopt any style or technique. The one and only quality denied to a work of art throughout the ages is privacy. Unless participation is allowed the spectator, it becomes a hopeless riddle and ceases to be any work of art at all.*" [9]

From the quotations above and from the writings of Mondrian and Kandinsky, it seems clear that the problem of meaning, content, or communication is the basis of much of the conflict over abstract art. Each author, regardless of his position, holds fast to it by simple affirmation, by insisting that his ideas are valid and not simply the product of opinion. On the other side of the question, Naum Gabo, a prominent modern sculptor in the non-objective or Constructivist mode, has given a clear presentation of some of the themes available to an artist who prefers the abstract mode of expression. It is a summation by a mature artist, the more valuable as the sculptor was trained as a scientist and is certainly not turning his back on objective experience. He points out that abstract art continues the traditional responsibility for communication, but he insists that it has a range of meaning all its own.

Gabo defines art as "*the specific and exclusive faculty of man's mind to conceive and represent the world without and within him in form and by means of artfully constructed images.*" [10] Moreover, he suggests that "*This faculty predominates in all the processes of our mental and physical orientation in this world, it being impossible for our minds to perceive or arrange or act upon our world in any other way but through this construction of an ever-changing and yet coherent chain of images. Furthermore, I maintain that these mentally constructed images are the very essence of the reality of the world which we are searching for.*[11]

"*We have not discovered electricity, x-rays, the atom and thousands of other phenomena and processes—we have made them. They are images of our own construction. After all, it is not long ago that electricity to us was the image of a sneezing and ferocious god—after that it became a current, later on it became a wave, today it is a particle—tomorrow its image will shrink to the symbol of some concise mathematical formula. What is it all if not an ever-changing chain of images, ever true and ever real so long as they are in use—both the old one which we discard and the new which we construe.*[12]

"*With what right,*" asks Gabo, "*is the scientist allowed to discard views of the world which were so useful to mankind for so many thousands of years and replace them by new images entirely different from the old? With what right is the scientist allowed it and the artist not—and why? . . . It was taken for granted that when the mechanistic conception of the universe replaced the anthropomorphic one, it was quite all right; and when now our contemporary sciences are developing an image of the world so entirely different from both the previous ones as to appear to us almost absurd, incomprehensible to common sense, we are again willing to take it—we have already accepted it; we have gotten familiar with a world in which forces are permitted to become mass and matter is permitted to become light; a world which is pictured to us as a conglomeration of oscillating electrons, pro-*

Piet Mondrian (1872–1944), COMPOSITION IN WHITE, BLACK AND RED, 1936
The Museum of Modern Art, New York. Gift of the Advisory Committee.

Mondrian perfected asymmetrical balance. In his art, primary colors and lines meeting at right angles provided him with all the material he needed to create infinitely varied patterns. This self-abnegation, like the self-denials of the religious life, rewarded him with a quiet intensity and ritualistic power.

Wassily Kandinsky (1866–1944), DOMINANT CURVE, No. 631, 1936
The Solomon R. Guggenheim Museum, New York.

Kandinsky was the creator of non-objective painting. He was a mystic who imagined or evoked cosmic forces, of which color and form are but shadows or attributes.

Wassily Kandinsky (1866–1944), PAINTING (WINTER), 1914
The Solomon R. Guggenheim Museum, New York.

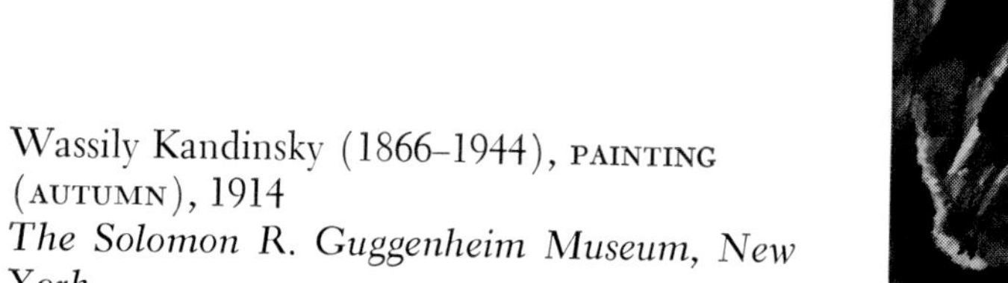

Wassily Kandinsky (1866–1944), PAINTING (AUTUMN), 1914
The Solomon R. Guggenheim Museum, New York.

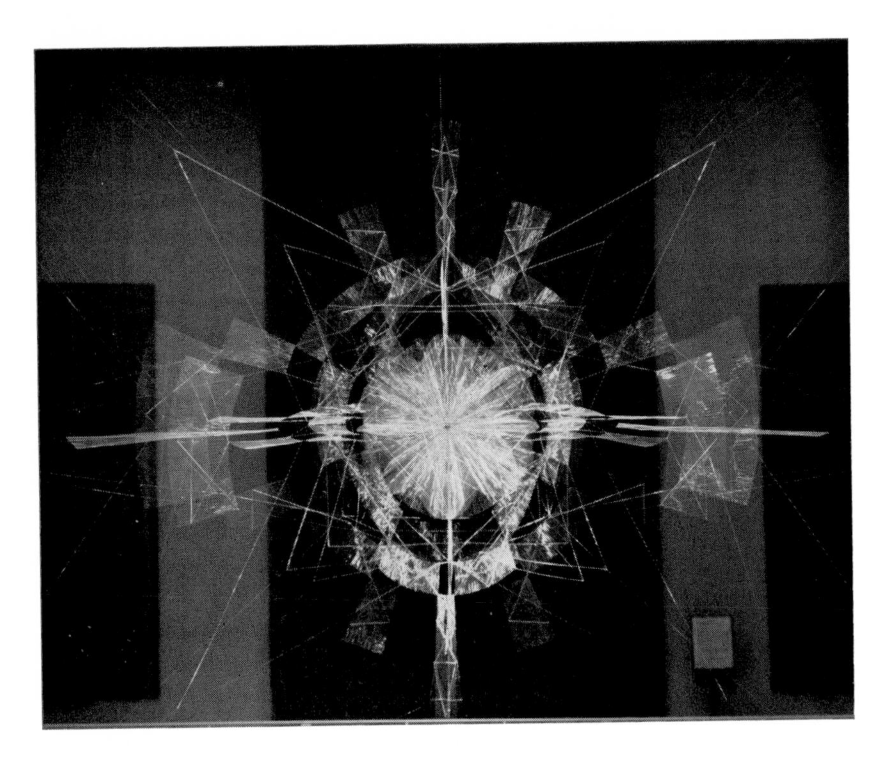

Richard Lippold (1915–   ), VARIATION WITHIN A SPHERE, No. 10: THE SUN, 1953–56
The Metropolitan Museum of Art, New York, Fletcher Fund, 1956.

Like the physicist, the modern sculptor concerns himself with space and presides over the disintegration of mass. Lippold offers us an aesthetic astronomy, as did Kandinsky before him. His art is half engineering, half jewelry, but a large conception lifts it into mystical significance.

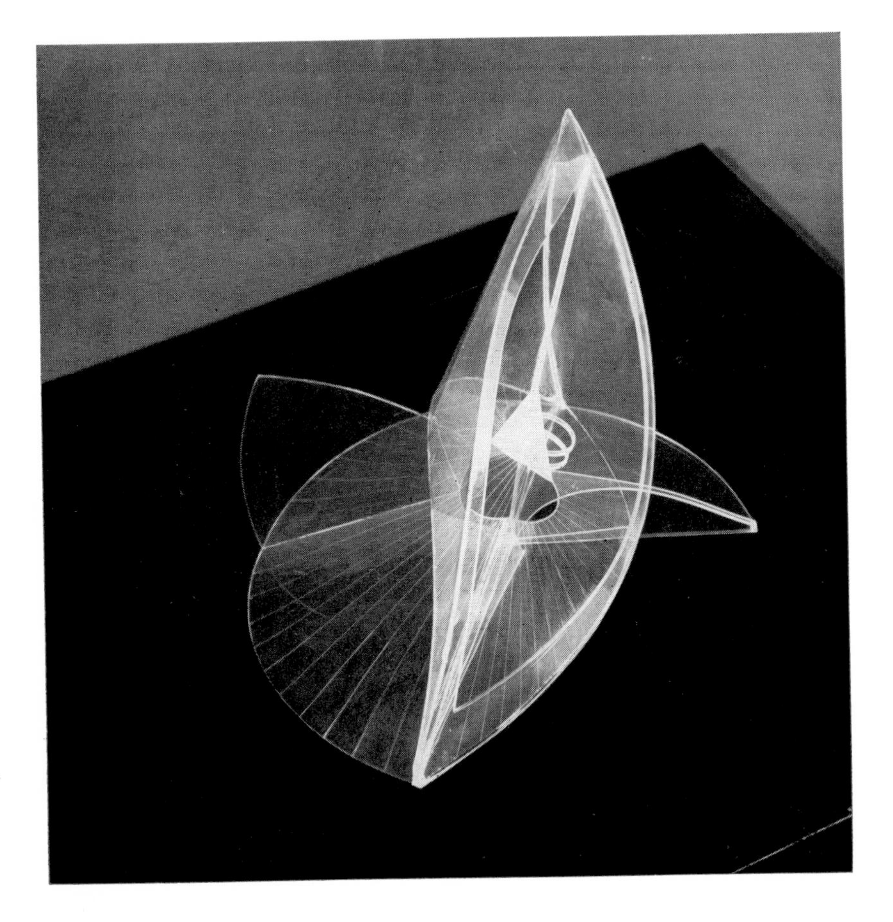

Naum Gabo (1890–   ), SPIRAL THEME, 1941
The Museum of Modern Art, New York. Advisory Committee Fund.

Gabo is one of the pioneers in creating a sculpture that parallels the world of the physicist, a world where loci and fields of force are at once reality and conceptions of man's mind. But it is not enough to visualize an art; it must be created. Gabo has found the material that suits his needs in metal, transparent plastic, and threads in tension.

Constantin Brancusi (1876–1957), BIRD IN SPACE, 1919
The Museum of Modern Art, New York.

This sculpture is a plastic diagram of flight, of motion, created long before "streamlining" became a commonplace of industrial design. Whereas the Cubists triangulated their way into the abstract, Brancusi found a dynamic spherical geometry, closer to organic form.

tons, neutrons, particles. . . . If the scientist is permitted to picture to us an image of an electron which under certain conditions has less than zero energy . . . and if he is permitted to see behind this simple common table, an image of the curvature of space—why, I ask, is not the contemporary artist to be permitted to search for and bring forward an image of the world more in accordance with the achievements of our developed mind, even if it is different from the image presented in the paintings and sculptures of our predecessors? [13]

"*Science in conveying a new image or conception can but state it; it can make it cogent by its own means, but, it cannot, however, by its own means alone make this image an organic part of our consciousness, of our perceptions; it cannot bring that new image to the stream of our emotions and transfer it into a sensuous experience. It is only through the means of our visual or poetic arts that this image can be experienced and incorporated in the frame of our attitude towards this world.*[14]

"[*These visual*] *means being shapes, lines, colors, forms, are not illusory nor are they abstractions; they are a factual force and their impact on our senses is as real as the impact of light or of an electrical shock. This impact can be verified just as any other natural phenomenon. Shapes, colors, and lines speak their own languages. They are events in themselves and in an organized construction they become beings—their psychological force is immediate, irresistible and universal to all species of mankind; not being the result of a convention as words are, they are unambiguous and it is therefor that their impact can influence the human psyche; it can break or mold it, it exalts, it depresses, elates or makes desperate; it can bring order where there was confusion and it can disturb and exasperate where there was an order. That is why I use these elemental means for my expression, but far be it from me to advocate that a constructive work of art should consist merely of an arrangement of these elemental means for no other purpose than to let them speak for themselves. . . I demand that they shall remain only means for conveying a well-organized and clearly defined image—not just some image, any image, but a new and constructive image by which I mean that which by its very existence as a plastic vision should provoke in us the forces and the desires to enhance life, assert it and assist its further development.*" [15]

This group of painters, searching for the absolute, has thus created a new artistic image of reality in place of the traditional "natural" images. Perhaps we should modify the statement in Chapter I that abstract art has no subject matter. Its subject matter may be this newly created image; and we discover it not by referring to objects outside of the painting, but simply by looking into the painting itself.

1. Piet Mondrian, *Plastic Art and Pure Plastic Art*, Documents of Modern Art Vol. 2, New York, Wittenborn and Company, 1945, p. 10.
2. *Ibid.*, p. 13.
3. Wassily Kandinsky, *Concerning the Spiritual in Art and Painting in Particular*, 1912, Documents of Modern Art Vol. 5, New York, Wittenborn, Schultz, Inc., 1947, p. 77.
4. Wassily Kandinsky, *The Art of Spiritual Harmony* (trans. by M. T. H. Sadler), London, Constable and Company Limited, 1914, p. 48.
5. *Ibid.*, p. 52.
6. Katherine S. Dreier, James Johnson Sweeney, Naum Gabo, *Three Lectures on Modern Art*, New York, Philosophical Library, 1949, p. 6.
7. Huntington Hartford, *The Public Be Damned*, privately reprinted 1955, p. 4.
8. Selden Rodman, *The Eye of Man* (*Form and Content in Western Painting*), New York, Devin-Adair, 1955, p. 3.
9. Francis Henry Taylor, "Modern Art and the Dignity of Man," *The Atlantic Monthly*, December 1948, pp. 31–32.
10. Gabo, *op. cit.*, p. 70.
11. *Ibid.*
12. *Ibid.*, pp. 73–74.
13. *Ibid.*, pp. 75–77.
14. *Ibid.*, p. 80.
15. *Ibid.*, pp. 82–83.

FOUR

The Dominance of Emotion

THE TERM "expressionism" has been applied to works of art in many periods. In this chapter we shall talk of Expressionism as a kind of painting that emerged in the first decade of the twentieth century. We shall see that it has much in common with expressionistic works of earlier periods, but as a contemporary style it is unmistakably different from its forerunners.

Herbert Read explains this style as *"a form of art that gives primacy to the artist's emotional reactions to experience. The artist tries to depict, not the objective reality of the world, but the subjective reality of the feelings which objects and events arouse in his psyche, or self. It is an art that cares very little for conventional notions of beauty; it can be impressively tragic, and sometimes excessively neurotic or sentimental. But it is never merely pretty, never intellectually sterile."* [1]

With this explanation in mind, let us analyze the paintings considered here on the basis of subject matter, form, and content. We see readily that the Expressionist painter makes clear references to subject matter. He uses definite thematic material.

Yet this material is presented not as a reality or a simulacrum of it, but clearly as a painting or a symbol. His approach is to use, not realism, but a free distortion. He uses color, too. But he is not using it primarily as an aid to representation.

Expressionistic form—distortion and a special use of color—is the means of conveying a particular kind of content. For the Expressionist is dealing, in Read's words, with "the emotional reactions to experience." He confronts the observer not with an accurate representation, but with a two-dimensional image whose lines and colors are intended to force an emotional and personal reaction.

But there would be nothing new about Expressionism if it were simply the communication of intense emotion. We can go back as far as the Hellenistic period in Greece (the fourth to second century B.C.), and find artists who were preoccupied with the expression of strong emotions. The complex statue of Laocoön in the Vatican Museum is a good example of the style of this time. It illustrates the death of Laocoön and his two sons in the writhing coils of a python, sent to devour them because Laocoön's attempt to warn the Trojans against the great wooden horse had offended the gods who favored the Greek side of that controversy. Strong passion again became a dominant characteristic during the Baroque period in Europe in the seventeenth and eighteenth centuries. A glance at almost any painting by the Flemish artist, Peter Paul Rubens, affords an insight into the Baroque projection of emotions. His bold swinging rhythms enmesh in a brilliantly-colored context all the aspects of sensuous reality that served his purpose.

Expressionism can be, says Read, "impressively tragic." So was the *Crucifixion*, attributed to the great sixteenth-century artist, Matthias Grünewald. The body of Christ is displayed on the cross in a state of putrefaction, and His hands and feet are being slowly torn as His weight presses down on the great nails which fasten Him. His flesh is punctured by great running sores and ripped by the lashing He suffered during the Tormenting. This comes close to the twentieth-century

Expressionist tragic mood.

We come closer still to Expressionism with the Romantic movement of the nineteenth century. Eugène Delacroix's portrayal of Hamlet as a sickly introspective and tormented figure walking around with a skull in hand, the Baron Gros' studies from a morgue or from an insane asylum, Holman Hunt's *Ophelia* drowning in her flowery stream, Caspar David Friedrich's landscapes with monks performing their liturgies among the snowy crags of an alp or among the ruins of a medieval court: all these exemplify the Romantic temperament in search of topics which plumb the depths of despair or the somber peripheries of human experience. Romanticism as a movement trusted to the power of emotion.

Yet there is an essential difference between the Romantics and the contemporary Expressionists. The nineteenth-century world was still comparatively rational, stable and optimistic. It was still possible to retreat from the morass of emotional experience to firmer ground. Not so for the Expressionists. Their sense of tragedy is not that external fatality of the Greeks, which Aristotle said purged the beholder; it is rather a sickness of soul which has afflicted many men in the twentieth century.

If we are to judge by their art, the people of no other region have felt this malaise so intensely as those of northern Europe, especially Scandi-

Matthias Grünewald (attributed to) (1470–1530), CRUCIFIXION
National Gallery of Art, Washington, D.C.

navia and Germany. Historically the earliest Expressionist movement, *Die Brücke* (The Bridge), began in Dresden in 1905; and its foundations were laid by the Norwegian, Edvard Munch. His painting, *The Scream* (1893), together with his woodcut, *The Cry*—variants on a theme—shows a cadaverous head with open mouth and ghost-like torso, intimately caught up in the swirling rhythms of the landscape—bridge, harbor, and sunset—so that everything in sight, whether of man or nature, seems burdened by terror.

Elsewhere in Europe, too, painters in the twentieth century have expressed terror and tragedy. Yet terror and tragedy were not the preoccupations that they were in northern Europe. For an instructive contrast, let us turn for a moment to the Fauve school, which started in Paris at the same time as *Die Brücke* was getting under way in Dresden. The Fauve movement, which achieved identity and a title because of the "wildness" of its style, developed out of the work of Seurat, Gauguin, and the Neo-Impressionists, taking its departure from the technical aspects of their painting and, specifically, their non-representational use of color.

The leader of the Fauve group was Henri Matisse. *The Red Studio* (1911) is a late example of his Fauve style, with all the brilliance and vitality of color for which Matisse is noted. The strident colors seem to lead a life of their own, independent of any psychological quality latent in the subject, and force the observer to consider the technical aspects of the painting above all else. Note, for instance, the kinds and variety of reds which the artist used, resulting in a jangling, unquiet surface charged with intensity. But this intensity was wrought more for itself than as an interpretation of a state of mind.

The earlier *London Bridge* (1906), by André Derain, is another example of Fauve painting

André Derain (1880–   ), LONDON BRIDGE, 1906
The Museum of Modern Art, New York. Gift of Mr. and Mrs. Charles Zadok.

that can be effectively contrasted with Munch's *The Scream*. Both are somewhat similar scenes, yet for all the violence, the vivid contrasts of blue, orange, yellow, and green, Derain does not create an atmosphere such as Munch provokes. In *London Bridge* Derain achieves a compositional unity by pitching all colors at their highest intensity, an effect heightened even further by the blatant juxtaposition of complementaries. But his bold mosaic of color disturbs no human being. Note that we cannot really be sure whether this painting represents a sunset, dawn, or even a murky London day, since the colors do not follow any particular law of representation. They are joined together primarily as a composition of extremely high color intensity; yet this Expressionist vocabulary is not used for the Expressionist's purpose. In Munch, color, distortion, and subject are coordinated to create a strong emotional response in the observer, and they most hauntingly succeed. *The Scream* (like *The Cry*) is an Expressionist work; none of the Fauve paintings is. In all respects except one, the Fauve style would qualify as Expressionism

Henri Matisse (1869–1954), THE RED STUDIO, 1911
The Museum of Modern Art, New York. Mrs. Simon Guggenheim Fund.

Edvard Munch (1863–1944), THE CRY, 1895

—it lacks the sense of tragedy.

The preoccupation of the Expressionists with tragedy and horror raises a fundamental problem. Along with the general characteristics of Expressionism there was another unsought characteristic which was probably responsible for a lack of popular appeal and the scandals which the new style provoked. This was, to quote Read, the absence of "*conventional notions of beauty.*"

In the tradition of Western European art the concept of beauty has, with many variations, normally contained an element of idealization, tracing its ancient lineage from Greece and Rome, through its codification in seventeenth-century France in the work of Poussin, to nineteenth-century Academicism. But with the advent of twentieth-century art this concept of beauty underwent a profound change. The Expressionists, even more than the Fauves, repudiated all idealization, both in the selection of subject matter and in its interpretation. Beauty idealized was basically antithetical to their attachment to a subjective emotional interpretation of experience.

Here again, however, historical parallels come to mind. The great Spanish artist, Francisco Goya, portrayed the impact of war on Spain during the Napoleonic period. His series of etchings entitled *The Disasters of War* shows all the horror

Francisco Goya y Lucientes (1746–1828), LOS DESASTRES DE LA GUERRA, No. 26, No se puede mirar
The Cleveland Museum of Art, Dudley P. Allen Collection, 1922

of physical mutilation and death as well as the loss of moral responsibility in a society caught in a titanic struggle. Other examples of sinister or horrific subject matter successfully wedded to art are Gros' *Pest House at Joppa,* Mantegna's *Dead Christ,* Daumier's *Rue Transnonain,* and many a scene of medieval martyrdom in Flemish, Italian, and Spanish art. But these examples are too literal for Expressionism; only in our times does the tragedy turn inward, the artist offering himself as the martyr of his own experience.

Frequently, critics attached to conventional beauty attack Expressionist work obliquely in terms of what they consider technical shortcomings, rather than for the choice of subject matter. In such instances, the innovations developed by the artist are brought under fire. Such criticism, for example, might concentrate on the rough, unkempt, and unfinished lines of the woodblocks in Ernst Ludvig Kirchner's *Peter Schlemihl* * series; yet the uncomfortableness of subject matter and the shock of unconventional technical devices are indivisible elements in Expressionist work. As such they must be discussed at some length.

At first sight Kirchner's prints may look like welters of confusion, somewhat messy conglomerations of forms. The roughness of execution, the complexity of shapes, and the broad sloppy smears of color are all nevertheless helpful in creating the total impact and in clarifying the theme of the pictures. The *Peter Schlemihl* prints distinctly

* Plate 8.

Honoré Daumier (1808–1879), RUE TRANSNONAIN, LE 15 AVRIL 1834
The Cleveland Museum of Art. Gift of Ralph King, 1924.

Daumier spent a lifetime as an illustrator; his medium was the lithograph. He began with bold political commentaries, such as our powerfully drawn illustration of needless police brutality. He was imprisoned for his attacks on the government of Louis Philippe and changed to themes of social satire. In his old age he gave up illustration to become one of the nineteenth century's greatest painters.

show the marks of the cutting tools used to gouge the surface of the wood block. The artist apparently wanted this unfinished effect, just as he needed the stark contrasts between the black and white of the ink and paper to vivify his impression of his work, to catch the unrefined violence of the passion which is the theme of the series. As van Gogh exploited the brush strokes of his oil technique for his own expressive purpose, so Kirchner exploited the qualities of the woodcut. He was one of the first modern artists to revive the woodcut technique and to make out of it an artistic medium powerful enough to compete with the more traditional oils.

When we come to the subject matter of this print, the seventh and last of the series of illustrations, *Schlemihl's Encounter with the Shadow*, the two important elements are certainly the pallid blue figure, his arms outstretched, knees bent, and feet pointed down in a posture of jumping or leaping, and the elongated black figure, legs flung wide apart as though bounding away from the blue figure. From the latter emanate diagonal bright red lines like an extra pair of arms to aid him in catching, in overtaking the elusive dark phantom. The slashes of black and

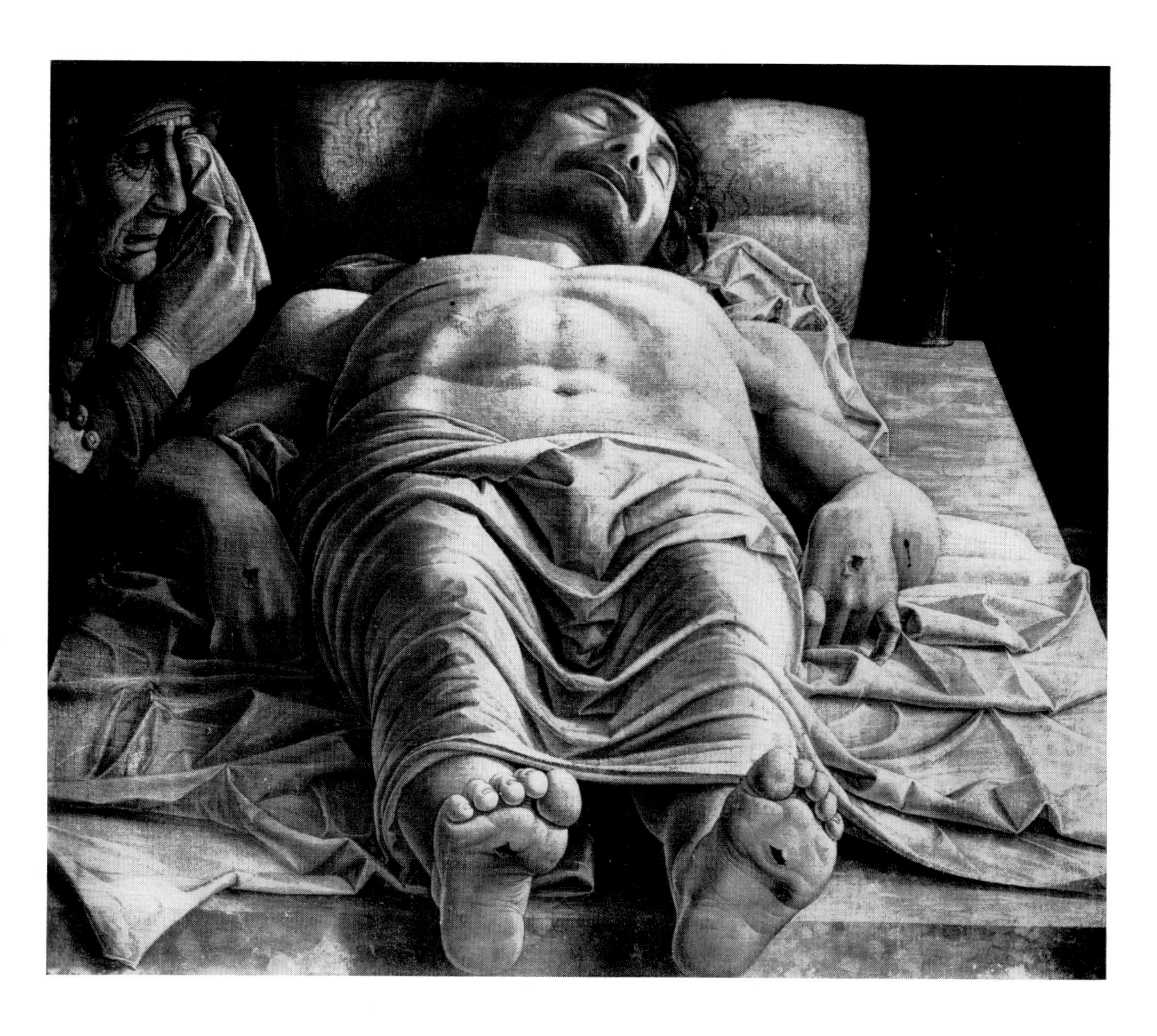

Andrea Mantegna (1431–1506), DEAD CHRIST AND MARY,
The Brera Gallery, Milan.

hot yellow, splotches of intense green and accents of vermilion, form no recognizable setting yet heighten the violence of the central action. The quarry evades the desperate pursuer and remains just out of his reach; certainly the scene is a tragic one—the pursuit is shown to be fruitless and frustrated.

Kirchner's print is sufficient in itself without needing additional explanatory material, but since it was made as an illustration, it is interesting to know the plot of the story. *Peter Schlemihl* was written in 1813 by Adalbert von Chamisso, an expatriate Frenchman in Prussia at the time of the Napoleonic wars. The story is a romantic nightmare dealing with a poor scholar, Peter Schlemihl, who sells his shadow to a devilish old gray-man in return for an inexhaustible purse of gold. In the course of his travels, Peter falls in love with a peasant's daughter, but he cannot consummate his passion because the girl's parents discover he has no shadow. The gray-man appears at this moment and provides the moral climax of the plot by offering to return Peter's shadow in exchange for his soul. The victim, ravaged by conflict, ultimately refuses and saves his soul at the expense of his desire, even though he knows that he will never be accepted again as a member of human society. This is the psychological drama of conflict and tragedy that Kirchner compressed into his woodcut. The Expressionist means, so effectively employed here, evoke our sympathy for Peter's torment and anguish as he vainly attempts to jump into his shadow and recapture his own humanity in order to gain the happiness he forfeited by selling his shadow for gold.

The Departure * by Max Beckmann was painted some twenty years later. An outstanding example of Expressionist painting, it shows the impact of the intervening developments in European art, particularly those concerned with symbolism and psychology. Nevertheless, the emphasis on recognizable thematic material and the subject matter chosen, point to the artist's concern with the interpretation of events through evoked emotion.

Beckmann is indebted to his German predecessors of the sixteenth century, who worked in the highly emotional yet conventionalized style of the late Gothic. The particular way in which Beckmann breaks up the even flow of space and keys all objects together in relation to the picture plane, rather than to depth, is the result of his intimate knowledge of the work of such a man as Martin Schongauer. The very fact that his picture is divided into three parts is indicative of his allegiance to the earlier German school. During the Middle Ages and up through the Baroque period it was not uncommon for altar pictures to have several painted wings which could be closed and opened, covering or revealing the pictures on certain religious holidays. It was certainly no accident that Beckmann selected the format of a triptych, or three-paneled picture, not only for *The Departure* but for many of his other important and mature works. This form, because of its traditional role, suggests that the painting reveals a major truth or message concerning matters of ultimate moral import. The following quotation from Beckmann's writings indicates the artist's obsession with moral problems, and describes his attitude both towards his own work and towards himself as an individual.

"*And then I awoke and yet continued to dream —painting constantly appeared to me as the one and only possible achievement. I thought of my grand old friend, Henri Rousseau, that Homer in the porter's lodge whose prehistoric dreams have sometimes brought me near the gods. I saluted him in my dream. Near him I saw William Blake, noble emanation of English genius. He waved friendly greetings to me like a super-terrestrial patriarch. 'Have confidence in objects,' he said, 'do not let yourself be intimidated by the horror of the world. Everything is ordered and correct and must fulfill its destiny in order to attain perfection. Seek this path and you will attain from your own ego even deeper perception of the eternal beauty of creation; you will attain increasing release from all that which now seems to you sad or terrible.'*" [2]

Max Beckmann started work on *The Departure* in Frankfurt, Germany, in 1932, just after the Nazis came to power. Forced to stop working publicly as an artist, Beckmann, out of a job, retreated to the great city of Berlin, where he lost himself in the multitudes and for a while was left alone. He finished the picture in 1935 and labelled it *Scenes from Shakespeare's "Tempest"* to confuse any Nazi investigators. He stowed the picture in his attic until 1937, when he was suddenly obliged to flee to Holland. Later he escaped Nazi persecution by seeking asylum in England, and eventually he found a haven in the United States.

Although the general theme of the picture is departure, there is very little specific action in any of the panels. In the central one, for instance, the hooded figure only makes an ambiguous gesture; on the right the drummer is the only one in

* Plate 9.

motion; and on the left a man holds up a bludgeon, but whether its arrested movement is upwards or downwards is not determined. The general vertical lines strengthen the effect of stillness. The violence of action and emotion have passed their climax; only the conclusion, or conclusive act, remains.

The three panels depict "the horror of the world" and possibly the "release from all that which now seems to you sad and terrible." On the left is an interior with three columns at the back. Facing one of these is a man standing in a barrel of liquid which rises to his crotch and barely touches his manacled hands. Next to him sits a gagged male figure whose mutilated arms are stumps strapped together over his head. Below, and to the left, is a pleasant still-life of an apple, a bunch of grapes, and a green pear. To the right, a dark man wields a bludgeon, and at the bottom, bound and kneeling over a round green object, is the figure of a young woman.

The panel on the right is just as hallucinatory. At the bottom a man with a drum passes before a yellow balustrade. On the platform above stands a woman, holding an oil lamp, lit, but shedding no light. So tightly bound to her as to be mistaken for part of her body is a man upside down, whose feet flap against her face. On the right, a blindfolded bellboy holds an enormous green fish. Behind is an arch-like proscenium with a series of verticals which look like a theater curtain and to the left are flights of steps. Almost unseen on the stage is a nude little boy.

The central panel contrasts with the others in its simplicity of organization and its broad areas of harmonious color. The people here are neither tortured nor bound. The woman's face is the only one of the entire picture to be seen fully and clearly. In front of her is a golden-haired child standing on the lap of a half-glimpsed attendant; while on the other side of the boat, a man in a blue mantle, a crown on his head, trails a net of fish over the gunwale. To his left is a heavily shrouded male figure stretching out a hand over an unused oar.

The painting itself offers no further specific clue to explain the drama or to clarify the relations of the figures. The most that can be definitely said is that the scene on the left of revolting physical torture is a pendant to the maddeningly illogical episode on the right. These contrast strongly with the central event of the departure. But who is traveling, and with whom, and in what direction? These questions are not answered. In spite of these baffling ambiguities, however, we cannot escape the sense of import, of moral judgment. All action seems arrested by the intensity of the artist's feeling. The painting cries out mutely, perhaps offers release, barely suggests the existence of hope.

Whatever the specific meaning of *The Departure* may be, it will have an additional, different meaning for each observer. Beyond such general statements as those made above, we cannot go with certainty. The ambiguity in the painting need not obscure the issues of the discussion, for we have been considering the nature and the claims of "beauty," as they may fuse or conflict with emotional content. We may well go on from here to a more profound matter—the relation of art to morality, and indeed the relation of art to life itself.

1. Herbert Read, *The Philosophy of Modern Art,* New York, The Noonday Press, 1955, p. 51.
2. Perry T. Rathbone, *Max Beckmann* (catalogue of exhibition), St. Louis, City Art Museum of St. Louis, 1948, p. 43.

Oskar Kokoschka (1886–),
SELF PORTRAIT, 1913
The Museum of Modern Art, New York. Purchase.

Kokoschka shows us a gaunt and haunted self, painted with the exaggerated freedom of the Expressionist. A moonlit quality and attenuated forms are owing to the influence of El Greco.

Henri Matisse (1869–1954), THE BLUE NUDE, 1907
The Baltimore Museum of Art. Cone Collection.

Matisse lived in a brilliant world of color and freedom. His forms are exaggerated, spontaneous generalizations. With great artistry he created the impression of impulsiveness and concealed a deliberate control.

FIVE

The Creation of New Symbols

THE ISSUES of this chapter are best raised by starting with a specific painting —Picasso's *Girl Before a Mirror.** The preoccupation with formal spacing and pattern which is characteristic of Cubism here seems to have a rival interest: we find an image charged with sensual elements, and with a curiosity about itself which gets only an ambiguous response. A distorted two-faced image confronts an answering image further distorted by the mirror. Does this image add up to a personality? An individual? An archetype—All-Women? Why are the colors bold, the forms violent? Does the painting seem essentially disquieting?

These questions are raised by the intense contrasts. We are struck by the painting's basic division or split: the composition is in two lobes. This division is carried further in the left (or real) head, which presents two contrasting faces, one silver, one gold, one full face, one profile, a sun face, and a moon, night face. There seems also a contradiction between clothed and naked: although the figure is clothed, symbols of nudity force themselves on our attention. The contrasts of harsh color, of light against dark, underline these basic dualities. Either the painting must be left in conflict with itself, or the conflict must be resolved by the psychological tying together of the two images.

In a personality, the harmonious unity of conflicting elements is called sanity. We are led to ask if the artist has healed the split in the composition; and if the images fuse, is it not precisely because they are different, because they do not reflect, as much as they complement, each other? —because the girl (perhaps already a symbol) sees a symbol of herself, rather than a reflection? (See also pp. 135–136.)

Let us turn to the contemporary philosopher, Ernst Cassirer, whose contribution to modern thought is the redefining of man as the user of symbols. "*Man cannot escape from his own achievement. . . . No longer in a merely physical universe, man lives in a symbolic universe. Language, myth, art, and religion are parts of this universe. They are the varied threads which weave the symbolic net, the tangled web of human experience.*" [1]

Webster defines the symbol: "*That which suggests something else by reason of relationship, association, convention, etc.: especially a visible sign of something invisible, as an idea, a quality, an emblem; as, the lion is the symbol of courage.*" Or, as white is the symbol of purity, red of love, green of happiness. These are general symbols. There are also private symbols which only work for the artist. In a sense all symbols are private, in that nothing means the same thing to any two people. For instance, literature is an experience shared, but every family has certain anecdotes or experiences which have charged a few expressions with private meaning; and so it is with artists. Even though private symbols do not communicate directly, they are rich in implication: they give away personality, they convey character or mood, they betray the artist's compelling interest.

Some periods of art are rich in symbolism, others in naturalism. Symbolism seems to have grown with this century's interest in the mind. The nineteenth century was more literal. Its confidence was in the literary, or the photo-

* Plate 10.

graphic, or in the scientific view in the days when science still gave us a world we could recognize. Still, there were nineteenth-century symbolists—take the French painter, Odilon Redon, who was born in 1840 and lived until 1916.

In Redon's *Silence* we have an image standing for an invisible thing. "*No one can deny me the merit*," wrote Redon, "*of having given the illusion of life to my most unreal creations. My whole originality, therefore, consists in having made improbable beings live humanly, according to the laws of the probable, by as far as possible*

Odilon Redon (1840–1916), SILENCE
The Museum of Modern Art, New York. Lillie P. Bliss Collection.

putting the logic of the visible at the service of the invisible." [2]

In this painting, Redon creates his effect quite simply, by gesture and the expression of the face. Yet the heavy oval frame or enclosure certainly plays a part in giving the painting its withdrawn, secretive air. The oval enclosure has an old history in art and reminds us of the Byzantine mosaics. The oval symbolized the enshrinement of an image and made it sacred, just as a niche enshrined a statue. It symbolized what was eternal, of another world. By contrast, the modern psychologist would say that this heavy oval framing is a symbol of life in the womb, offering us an image at once quieting (because unborn) and disquieting (because observed).

Similar heavy oval framings occur in Picasso's painting; this is worth noting, however the works may differ in other respects; and perhaps these ovals make the image prisoner and add a certain mystery. Picasso was at one time strongly influenced by the art of Byzantium, and *Girl before a Mirror* has the dramatic coloring and bold outlines of a Byzantine mosaic. Byzantine in influence or not, Picasso's painting seems much nearer to us than Redon's; and it is doubtless the literary quality of Redon's symbolism, as though it illustrated a poem of the time, that takes the work back into the nineteenth century. You may want to consider the extent to which *Silence* depends for its other-worldly effect on its title.

Van Gogh's *The Starry Night* is closer to the painting of our time in its heavy plastic qualities, yet its literary symbolism holds it in its own epoch. Van Gogh preaches a sermon on man's condition, a sermon raised to the level of Biblical language by the intensity of his genius. The church spire, the cypress that rivals the spire and for van Gogh symbolizes death (as he confessed in his letters), both point to the stars that gyrate and spin with the artist's ecstasy—which is his anxiety transformed. In van Gogh's late work the principle of composition is the vortex, a pattern that emerges from the pressure of powerful emotion, as psychologists tell us. Note that we also find vortices, although in quite different terms, in *Girl before a Mirror*. Circular forms rotate within larger circular forms. Perhaps *The Starry Night* helps us to feel that Picasso's painting owes some of its intensity to these gyrations.

The "visible at the service of the invisible" was also the essential subject for de Chirico, whose early paintings, typified by his *Delights of the Poet*, are a chapter in psychological autobiography. This Italian painter, born in Greece, lost his father at an early age, and whatever the family drama or circumstances may have been, the artist's vision was turned toward the past. There is everywhere an anxious search for security, and we often feel the presence of some menacing figure who is just out of sight and only known by the shadow he casts into the picture. The painter's anxiety calls for immobility—we pray that nothing will happen—and in de Chirico everything is static and transfixed at a late hour of the afternoon, as though the observer were warding off the shadows of night.

Architecture serves de Chirico as the symbol for an imposing Italianate past, and empty architecture for loneliness and quandary. Endless arcades lead nowhere. Clocks are a frequent reminder of time; and, in fact, time seems to be the basic subject matter. "Too late" could be the title of most of these paintings; and a train or locomotive is frequently introduced in the background, symbolizing departure, a word which also comes into the artist's titles. The one figure on the scene is solitary and bewildered. There is no clear direction for him. Even the perspective is strange.

What impression do you take away from this picture? Face yourself with moral antitheses: Are you here free or fated, fearless or fearful, innocent or guilty? Is there any exit? Is any motion possible at all?

Does the painting suggest any experience of your own, recent or remote? We might consider how it is that we can be moved by an image of things that may never have entered our lives. Has the artist "put across" his private experience in terms which speak to some private experience of yours?

By the time you have turned over such questions, you will surely find yourself thinking about symbols. However the artist has managed it, he seems to raise the question of the flight of time and what it can mean to us. The language is *space*, but the communication is *time*. What cannot be seen has to be shown by what can be seen.

De Chirico's fear-ridden symbolism is very different from Picasso's. Yet in Picasso's painting we also are confronted with some tension between seen and unseen. The relation between face and mind has its own ominousness; the face which looks back from the mirror is significant to the degree that it differs from the face that looks in. Something far more primeval than the world of de Chirico stares back from the mirror.

For most of the human race, childhood seems

a relatively blessed time, at least in retrospect, and people are loved for being childlike. Chagall is homesick for his childhood, and in his early *I and My Village,** it is a real, remembered childhood, not de Chirico's anxious state which the psychologists relate to forgotten experiences. Chagall tells us his recollections with the innocence and frankness of a guileless poetic nature, and in this he resembles the Danish story-teller, Hans Christian Andersen.

A great deal is taking place in his painting. We have only to add up the incidents. Most seem fantastic, but it is true that man and animal live in the same world and recognize each other at sight, so there must be some common denominator of personality which allows them to communicate. Chagall gives us the resemblances between living creatures which a child sees and accepts. An animal is a person, too, and it is true that there is something animal about us all. But here the artist goes beyond mere confrontation of beast and man. For the child, people and animals are on a common footing, leading their daily lives together. Chagall even shows us, literally, what is in the animal's head. The animal and the child Chagall can even share a joke: people and houses, too, can be stood on their

* Plate 11.

Giorgio de Chirico (1888–), DELIGHTS OF THE POET, 1913
The Museum of Modern Art, New York. Acquired through the Lillie P. Bliss Bequest.

heads. Grown people imagine they have ordered the world, but child and animal know better. We are beginning to see whose world it is in the picture—whose world is right side up. It is diverting to discover the pictorial means that tie these anecdotes and incidents together. We can enjoy the arbitrary use of color. The color, like the little figure, is simply inverted. Perhaps the man's head is green because green is an inviting color to the animal.

All this seems in innocent contrast to Picasso's painting. Yet in Chagall, the confrontation of the large heads of man and animal is profound as well as innocent. The sheep or goat has an eye that is primarily human. The man has something of a sheep's eye. Recognition moves from one to the other on the dotted line. The sheep's mouth, too, has a human expression. We are not so far, perhaps, from the figure confronting itself in the mirror. We are again dealing with visible signs of mysterious relationships.

At first, the symbols in *Around the Fish* by Paul Klee seem very private indeed. He offers us a number of objects, which appear to be treasures of arbitrary value, like the things which collect in a small boy's pocket. This is doubtless true enough, but Klee is the sympathetic adult who leads his juvenile self by the hand. He is always slipping in some wry, mature philosophy by way of self-education.

To begin with the fish:—it is worth remembering that when the young Klee went to Italy to study, what struck him most was the aquarium at Naples. Klee is reminding us that life itself comes from the sea, that there was once a "sea around us" in the closest sense, and that we do begin with the fish. The painting seems to center on two fish which may well stand for our remote first parents.

Underwater images floating and luminous were convenient symbols for this sensitive artist, who gave us the silent world of the fantasies and impulses which float through the mind. What is *submerged*, we are told, is a universal symbol of what is less than conscious. Our ancestral fish, in his blurred, nearsighted universe, has not been left behind, after all.

Yet we emerged, and this emergence Klee dramatizes with an exclamation point. Suddenly, there is *man*, with gaunt features, as though already the victim of thought. After this miracle, man begins his counterclockwise voyage around the fish. The column on the left, if column it is, tumbles and lets man down; another column climbs on the right. Are these columns first pagan and then Christian, since we climb toward a cross in the upper right of the picture? Doubtless this is explaining too much and overriding the private symbols which give Klee's art such a personal quality. Yet it is clear that this evolutionary cycle from fish to man reaches a symbol of the Trinity along with the cross, before we come to the heaven of sun and moon. So Klee gives us a little history of man, beginning with zoology and ending with religion.

Circle and crescent, sun and moon as they undoubtedly are here, are persistent images in the painting of Klee, which suggests that they are private as well as general symbols and that they mean something special to him. Sun and moon, close together as here, are often presented with the crescent set horizontal, a wide cap over the circle, the combined image inescapably that of the eye and its lid—in any photograph of Klee, his dominant eyes are the feature which seizes our attention. So we suspect that we are not faced with a choice between obvious and private symbol, but that circle and crescent are always in some degree sun and moon, the sources of light, and in some degree the organ of sight. Symbols, however private, add meaning to the work of art.

The artist, says Klee, "*is, perhaps unintentionally, a philosopher, and if he does not, with the optimists, hold this world to be the best of all possible worlds, nor to be so bad that it is unfit to serve as a model, yet he says:*

"*'In its present shape it is not the only possible world.'*

"*Thus he surveys with penetrating eye the finished forms which nature places before him.*

"*The deeper he looks, the more readily he can extend his view from the present to the past, the more deeply he is impressed with the one essential image of creation itself, as Genesis, rather than by the image of nature, the finished product.*" [3]

Ask yourself if Klee is altogether serious in *Around the Fish*. Is this satire? Is his painting religious or irreligious? If you wish to argue this point, Klee will offer support for either side. A temperament with perceptions so subtle is not content with a single answer. To be all things to all people is one of the virtues (and vices) of the sophisticated; and it has kept Paul Klee a genius in a minor key.

Once more, let us disregard great differences in temperament to see if our experience with Klee helps us to discover something more in Picasso's *Girl before a Mirror*. Sun and moon for Picasso equal face, for Klee equal eye. For both, there is an equation between light and sight. As in Genesis, the creation of light leads to our creation.

But Picasso opens up something which Klee passes over. Face is a symbol of mind, and mind contains all history. The shining, day and night face of the woman is not the deeper face which looks back from the mirror. The glass gives back a proud predatory beak, akin to the Egyptian hawk-headed deity. Picasso begins with surface, only to move inward. He makes it his task to reflect back the basic aggressive impulses which he feels must be our deepest definition—or we would not have survived at all.

Picasso's *Seated Woman* was painted five years earlier than *Girl before a Mirror,* and they are similar in style. The heavy ovals, the same fluent indications of arms and hands, suggest an established procedure (and therefore a purpose) rather than the result of unconsidered spontaneity. *Seated Woman* is if anything the more distorted of the two examples.

Consider the number of heads, or positions of head. There are at least four: two facing each other and sharing the same profile, and two full face—or perhaps one head is seen from the back, so that the figure accomplishes a full revolution.

We are now familiar with stroboscopic photographs showing many stages of a single act: for instance, a man swinging at a golf ball. We know that it was part of Picasso's Cubism of an earlier date to show more than one aspect of an object.

Paul Klee (1879–1940), AROUND THE FISH, 1926
The Museum of Modern Art, New York. Mrs. John D. Rockefeller, Jr., Fund.

So when we ask ourselves what is gained by this multiplicity, this doubling or trebling of an image, we are probably ready with the one-word answer, "motion," or the shorter word, "life."

Yet this painting also differs from Cubism. One obvious difference, of course, lies in the flowing and sweeping lines and contours found here, so at variance with the use of straight lines and precise planes in Cubism. This formal difference is overshadowed by a different degree of vitality. The Cubist forms seem much more passive—at most they flutter a little. Here, on the contrary, there is a figure which appears to move and swirl of its own accord. There is a shift from passive objects—the chessmen in a game of ideas—to an active entity, not an individual to be recognized, yet somehow a living creature.

Do you agree with this statement? In other words, do you feel that this figure has the capacity to move? Do you feel that she is a generalization like womankind, rather than an individual? If a generalization can live for you, the world of symbols lies open before you.

With this in mind, come back to the *Girl before a Mirror*. Here there is gesture in the arms rather than motion in the head, and the gesture makes the arm lines sweep, or the sweep of the brush makes the arm move in imitation. The head has more definite features, since it has the employment of looking; yet somehow it still escapes being a particular person. If this seems strange, think of the world of Greek divinities with their idealized faces. A little reflection will suggest that image makers were not primarily concerned with portraiture until the time of the Renaissance.

The girl looking, then, is a type; and the girl who looks back at her is an *archetype*, as the psychologist would say. This painting is a kind of psychological Cubism showing us simultaneously more than one aspect of ourselves. The White Queen on the Cubist chessboard looks and sees that she is also the Dark Queen.

At this point, we may well ask: does this essay, in its endeavor to provide meaning for *Girl before a Mirror*, only go to prove that the meaning of the painting is lacking, or so inadequate that we are driven to such far-fetched explanations? It is well known, for instance, that the psychoanalytic experience presents (among other effects) the experience of progressive discoveries dealing with human nature. It may be argued that this sense of psychological illumination parallels or resembles the experience which the artist provides, but has little to do with art. Many other things besides works of art are symbolic. Such a discussion—or dissection—as ours, may only take the interest away from the essential art aspect in the painting.

Perhaps we have traveled away from the painting, led, or misled, by our absorption in unraveling symbols, when symbols are everywhere, in good painting and bad, and in man's every gesture. Perhaps it takes quite different considerations to bring us back to the painting. Value and quality, we may argue, have nothing to do with symbols. They depend more on the painter's technical resources, and on the character of his genius.

Let us catalogue some of the qualities or characteristics of these paintings and painters. *Girl before a Mirror* has a violence, an incisiveness, a boldness of execution which convey precisely the concentration and tension which makes this painting a great work of art. Nothing is diffuse or indirect. Everywhere we feel the dominance of Picasso's creative will. Judged in terms of strong purpose, this is a work of technical excellence.

So it is with Redon, who possesses the skill necessary for a contrary effect: all seems done without effort. It is creation by means of (apparent) ineffable accident—the pollen brushed off from the butterfly is enough to insure the immortality of the flower.

De Chirico, more literary, speaks to us with images which are almost half-forgotten episodes; Chagall offers anecdotes. Space is none the less controlled, the eye is guided from incident to incident. We are never allowed to pause, or stumble.

The subtle surfaces of Redon, the organizational qualities of de Chirico or Chagall, combine in Paul Klee. He must be effortless, since he chooses to be sardonic; being sardonic, he must be profoundly aware of relationships on all levels, not to be trivial; he must be "one who understands"—to quote one of his titles.

Yet all these qualities cannot be assessed without considering the artist's overriding purpose, and in our selections it is the conveying of *meaning* which seems to be the artist's intent. He must be *judged* as a symbolist if he is one; hence value and quality can have something to do with symbolism, after all.

Finally, it is the balance between private and universal meaning which provides a work of art with the equivalent of a total philosophy. We shall reach, in the next chapter, works in which the private aspect is stressed still further—almost to the point of breakdown in com-

Pablo Picasso (1881–   ), SEATED WOMAN, 1926–1927
The Museum of Modern Art, New York.

munication. But it is understandable that man should struggle to preserve his personal entity as the world of his own making grows larger about him—as though it were better to be mad than to be a cipher. One of the great contributions of the modern artist is that he saves the individual through privacy, that is to say, through uniqueness; and it is only in his work, which is completely untrammeled, that he preserves the ideal of unconditional freedom.

We have given, granted, a partial account in our consideration of symbolism. But we should not be afraid to take apart a major work and contemplate an aspect. It is only a lesser work which stays in fragments; the great work miraculously restores itself, and re-establishes its unity.

If we are impelled to take a thing apart, it is to find out what it means. And as surely as we ask what a thing means, we are treating it as a symbol of something else. Artists, however, are like mystics: they do not care for intermediate steps. They relate bird to man not like Darwin, but like Saint Francis.

1. Ernst Cassirer, *An Essay on Man: An Introduction to a Philosophy of Human Culture*, Garden City, New York, Doubleday & Company, Inc., 1953, p. 41.
2. Robert Goldwater and Marco Treves, Eds., *Artists on Art*, New York, Pantheon Books, Inc., 1945, p. 361.
3. Paul Klee, *Paul Klee on Modern Art*, London, Faber and Faber, Ltd., 1948, p. 45.

Jean (Hans) Arp (1888–), MOUNTAIN TABLE, ANCHORS, NAVEL, 1925
The Museum of Modern Art, New York. Purchase.

Arp goes back to the Dada revolt that ushered in the cult of the irrational, during the First World War. He produced images that suggest organic growth, rather than construction, at a time when abstract art was still dependent on geometric forms.

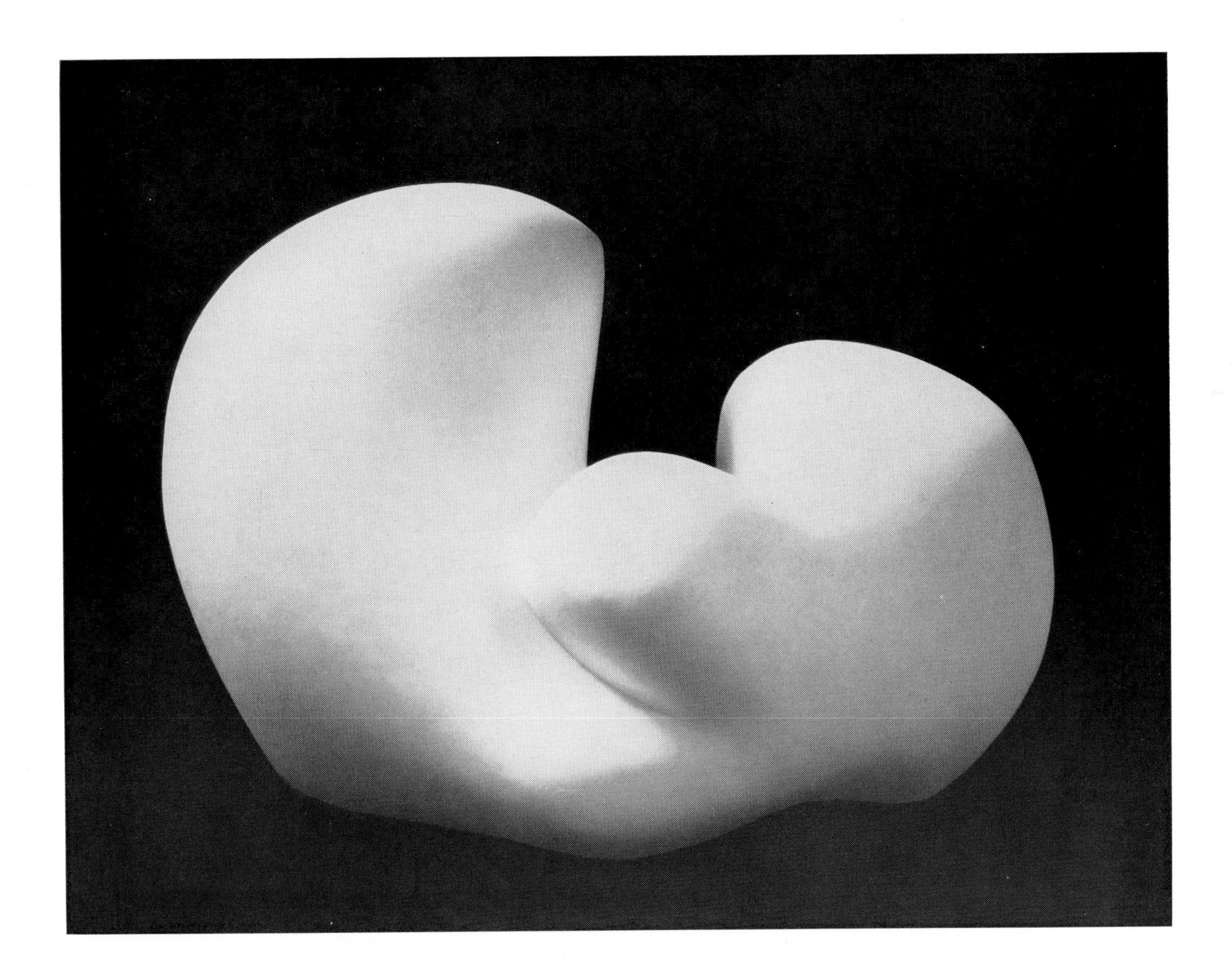

Jean (Hans) Arp (1888–), HUMAN CONCRETION, 1935
The Museum of Modern Art, New York. Gift of the Advisory Committee.

The organic metaphor is still more in evidence in Arp's work as a sculptor: he creates forms which have a living quality and yet are far removed from representation. They suggest that an emotion itself, at once imperious and blind, is their real content.

Marcel Duchamp (1880–   ), NUDE DESCENDING A STAIRCASE, No. 2, 1912.
Louise and Walter Arensberg Collection, Philadelphia Museum of Art.

SIX

Making the Mind Visible: Surrealism

THE PAINTING by Max Ernst, *Woman, Old Man and Flower,** is filled with images that are outside experience and logic. You may find yourself questioning the sincerity of the artist's motives, or even suspecting that his painting is a gag. But if you are taking the artist seriously, you will probably find yourself asking the meaning of his painting: Is the artist by any chance painting a dream?

This last question comes near to the problem of the painting. If the artist is drawing his material from the dream world, you may well go on to ask, "What do we know of the nature and meaning of dreams?" We recall what we may have read of the writings of Sigmund Freud. Not everyone has read Freud, but everyone has read about him. However, to bring in Freud is not a simple and direct answer to a question, and it is wise to get solid historical ground underfoot. If Freud has the credit for revealing certain obscure and powerful drives, artists, writers, and critics have always sensed that the rational was a very limited account of experience.

Take Marcel Duchamp's *Nude Descending a Staircase:* painted in 1912, ostensibly Cubist, the canvas gives us a series of successive images describing continuous motion, quite like stroboscopic photographs. But these successive stick figures are more than a sequence in time. They convey an uneasy impression of the unity of the figure dissolving, much as the psychiatrist resolves personality into its elements. When this picture was painted, the subconscious was beginning to break the surface, in poetry and prose, in medicine—and in art. There is no doubt that the tensions of war, when they came, added to the appeal of the irrational. In self-defense, the arts, too, strove to provide shock.

During the First World War, a deliberate obstreperousness broke out among the intelligentsia of both sides—refugees from the holocaust. Advanced writers and painters chose the meaningless word, "Dada," for a cult of unreason. They attacked all patterns of culture in a revolution intended to revolt others. Absurdity was essential, and for method they made use of "automatic" writing or painting, in which the unconscious was invited to guide a hand freed as far as possible from deliberate direction. The result was a symbolism of diagram, devoid of the atmosphere and depth which account for the plausibility of dreams.

Dada went beyond painting: "ready-mades"—objects, tools, or artifacts—were signed and exhibited. Doubtless the artists were jealous of the war which had robbed them of their audience, but at this distance the Dada absurdities and pranks, in literature, sculpture, and paint, can be seen as a significant interlude. The sculptor, Hans Arp, who was in the midst of the movement, gives an account in retrospect of the artists' intentions: *"In Zurich in 1915, losing interest in the slaughterhouses of the world war, we turned to the Fine Arts. While the thunder of the batteries rumbled in the distance, we pasted, we recited, we versified, we sang with all our soul. We searched for an elementary art that would, we thought, save mankind from the furious folly of these times. We aspired to a new order that might restore the balance between heaven and hell."* [1]

* Plate 12.

The face of appearances had become hideous and meaningless to the artist, and solid logic seemed to him no more than a habit of thought. But the realization that the subconscious, looming underneath, had its own ominous nature, which was far from absurd or meaningless—this had yet to take hold. The cult of Dada spread to Paris and Berlin after the war, and then died. By 1924 a more adult movement, Surrealism, took its place.

Surrealism was born in Paris, complete with a Manifesto written by the poet-spokesman for the painters, André Breton. The movement was literary as well as pictorial, and it undertook to systematize what was said to have no system. To do this it leaned heavily on the new psychology of Freud.

The Surrealist movement has had remarkable staying power. Max Ernst (who was also associated with Dada) has an enduring reputation, as have the Spaniards, Dali and Miró. The Surrealists claimed the early work of the Italian "metaphysical" painter, de Chirico, and the post-Cubist painting of Picasso—although Picasso had his own development and resisted such classification. Paul Klee more nearly falls into the Surrealist pattern, but Klee is a satirist who skirts the unconscious realm without trusting himself to its depths.

Max Ernst was a German student of philosophy before the First World War. After the war he was an international painter. In the Dada days he pursued the irrational with a pair of scissors, producing collages out of nineteenth-century prints by cutting out images and reassembling them in implausible and evocative compositions. These free-association essays in the odd soon gave place to more personal creations. *Woman, Old Man and Flower* is a mature work done at the very beginning of the Surrealist movement, and its muted color, its subdued, suppressed tonalities, contribute to its unity and beauty. Its themes repeat themselves like musical motifs. The painting is at once sensuous and cerebral, inhibited and filled with desire.

If we search for the title in the painting, *Woman* and *Old Man* are apparent, and we may suppose that the *Flower* is the figure whose head is a fan. The scene is a stony, barren shore, with a sea in the middle distance and an island on the horizon. There is a progression of mysterious verticals, from the pole on the left, to a vertical shaft which hides the old man's face and perhaps continues his nose as though he were an anteater, to a short turned post on the right.

The entity most alive in this picture is certainly the old man, who at least has a face. His eyes are shut, and perhaps this painting is *his* dream. He has a shell like a crustacean, cut away to show that his interior is hollow. He both holds and contains the small figure of a woman in this void in his side. We have a curious inversion here, as though it were man giving birth to woman, after the fashion of Adam, the woman here being the old man's rib.

We may suspect that the old man is a symbol of genius, of the creative. The female figure within him is then—inspiration? But that is a nineteenth-century word. She would be better named his persisting desire.

Ernst dramatizes the strangeness, the unnaturalness of masculine birthgiving via the imagination, and we may go on to ask the meaning of the old man's wooden leg. This is a common castration symbol in Freudian language. Here it serves as a check on the presumption of creative desire. On the other hand, the shaft or staff which at once supports the old man and seems to join with his head perhaps compensates him in some strange way by adding a creative dimension to his thought, or his brain.

We can now see the phantom figure in the foreground as the creation of the old man. If so, she is much stranger, more fictitious, than the woman whom he carries within him. If woman, we only surmise it from the head which is a woman's fan.

The arms are in outline: perhaps we have surprised the artist (in the painting) with his work incomplete. The image he has made remains partially drawn in. The woman's gesture although exuberant, is self-centered, turning back toward the fan, symbol of vanity and concealment.

What more can we say of this figure? As a female Frankenstein, she has little concern with her creator. She is curiously dressed, with a dream-like immodesty. It is her head that is most concealed; the upper part of her body is a jacket —which may even be a sort of lock-and-key device. And how do you explain the fact that we see right through her, each lung area cut out? She, too, is hollow, like her creator. Hollowness appears to be a major theme in this painting. It is the one thing which creator and created share.

This figure is most hollow and void where her breasts should be to indicate that she is not meant to nourish or sustain further life. She gives nothing in return for her existence. She rejects her creator. There is a similar rejection for us, in that we only see her back. In fact, she is so self-centered that she only looks at us with stud-like ornaments on the back of her headdress, or head.

Do you accept this explanation of a nightmare fantasy of the creative man and his creation? Would it be in keeping with the painter's intention if his painting meant something entirely different to you?

When we come to the painting, *Catalan Landscape (The Hunter)*,* 1923–24, by Joan Miró, a work of the same date, we find it is as frolicsome as the *Woman, Old Man and Flower* is somber. Everything in it suggests movement, gaiety, irresponsibility. These objects have a life of their own, and if they are caricatures of people, they are so distorted, so far-fetched that they are hardly recognized as such. Perhaps this is just as well. The artist is able to smuggle in a certain amount of sexual imagery under this general disguise—quite as in dreams.

So much is going on that we look for a locale, a setting for this carnival, and Miró provides one in his title: *Catalan Landscape*. Catalonia, with its capital, Barcelona, is on the Mediterranean, and this is a seaside landscape. There is a definite wavy shore, with a straight horizon line, indications of waves to the right, sea gulls winging (still to the upper right) and perhaps a flagged buoy. The sun in this sky is hot as a scorpion. The light undulates with the heat, and the sun seems to provide out of itself whatever shadow there is in the blazing scene.

The apparatus in the upper left seems to provide us with the ladder, wheel, and balancing pole of the tightrope artist. The horizon line may serve as a tightrope. Perhaps we are witnessing a circus. But we must not generalize from a single incident which may be only one of many cheerful recollections.

In any case, here is a man on the left, a large stick figure, straddle-legged. He is angular, and his head is triangular, but he has an eye, a moustache, a straggling beard, and a flaming pipe. He has hair and an ear, and the slant of his head will serve for a nose. His arms wave; one points toward the head of a child, the other waves a flag and indicates the cone and ball symbols which recall to some of us the trylon and perisphere of the pre-war New York World's Fair.

The man's gesture is clearly for someone's benefit, but the creature to the right seems quite simply an egg. At least she is feminine and she has definitely something to offer: a beam of eye, and a green heart that flies out of her body. It is obvious that she eyes the gifts he offers—she is not indifferent to the conversation.

* Plate 13.

There is a lower level to this painting. A long figure lies prone, with a head, hair, eye and perhaps a tongue to the right, perhaps a triangular skirt to the left. Somewhere in between swims a tadpole form. To the far lower left someone has set up his flag. As you look to right and left in the middle distance, there are other pyramids and spheres staked out, and other tadpoles—a favorite entity in Miró's painting. We do not have to tax our imaginations to see the paraphernalia of a cheerful, erotic dream.

Catalan Landscape has, however, received quite a different interpretation, more closely based on its subtitle, *The Hunter*. This interpretation is provided by the museum which owns the painting: "*The letters SARD refer to the sardana, a Catalan dance, and from a top-shaped ship at sea flies the Spanish naval flag. The picture's subtitle,* The Hunter, *identifies the principal human figure who stands moustached and bearded, a pipe in his mouth, a heart palpitating in his breast; his right hand holds his leashed dog, his left a flaming gun; a trail winds before him. Across the foreground races a rabbit with frightened eye and triangular tail. In the distance is a round tree with a leaf and beyond that the hunter's eye or perhaps the sun, the 'eye of day,' as Shakespeare put it.*" [2]

This interpretation returns us to the painting with misgivings, making us pause in our free translation of private symbols. Is the egg of the first interpretation some bovine domestic animal dreaming of a green leaf as the hunter passes? On second thought, the museum seems right. The figure in the foreground becomes definitely a rabbit—what we took for a tongue is an ear. The rabbit is elongated into a line because it is going all out. But it runs in dotted circles.

An element of composition holds the whole painting together: gay little red gestures that are flags, a bright red tongue for the rabbit, and pipe and gun have their own red tongues, too.

In logic, such contrasting views of the same work are irreconcilable. And yet it is possible that the artist is inviting us into a realm where such diverse interpretations are equally acceptable. Is it essential to differentiate, in a painting such as this, between erotic pursuit and the chase of the hunter? The special virtue, or justification, of Surrealist art is its capacity to provide pliable symbols, to have different meanings on different levels.

Nearly a decade of Surrealist painting went by

before the young Dali produced *The Persistence of Memory* * in 1931. Dali, like Miró, had come to Paris from Catalonia and had found his opportunity in the Surrealist movement. Essentially an illustrator of Freudian ideas, he must be classified as an interpretive artist. Perhaps this is why he is also close to the actor: he has a theatrical temperament, and has compounded dramatic painting with spectacular behavior. More than anyone else, he has both exploited and exhausted Surrealism, providing shock until there is no longer response. The excitement in his paintings is in inverse ratio to their size. The early small paintings, like our example, are intense; the late large paintings are of low voltage.

The Persistence of Memory offers images which invite the same approach used with *Woman, Old Man and Flower*. We have here, too, a sterile scene, with distant water, and a forbidding landscape beyond. The one tree is dead, or is a symbol of death and sterility. The plank to the left, the box-like form at the lower left, seem theater props for the drama of the tired watches and the drowned head. The draped watches, limp as bacon, are literally fly-blown, or (lower left) covered with insects, a fantasy perhaps suggested by the jewels visible in the works. In short, time is dead. No wonder the strange head is dead, too, and appears as though seen at the bottom of shallow water. Its tongue protrudes: is it death by drowning, or by thirst?—for it is not absolutely clear whether the head is on the desert or in the sea. Perhaps it is only a sleeping head: the dreamer of the painting.

If you are familiar with other Dali paintings (for he repeats himself) you will identify these watches, and the head, too, as partaking of the form of *tongues*—the protruding tongue is the key to the painting.

Perhaps this protruded or detached tongue is a symbol of death, or a sensual symbol, or both at once. If of death, remember that it is imagined or *dreamed* death.

Dali has an amazing ability as an academic draftsman: he is a counterfeit old master in the twentieth century. His skill carries him to the point of illusion and allows him to create hallucinatory paintings which rival reality. His facility with symbols has worn out Surrealism, or perhaps the subconscious world of rudimentary impulse has very few drives to illustrate. The fact remains that Surrealism has turned out to be a relatively shallow movement, although it undertook to give us the deepest perception of all.

* Plate 14.

When the Surrealists' self-explanations were over, it became clear that the writings of Sigmund Freud were their most valid text. The writings of Freud, as an imaginative achievement in the twentieth century, tower above the writings and paintings of the Surrealists; hence the derivative air of Surrealist painting, its early flights of sophistication, its use of science to enforce belief. Perhaps Dali also unconsciously wrote Surrealism's epitaph: "*Let some huge motor-cars three times as big as actual ones, be made in plaster or onyx with a thoroughness of detail greater than the most faithful moulds, let them be wrapped in women's underwear and buried in a graveyard, the spot being indicated merely by a thin yellow-coloured clock.*" [3]

Picasso and Klee were wiser in limiting their explanations of the subconscious so that they extended frontiers without losing themselves in desert mirage. Picasso, in the forefront of the ideas which were stimulating the artist after the First World War, is already in the realm of the mystery-charged with his *Three Musicians*, painted in 1921. It is a painting of contradictions, with a knife-edge balance between Cubism, which had a dying or concluded interest for Picasso, and a world of fantasy and symbol. The images are paper thin and they have no more body than if they were paper collages, but they are no less alive on that account. They have the vitality of the totem. They stand for activities—for classifications of people. We are at a carnival: the costumes suppress the bodies underneath, which are here nonexistent. Life goes over into the costumes as they put on their act.

Mask and music: disguise, and therefore irresponsibility with its attendant release. The clown, the harlequin (no new figure for Picasso), the mummer disguised as a monk, suggest the world of impulse, which has always absorbed this artist. It is his function to bring irrational life to the surface, just as did James Joyce in *Ulysses* at almost the same date. Perhaps that is why this painting is all surface.

The comedy in the painting is not far from tragedy. The Spaniard loves outward forms: they heighten his life, he will sacrifice his life for them, he will be hypnotized by cruelty in the form of a pageant—if this is comedy it is not far from the gaiety of the attendants at an *auto-da-fé*. Blacks and browns are the colors of suppression, of restraint, sober costume, and good manners.

The painting presents a paradoxical and sardonic view of life itself. We have the feeling that we are confronted with a vast disguise, that nothing is what it seems. But were we to ask what is disguised, what lies underneath, we are told "nothing." The mask is all.

Is this over-reading the painting? Certainly here is a disturbing factor: animation without embodiment. Or is this no more than a striking poster for a carnival?

Paul Klee's *The Mocker Mocked* (1930) is infinitely slighter than the Picasso. It brings out Klee's capacity to create the impression of significance with the frailest means. That this is a mocker the ironic laughing face makes clear: Klee has given us a diagram of a tangled, involved personality, turned back upon itself. Everything is re-entrant. The lines present no beginning and no end. If you follow a line, you discover that you come back to your starting point, but you have not been anywhere. It is worth while

Pablo Picasso (1881–), THREE MUSICIANS, 1921
The Museum of Modern Art, New York. Mrs. Simon Guggenheim Fund.

making a separate tracing of each line—or loop —for there are several. The mocker is composed of several loops which mean nothing in themselves. Combined, they add up to a schizophrenic diagram—a compulsive laugh—for nothing else is there. The mockery is composed of meaningless elements.

This painting must be seen in relation to Klee's thought on the line and its functions. Klee tended to see line as the basic element of form: it is the line which describes a plane. For Klee, lines are active, passive, and median or neutral. He begins with "*an active line on a walk, moving freely without goal. A walk for a walk's sake.*"[4] A median line is a line which encloses a plane; it exists not for its own sake but for the plane it describes. When a plane moves, it leaves linear traces, or passive lines. This is only a rudimentary account, but it includes a basic characteristic of Klee's thought. The artist tends to see everywhere a division into active, median, and passive: for instance, a single physical act goes from active (brain) to median (muscle) to passive (bone— upon which the muscle acts). In this drawing,

Paul Klee (1879–1940), THE MOCKER MOCKED, 1930
The Museum of Modern Art, New York. Gift of J. B. Neumann.

the rambling lines describe no plastic forms whatever. They are "median lines," and they produce a face quite literally by coincidence.

There is, of course, self-mockery in this drawing. The artist is commenting on his own nature.

It should not be forgotten that Surrealism began as a literary movement as well as an art movement. It exploited free association, drew on irrational depths, and its source material, logically its *only* source material, was autobiography. If we are to understand such painting, we should add to it a fragment written by Max Ernst not long after he painted *Woman, Old Man and Flower*. Here the artist furnishes an antechamber in the haunted palace of Joyce or Kafka.

"I see before me a panel, very rudely painted with wide black lines on a red ground, representing false mahogany and calling forth associations of organic forms (menacing eye, long nose, great head of a bird with thick black hair, etc.).

"In front of the panel, a glossy black man is making gestures, slow, comical and, according to my memories of a very obscure epoch, joyously obscene. This rogue of a fellow wears the turned-up moustaches of my father.

"After having executed some leaps in slow motion, legs spread, knees drawn up, torso bent forward, he smiles and draws from the pocket of his trousers a fat crayon in a soft material which I find I cannot describe more precisely. He sets to work: panting violently he hurriedly traces the black lines on the panel of false mahogany. He quickly imparts to it new forms, forms which are at once surprising and abject. He accentuates the resemblance to ferocious or vicious animals to such a point that he extracts from it living creatures that fill me with horror and anguish. Content with his art, the fellow tosses his creations in the air, then gathers them in a kind of vase which he paints, intentionally, on the inside. He whirls the contents of the vase by stirring it, faster and faster, with his fat crayon. The vase itself, in whirling, becomes a top. The crayon becomes a whip. Now I realize that this strange painter is my father. He wields the whip with all his force and accompanies his movements with terrible gasps of breath, comparable to the snorts of an enormous and enraged steam-engine. With fiendish passion he causes the top to whirl and leap around my bed, that abominable top which contains all the horrors that my father is capable of evoking in an amiable panel of false mahogany by means of his frightful soft crayon. . .

"The well-known game of purely optical representations which obsesses us in half-sleep quickly becomes a procession of normally clad men and women which departs from a distant horizon toward my bed. Before arriving, the participants separate: the women pass to the right, the men to the left. Curious, I lean toward the right so that not one face shall escape me. Moreover, I am struck by the extreme youth of all these women; and later by the fact that the persons in question are always the same, only the head changing a little, the identity never. In scrutinizing them carefully, face by face, I realize my error: among these women many are of a 'certain age,' some really old and only two or three very young, perhaps 18 years of age, the age expedient to my puberty.

"I am too occupied by the women to give any attention to those passing on the men's side. But I know without seeing that I shall now commit the contrary error: all these gentlemen begin by frightening me with their precocious senility and their remarkable ugliness, but upon close examination only my father, among all these, bears the traits of an old man." [5]

It is a question how far we can go in interpreting imagery which only a psychoanalyst could trace to its source, and that only after hours and years of contact with the artist's mind. Perhaps we should respect the artist's need to be obscure, and not let ourselves be enticed by will-o'-the-wisp images into quagmires which cannot be traversed. If so, then Paul Klee may be right in staying on the subconscious margin—he puts one foot into the quicksands, and draws back.

Many psychoanalysts have chosen to comment on art and the artist. "No *analyst*," writes Daniel Schneider, "*can fail to recognize the special danger—the narcissistic danger threatening the artist—a danger which is closely connected with the content of art and with what might be termed the personal illusions and delusions to which the artist is subject.*

"Freud noted this particularly. The artist's predisposion to neurosis and perversion is a very real thing—notably in a world where artistically sensitive transformational powers may be cruelly mutilated by all kinds of ignorance, superstition and viciousness, from childhood up—let alone the fact that no society yet exists which makes full economic and intellectually liberated provision for artistic work in the formative years of an artist's life. Only the most powerful, stubborn and fortunate artists have come through the very real economic (and emotional) holocaust of their lives—and even these not without visible and invisible scars. . .

Joan Miró (1893–), DUTCH INTERIOR, 1928
The Museum of Modern Art, New York. Mrs. Simon Guggenheim Fund.

Miró was at one time influenced by the little Dutch masters, and he has transformed their sober domestic comedies into something as eye-catching and as artificial as a ballet.

"Freud stated that the artist is a man who cannot accept the renunciation of instinctual gratifications in the way it is first demanded of him, that this refusal to renounce is a constant source of fantasy, and finally that with his special gifts he knows how to find his way back to reality and so to mold his fantasy as to force the world to accord his art the merit of being valid and a source of joy." [6]

We are being led into very broad generalizations. If we pursue these ideas further, we must ask whether symbolism is characteristic of Surrealist art alone; or whether it is characteristic of *all* art, paradoxically most potent where it is least recognized (and therefore least conscious); giving meaning to the work of the abstract painter, and rational explanation to that difficult word, "form."

1. Hans Arp, *On My Way: Poetry and Essays 1912 . . . 1947*, Documents of Modern Art Vol. 6, New York, Wittenborn, Schultz, Inc., 1948, p. 39.
2. Alfred H. Barr, Jr., Ed., *Masters of Modern Art,* New York, The Museum of Modern Art, 1954, p. 142.
3. Max Ernst, *Beyond Painting and Other Writings by the Artist and His Friends,* Documents of Modern Art Vol. 7, New York, Wittenborn, Schultz, Inc., 1948, p. 22.
4. Paul Klee, *Pedagogical Sketchbook,* New York, Frederick A. Praeger, 1953, p. 16.
5. Max Ernst, *op. cit.*, pp. 3–4.
6. Daniel E. Schneider, *The Psychoanalyst and the Artist,* New York, Farrar, Straus and Company, 1949, pp. 139–141.

SEVEN

Abstract Expressionism

THE NEWEST type of painting in the modern tradition is Abstract Expressionism. It began in New York around 1944. Poured into the crucible of the city had been all the experience of Americans with modern art. Present were not only eminent native artists, but also Europeans with established reputations—refugees from Fascist Spain, Nazi Germany and Occupied France. Their meetings with each other brought about interchanges on all levels of thought and practice. Out of this ferment came not an adaptation of a trend formalized abroad but a new style of painting created in America.

In founding Abstract Expressionism painters broke with many traditional influences. Philosophically some of them were ranging far from the Greco-Semitic tradition of Western civilization. In the Pacific Northwest, for example, Mark Tobey had developed an interest in Oriental art and theology, particularly Zen Buddhism. His work shows the attempt to find unity and truth discoverable through intuition and contemplation. The work of other Abstract Expressionist painters has been interpreted as a statement of Existentialism.

Incessant innovation has been characteristic of twentieth-century art, and earlier schools of modern painting had lost their momentum by the forties. There were still numerous variations on Cubism, Surrealism and the superbly decorative work of Matisse. But many of the younger artists did not want to go on ringing changes on these styles.

Abstract Expressionism, then, represents a new approach. Yet it is very much related to the past. It derives directly from the revolution of man's visual experience which had already been accomplished by earlier twentieth-century schools. As Robert Motherwell said, "*Every intelligent painter carries the whole culture of modern painting in his head. It is his real subject, of which anything he paints is both an homage and a critique, and everything he says a gloss.*" [1] Technically the Abstract Expressionists owe their greatest debts to Cubism and to the German Expressionist movement, as we shall see further on. Philosophically they have been influenced by Mondrian, Kandinsky and the Surrealists.

At first the more important artists working in New York in the early forties were all grouped under the label, "School of New York." Not all of them, however, were Abstract Expressionists. Some of them, for example, sought to exploit the ultimate style of Mondrian, represented in this book by *Broadway Boogie Woogie*. But, as will become clear later in this chapter, Mondrian's technique did not point towards Abstract Expressionism.

A tremendous amount has been written concerning the characteristics of Abstract Expressionism. Indeed, one of the phenomena connected with the style is the amount of verbalizing done by artists, critics, and interested bystanders. The mere existence of works of this kind seems to have been a challenge to their creators and exhibitors to explain them in print. At this point, to avoid confusion and complicated terminology, a definition of Abstract Expressionism will be postponed until after analysis of the work of several artists who belong to the movement. This is all the more essential because there is more than one kind of painting which belongs to the style. Three types will be singled out, more in an effort to provide insight and comprehension than to be rigidly arbitrary about classification. Undoubtedly some pictures you will eventually examine will fit into more than one of the categories set up. In any event, an approach will be made to the paintings themselves in the hope that analysis of them will clarify such fundamental questions as: What should one look for in this kind of painting? What is their significance in the tradition of modern art? What standards can be used in judging these works?

1. *Structural Painting.* Hans Hofmann exemplifies our first category of Abstract Expressionists—those who emphasize structure. With him we may group Grace Hartigan, Philip Guston, Sam Francis, Theodoros Stamos, Willem de Kooning, Jack Tworkov and others.

Hofmann was among the first of the Abstract Expressionists. He was also its most brilliant teacher. It was in this capacity that he was called to the United States in 1930, at the age of fifty. Yet he did not receive the touch of fame until after his first exhibition in New York at Peggy Guggenheim's Art of This Century Gallery in 1944.

A first glance at his painting, X, *1955,** may suggest that there is no apparent order in the bright, stabbing colors and the broad swaths of paint. You might be reminded of several things simultaneously from paintings discussed in previous chapters, such as the blatant, bold color of the German Expressionists and the French Fauve artists. Most probably you may catch many resemblances to the *Improvisations* of Kandinsky illustrated in Plate 7.

Both Kandinsky and Hofmann paint non-objectively in the sense that all reference to the reality of the phenomenal world has been eliminated. Both are what we can call colorists, since their pictures are built up with the substance of color and achieve their particular effects as a result of it. To this extent Kandinsky could be classed as an Abstract Expressionist and of all the artists discussed up to now, his work is the nearest in style to it. Yet the paintings belong to two different worlds in spite of their similarities.

The surfaces of Kandinsky's *Two Compositions* are relatively smooth or flat compared to X, *1955.* The latter is built up of viscous pigment into almost three-dimensional relief, whereas the pigment of the former has been floated or drawn on the canvas and melted along the picture plane. The difference involved here is a basic one for all types of Abstract Expressionism. The pigment must be thick enough to preserve the stroke of brush or palette knife or of whatever instrument is used, even a finger, so that the trace of execution or performance remains on the surface. The act of painting, the actual process of creativity, is thus captured for us on the canvas.

* Plate 16.

Another distinction must be made between these two types of abstraction. Kandinsky manipulates his color areas and lines in such a way that the observer must keep his eye in continual movement; particularly strong are the directional axes which are curvilinear and flow into, around, in front of and behind each other, producing an effect of continuity or organic development. This effect should be seen in terms of the artist's stated intention of operating on two levels simultaneously—the aesthetic and the psychic. For Kandinsky sees the canvas as an arena for moral struggle. His forms and colors are contending forces of light and dark, good and evil. X, *1955,* on the other hand, deals solely with the elements of art, and does not demand moral interpretation of this type. The Hofmann is relatively static, as opposed to the kinetic effect of the Kandinsky; and this static, structural quality is characteristic of this first type of Abstract Expressionism. But if we are to talk about structure in X, our first impression that there is only chaos here must be re-examined. And as we look again, a wealth of detail—ordered detail—catches the attention. In fact, this painting has been so carefully built, so deliberately organized, that it may have a closer affinity to Cubism than to Kandinsky.

This may not be immediately apparent if we look back to Braque's *Man With a Guitar.* Compared to the Hofmann the Braque painting is strikingly limited in its use of color and motif, with monochromatic brown organized through predominantly short straight lines and sharp angles making planes which tilt, overlap and blend. The elements of design selected by the Cubist are not those of the Abstract Expressionist. The texture of his surface is entirely different. And Braque still holds on to references to visual phenomena, which have been banished from the Hofmann.

Yet there are important similarities. Both types of painting focus attention on the substance of painting as a medium. The composition is constructed in each case out of the qualities of the craft itself. In both cases there is carefully organized structure. Let us now examine Hofmann's X, *1955* to see how it is constructed.

In its representation of space visually on the

canvas, X, *1955* projects forward. All the pigments are at the same point in reference to the observer; they rest on the surface equally and move towards the eye rather than away from it. Even where one color is placed over another, as the great red swath cuts above the blue, the latter immediately springs to the same level as the red. This retention of all parts of the surface in the same plane is typical of Abstract Expressionism. The areas in X, *1955* do not recede, or tilt as in Cubism, or flow back and forth as in Kandinsky's type of composition. They stay on the surface and emphasize it.

To organize his surface, Hofmann has placed a huge "X" (the title of the picture) almost in the center of the canvas. The crossing of the two bars is, however, a little high and to the left of the center making the composition inevitably asymmetric.

In discussing his own work, Hofmann constantly uses such phrases as "the establishment of relationships," "development of tensions," "expansion-contraction," and "push-pull." All of these terms deal with color and the effect of different colors on each other as a result not only of the qualities of chroma, value and intensity, but also of direction and size of the areas in which they exist. They are certainly not new terms and can be equally well applied to the analysis of such a painting as the *Blue Vase* by Cézanne, which has many similarities of general structure to X, *1955*. The major force in the latter picture consists in the strong rising pull to the left along the bar of red. This is only partially counteracted by the more vertically placed blue swath. To hold the red in balance, Hofmann placed the very narrow sharp red arc at the top which carries the eye over to the right-hand edge of the canvas and to three lines dug into the thick green pigment, heightened by bits of red slashed in and over them. These establish or reinforce the vertical edge of the canvas as a force in the composition which helps prevent the red diagonal from tilting too far. The large yellow area to the right of center also aids in stabilizing the central masses as do the smaller yellow squarish areas to the left of center. In fact every block of pigment is carefully and superbly placed to maintain the structural tension and the push-pull of the varying color areas. What looks unorganized is very meticulously planned.

If this does not seem to be the case, it is because we are unaccustomed to the roughness, vagueness or unfinished quality of the shapes used. We have become so used to the definite shapes used by modern artists for the last fifty years that our eyes are somewhat startled by the lack of clarity or the indefiniteness of shape. This very lack, however, is a great help in making more obvious the process of organization; it is as though the artist had no time to go back and tidy up the edges and smooth out the planes with which he is dealing. The result has a much greater effect of spontaneity,

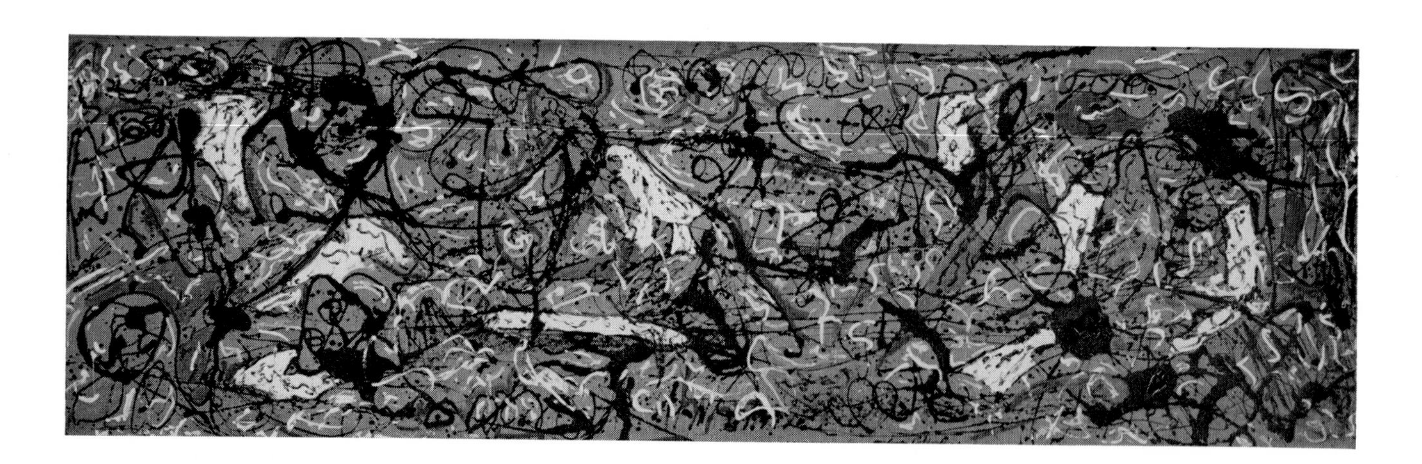

Jackson Pollock (1912–1956), THE COCKATOO, 1948
Courtesy Lee Krasner Pollock, New York.

Pollock introduced a new freedom with his celebrated drip technique. Painting on a canvas flat on the floor, he wove a pattern which relies on a blend of impulse and accident and captures the physical rhythm of the artist's performance.

and vivifies the concept of the creative process leaving its record on the surface of the artist's canvas.

Hofmann, himself, like most other well-known Abstract Expressionists, has indulged in a great deal of self-explanation. Typical phrases are: "*Pictorial life is a created reality. Without it pictorial communication—the appeal to the senses and the mind—is non-existent.*" "*Pictorial life is not imitated life; it is, on the contrary, a created reality based on the inherent life within every medium of expression.*" "*Color is, of course, not a creative means in itself. We must force it to become a creative means. We do this in sensing the inner life by which related colors respond to each other through the created actuality of intervals.*" "*Looking at a picture is a spontaneous act that reveals at once the quality or non-quality of the work. But what is quality? Quality is the essence resulting from convincingly established felt-relationships.*" [2] This is another way of saying that painting without verbal or visual references to visible nature is valid in itself; it is good if it hangs together as a composition, just as all pictorial art should. The meaning is highly personal and is definitely marked by the artist's own judgments and values.

2. *Action Painting.* The second category of Abstract Expressionism makes much more out of the concept of the act of painting than does the first type. So much so that it has been called "Action Painting." The spontaneous movements made by an artist, his involuntary reflexes motivated by long training, the exploitation of the accidental and the dependence upon intuition, coupled with new techniques of applying paint, are all part of Action Painting as opposed to the structural ordering of form illustrated by Hofmann. Jackson Pollock was the American most successful in developing this approach to the creative act, as Georges Mathieu has been in France. For both of them "*What was to go on to the canvas was not a picture but an event.*" "*A painting that is an act is inseparable from the biography of the artist . . .*" "*The act-painting is of the same metaphysical substance as the artist's existence. The new painting has broken down every distinction between art and life.*" [3]

With these artists the act of painting has become the overriding consideration; the creative act itself transcends all other considerations. At first reaction, we may feel that nothing at all remains of art except the elusive and ephemeral moment of action. Yet the object made as a result of the artist's actions is still with us and it is our task to comprehend and to approve or disap-

Georges Mathieu (1921–), NO. 7, 1955
Photograph courtesy Kootz Gallery, New York, New York.

prove of this record.

To help us we may refer to the aesthetic theory of Benedetto Croce: "*. . . intuitive knowledge is expressive knowledge. Independent and autonomous in respect to intellectual function; indifferent to later empirical discriminations, to reality and to unreality, to formations and aperceptions of space and time . . . : intuition or representation is distinguished as* form *from what is felt and suffered, from the flux or wave of sensation, or from psychic matter; and this form, this taking possession is expression. To intuit is to express; and nothing else (nothing more but nothing less) than* to express."[4] The works of Pollock and Mathieu are extreme illustrations of Croce's ideas; they record or express the passing moment of intuition (nothing more but nothing less).

The accidental occurrence as opposed to the conscious act was first recognized as a possible means of creativity by the Dadaists, who made of the fortuitous, the autonomous and the accidental a positive element for the modern tradition. Pollock and Mathieu raised this non-rational element of the creative act to the position of a major principle. In order to apply it fully, Pollock abandoned the more normal methods of manipulating paint, as can be seen readily in *The Cockatoo* and *Painting 49–9.** Taking cans instead of brushes, he dripped paint over the canvas in long arabesques interwoven across the total surface accompanied with blotches which contrast to the essential linearity of his effect. Partially because of the requirements of the gestures used to fling this paint across a two-dimensional surface, the artist resorted to ever larger canvases, until dimensions of ten feet or more were not unusual. These gigantic murals, which would take up most of an ordinary

* Plate 17.

Georges Mathieu (1921–), At work on the BATTLE OF BOUVINES, 1954
Photograph by Robert Descharnes.

domestic wall, afforded the means for a superb display of the movements of the painter, involving not only the hand and wrist but the arm and the entire torso.

The variety of possibilities which this technique opens up is revealed if we contrast the paintings by Pollock with the work of Mathieu. Immediately observable are differences in types of color, the uses of area against line, and above all, the configurations of stroke.

The following account of "Mathieu Paints a Picture" by Michel Tapié de Céleyran, is a good description of Mathieu's type of action-painting: *"But here are the facts: at the end of last winter Georges Mathieu was invited to participate in the* Salon de Mai. *He had decided in advance to refuse, being not unreasonably against such pointless exhibitions; however, he replied with a challenge; he would show an enormous picture or none. The gigantic canvas was accepted although, of course, not yet painted. Reading a treatise on heraldry one day, Mathieu's eye fell on the following passage: 'Mathieu of Montmorency, having seized twelve imperial standards at the Battle of Bouvines, his descendants changed the four eagles on their arms to seventeen eaglets . . .'*

"This phrase set off in him the unceasing excitement from which emerged the painting and the myth adventure of Bouvines. Sensing his subject, Mathieu began to read everything on Bouvines and on feudal strategy, and to gather all possible information about every personage involved, from Philip Augustus and the Emperor Otto to the least important participant who had suffered a wound in the fight. Mathieu's car was loaded with General Staff maps, schemes of battles, lists of genealogies.

"He rented the enormous Calmels studio on the Rue Marcadet, where the biggest sets for Paris films are painted. Since the Battle of Bouvines took place on a Sunday, early in the afternoon, it was on a Sunday, just after lunch, that he set to work. Present were the Flemish poet, Emmanuel Looten, representing the Count of Flanders, and myself representing the Count of Toulouse. Mathieu was dressed in black silk; he wore a white helmet and shoes and greaves with white cross-bars. The film maker, Robert Descharnes, shot the entire execution of the Battle in color to commemorate the event. And it was our good fortune to witness the most unpredictable of ballets, the dance of dedicated ferocity, the grave elaboration of a magic rite.

"In the hodge-podge of paint-tubes and the hundreds of brushes as long as halberds, of spilt oil cans, Mathieu, demiurge of destiny, summoned onto his canvas in a few hours (exactly the time taken by the fighting) first the army of the king of France, with the communal militias (to the left of the picture), and then the armies of the coalition; above there spurted onto the canvas splashes of larger characters and many colors, used for their own sake just as much as for the pure joy of the symbol. These represented wherever and whenever necessary the Bishop of Beauvais, the Bishop of Laon, the Count of Boulogne, etc. etc., . . . and Otto IV, Holy Roman Emperor, whose flight was finally indicated by a trail of black, almost ten feet long, beginning at the center of the canvas and descending to its lower right-hand corner. Mathieu's motions . . . which he himself admits are impossible to describe in words . . . cannot by any stretch of the imagination be integrated in the ordinary terminology of a 'technique.' They will be recorded as such in the film.

"When, by evening, the painting was completed, the magic world determined by it evoked in its turn the spell of this extraordinary adventure, linked in the most suggestive equivocation to historical fact and its reverberation in a work of art." [5]

No doubt this reveals a flair for attracting attention reminiscent of Salvador Dali. Yet it is the result that counts. And Mathieu's results are highly decorative and elegant.

3. *Symbolist Painting.* There is a third variation of the Abstract Expressionist style—a variation whose particular qualities are the result of an interest in symbolism. Because of the apparent vagueness of meaning derived from an Abstract Expressionist painting, it may seem that an emphasis on symbolism might be a contradiction of the purpose of the style. But just as the other characteristics have been taken from the modern tradition, so this one follows from Dada or Surrealist precedents.

Robert Motherwell in particular has done research in the area of signs and symbols and arrived at an effect generically different from those of Hofmann or Pollock. There is not much regard for great complexities of color relations nor, relatively, is much achieved by the manner in which the surface of his painting is developed in tactile terms. Both these factors are certainly present; but what counts are the implications of meaning. It is the possibility of a more definite meaning which attracts the observer to the few and simple areas, strips and lines, to the directions, attractions and counter-attractions, and finally to the interrelationships of these elements.

Confronted by a Motherwell painting, the observer will begin to search for associational values partially implied by the "images" he sees on the canvas. But they are highly ambiguous images. No positively recognizable reminiscences of experience occur in the painting and yet we are haunted by the possibility or implication of meaning it proffers. On the one hand, an experience of this type may be intensely frustrating; on the other, the process of creating meaning out of the pictorial elements may be deeply satisfying.

What has been said above concerning the symbolist category of Abstract Expressionism can be effectively demonstrated by looking at Motherwell's *The Voyage*, 1949. The reproduction is not sufficiently delicate to catch the quality of surface, so we will have to confine our observations to the general effect of the painting. With respect to the method by which the picture is organized, it is clear that it parallels the approach of structural Abstract Expressionist painters rather than that of the Action Painters. A very definite, almost symmetrical, balance is developed around the center circle and vertical black band. A green strip at the bottom right and the angle of the white line on the left, diagonally across the black rectangle, hold the other areas and colors in a typical tension, assisted particularly by a tall yellow rectangle to the right of center. The method is essentially structural in effect but the interrelation of the areas and the greater definition of shape elicit a response from the observer in terms of such questions as: What is happening? Why are these shapes in this context? This leads to the conclusion that there must be some meaning, which is as yet elusive, but which may be trapped if only more could be known about or seen in the painting. In this way the relationship of shapes in a composition implies significance other than the kind to be found through an analysis of structure or through the evidence of the creative process.

In contrast to this picture, which Motherwell painted in 1949, is his *Je t'aime, IV*, dated 1955–57. The background is in the structural Abstract Expressionist style. Superimposed upon this the words *"Je t'aime"* serve to wrench the spectator psychologically between two different and irreconcilable spheres of existence: that of the created object, and that of his everyday life. Placing the writing on the picture plane is, of course, a revival of an old idea; for it has the same significance as the bits of newspaper, wallpaper, theater tickets, and so on, which appear in the collages of later Cubism, typified by Gris' *Breakfast* and Picasso's *Man with a Hat*.

Franz Kline, Adolph Gottlieb, and Bradley Walker Tomlin all join Motherwell in attempts

Robert Motherwell, (1915–), THE VOYAGE, 1949
The Museum of Modern Art, New York. Gift of Mrs. John D. Rockefeller, 3rd.

to evoke meaning without permitting the elements of design or the technique of painting to complete a specific reference to the world of our visual sense. Each of these three artists refers to systems of conveying knowledge which are inherently abstract themselves. Either because of their exoticism for the Western eye or because their context has been transformed, the symbols used are bereft of definite significance. There are many such systems, completely arbitrary in nature, such as the symbols of mathematics, cuneiform, Demotic writing, Chinese calligraphy, pictographic writing, graffiti of any type, and petroglyphs. Removed from their contexts, exaggerated in scale and distorted, the motifs selected still show they were once shaped by the hand of man. They evoke qualities of meaning without possessing it.

Franz Kline's *Accent Grave*, 1955, has all the general qualities of Abstract Expressionism as well as the particular attributes of the symbolist group. The title apparently refers to the stroke of black pigment above the main "image" on the canvas, an accent symbol used in French. The "image," however, has no relation to any written language based on the Roman alphabet, so the observer is thrown back to begin a search for meaning all over again. Yet the more one's attention is focused on the grave accent the greater becomes the impression of impending impact between the shaft-like stroke and the black "image" below. One's eye is

Robert Motherwell (1915–), JE T'AIME, IV, 1955–57
Courtesy of the Artist.

Motherwell built a bridge from Surrealism to what has now become the Abstract Expressionist movement in American painting. His large plastic symbols replace the Surrealist clinical illustrations. In his skill in projecting forms which are consciously meaningless, but unconsciously meaningful, he resembles Miró.

forced to move along the swaths of pigment in search of significance to satisfy the mind's need of order. The suggestion that Kline derives his forms from the characters of Oriental calligraphy does little to help in attaining meaning but it does bring a flood of associational values to the painting, such as an appreciation for the secular Chinese tradition of writing with a brush.

If Adolph Gottlieb's *Exclamation*, 1958, is compared to his 1946 canvas, *Premonition of Evil*, the influence on the artist of the Abstract Expressionist movement will become quite clear. In the earlier example the composition is divided into a grid with little symbols in each resulting rectangle. The symbols may not be very specific, yet an eye here, a possible nose, a face, triangles, etc., are quite identifiable. The Bradley Walker Tomlin, *No. 20*, 1949, shows the same stage of evolution with its eyes and arrows. This kind of painting stems from the evocative work of such artists as Klee and Miró. In *Exclamation* Gottlieb has eliminated all the specific aids to recognition still retained in *No. 20*. What is left are two major conflicting areas whose relation suggests an idea, a program or situation.

The symbolic type of Abstract Expressionism

Franz Kline (1910–), ACCENT GRAVE, 1955
Private Collection, Courtesy Sidney Janis Gallery, New York, New York.

Edward Hopper (1882-), HOUSE BY THE RAILROAD, 1925 *Plate 1*
The Museum of Modern Art, New York.

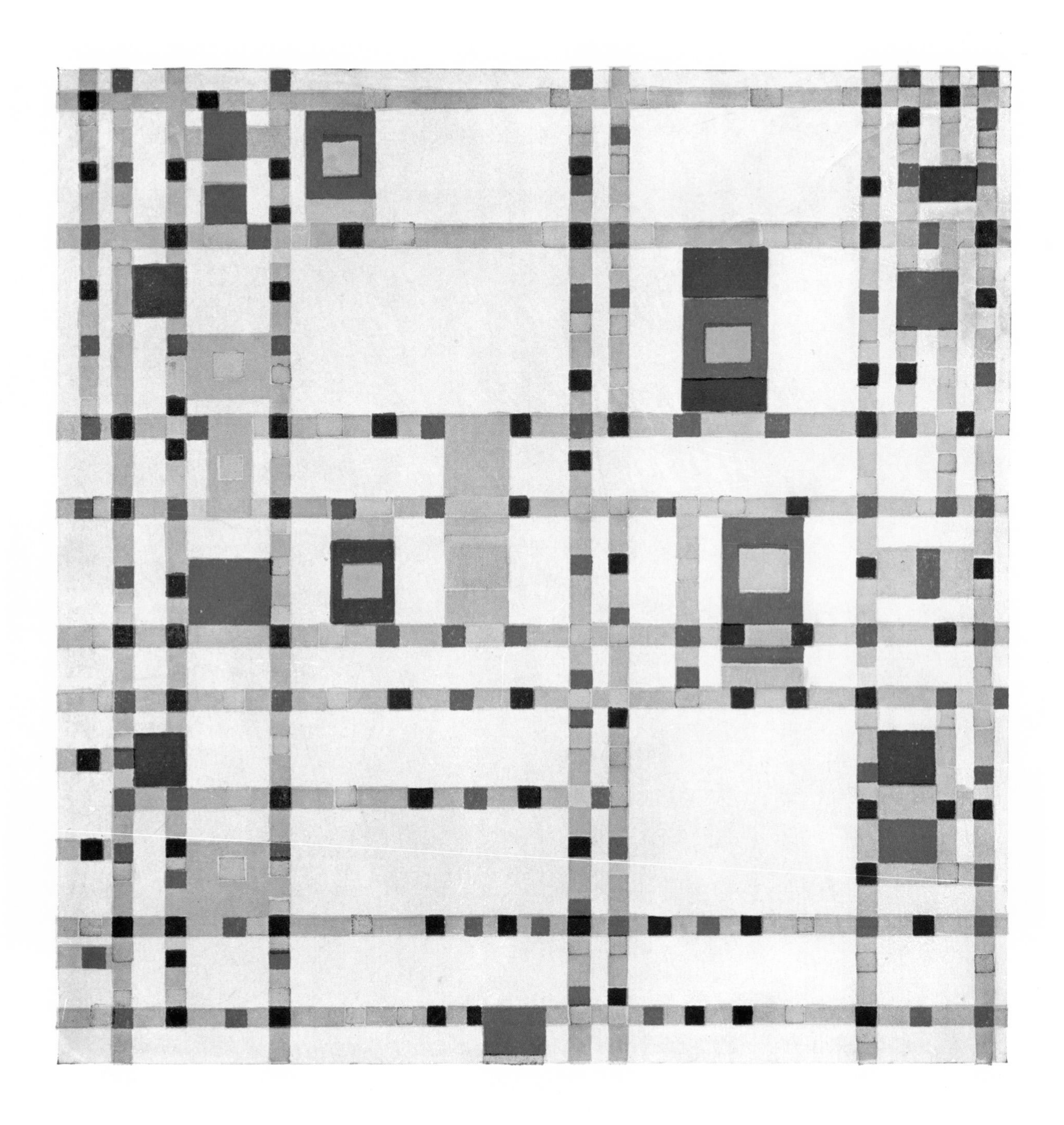

Plate 2

Piet Mondrian (1872-1944), BROADWAY BOOGIE WOOGIE, 1942-43
The Museum of Modern Art, New York.

Vincent van Gogh (1853-1890), THE STARRY NIGHT, 1889
The Museum of Modern Art, New York. Acquired through the Lillie P. Bliss Bequest.

Plate 3

Plate 4

Pablo Picasso (1881-), LES DEMOISELLES D'AVIGNON, 1907
The Museum of Modern Art, New York, Acquired through the Lillie P. Bliss Bequest.

Georges Braque (1882-), MAN WITH A GUITAR, 1911
The Museum of Modern Art, New York. Acquired through the Lillie P. Bliss Bequest.

Plate 5

Piet Mondrian (1872-1944), COMPOSITION, 1935-42
Collection: Mr. and Mrs. Burton Tremaine, Meriden, Conn.

Wassily Kandinsky (1866-1944), Two Compositions (Nos. 3 and 4 from a series of four), 1914
The Museum of Modern Art, New York. Mrs. Simon Guggenheim Fund.

Plate 8 Ernst Ludwig Kirchner (1880-1938), SCHLEMIHL'S ENCOUNTER WITH THE SHADOW, 1916

Max Beckmann (1884-1950), THE DEPARTURE, 1937
The Museum of Modern Art, New York. Given anonymously.

Plate 9

Pablo Picasso (1881-), GIRL BEFORE A MIRROR, 1932
The Museum of Modern Art, New York. Gift of Mrs. Simon Guggenheim.

Plate 10

Marc Chagall (1887-   ), I AND MY VILLAGE, 1911
The Museum of Modern Art, New York. Mrs. Simon Guggenheim Fund.

Max Ernst (1891-　　), WOMAN, OLD MAN AND FLOWER, 1923-24
The Museum of Modern Art, New York. Purchase.

Plate 12

Joan Miró (1893-   ), CATALAN LANDSCAPE (THE HUNTER), 1923-24 *Plate 13*
The Museum of Modern Art, New York. Purchase.

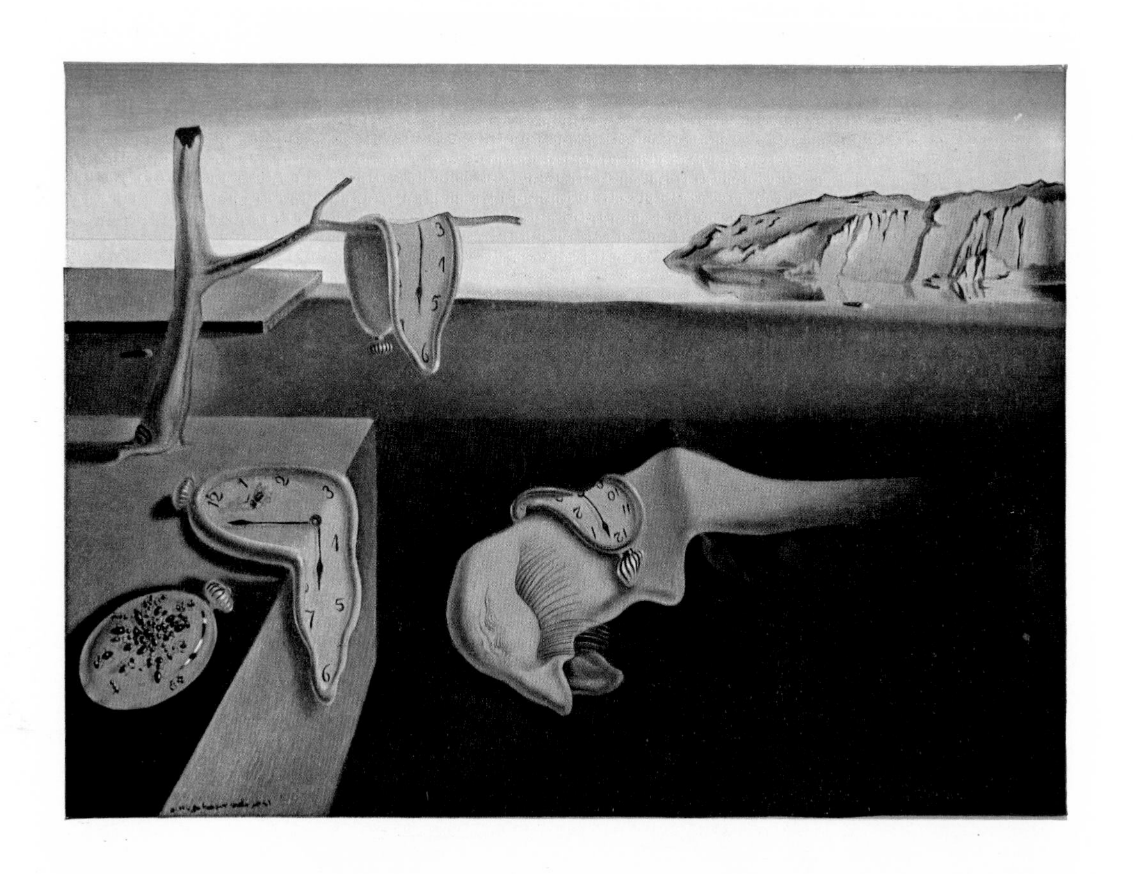

Salvador Dali (1904-   ), THE PERSISTENCE OF MEMORY, 1931
The Museum of Modern Art, New York. Given anonymously.

Plate 14

Joan Miró (1893-   ), PERSONNAGES DANS LA NUIT, 1940
Collection: Mr. and Mrs. Burton Tremaine, Meriden, Connecticut.

Plate 15

Miró, like Klee, skirts the Surrealists' realm of subconscious imagery, and like Klee, he is never wholly committed to it and tends to limit himself to fantasy. Miró is playful, and he is always able to turn the subject back to color, spacing, and design, which he handles with a sure instinct.

Plate 16

Hans Hofmann (1880-), "x-1955"
Courtesy Mr. Peter A. Rubel, New York.

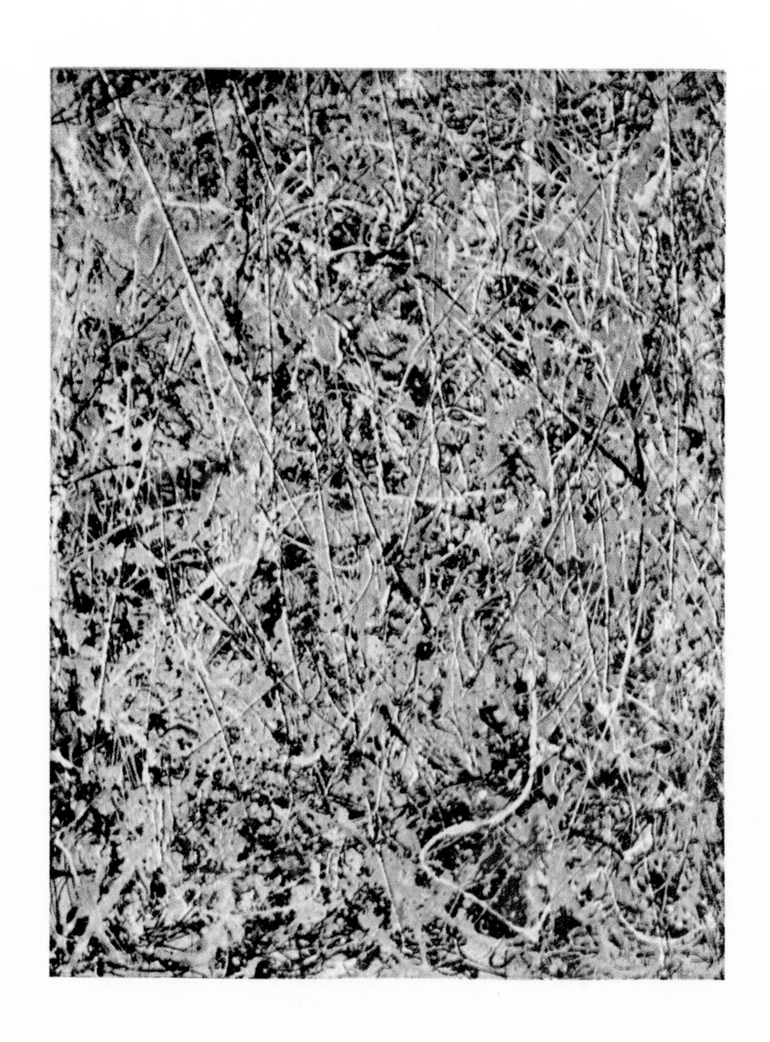

Jackson Pollock (1912-1956), "PAINTING 49-9," 1949
Courtesy Mr. Anthony Smith, So. Orange, N. J.

Plate 17

Plate 18

Georges Rouault (1871-), THREE JUDGES, 1913
The Museum of Modern Art, New York. Sam A. Lewisohn Bequest.

Yves Tanguy (1900-   ), SLOWLY TOWARD THE NORTH, 1942
The Museum of Modern Art, New York. Gift of Philip C. Johnson.

Plate 19

Plate 20

Fernand Léger (1881-1955), LA GRANDE JULIE, 1945
The Museum of Modern Art, New York.
Acquired through the Lillie P. Bliss Bequest.

Léger has to his credit the awareness of the impact of the machine age on our lives. A new conception when Léger mechanized even the female nude in his *Breakfast* paintings, it continued to dominate his art. Here, in a later work, is the typical metallic crispness, incision, and legibility.

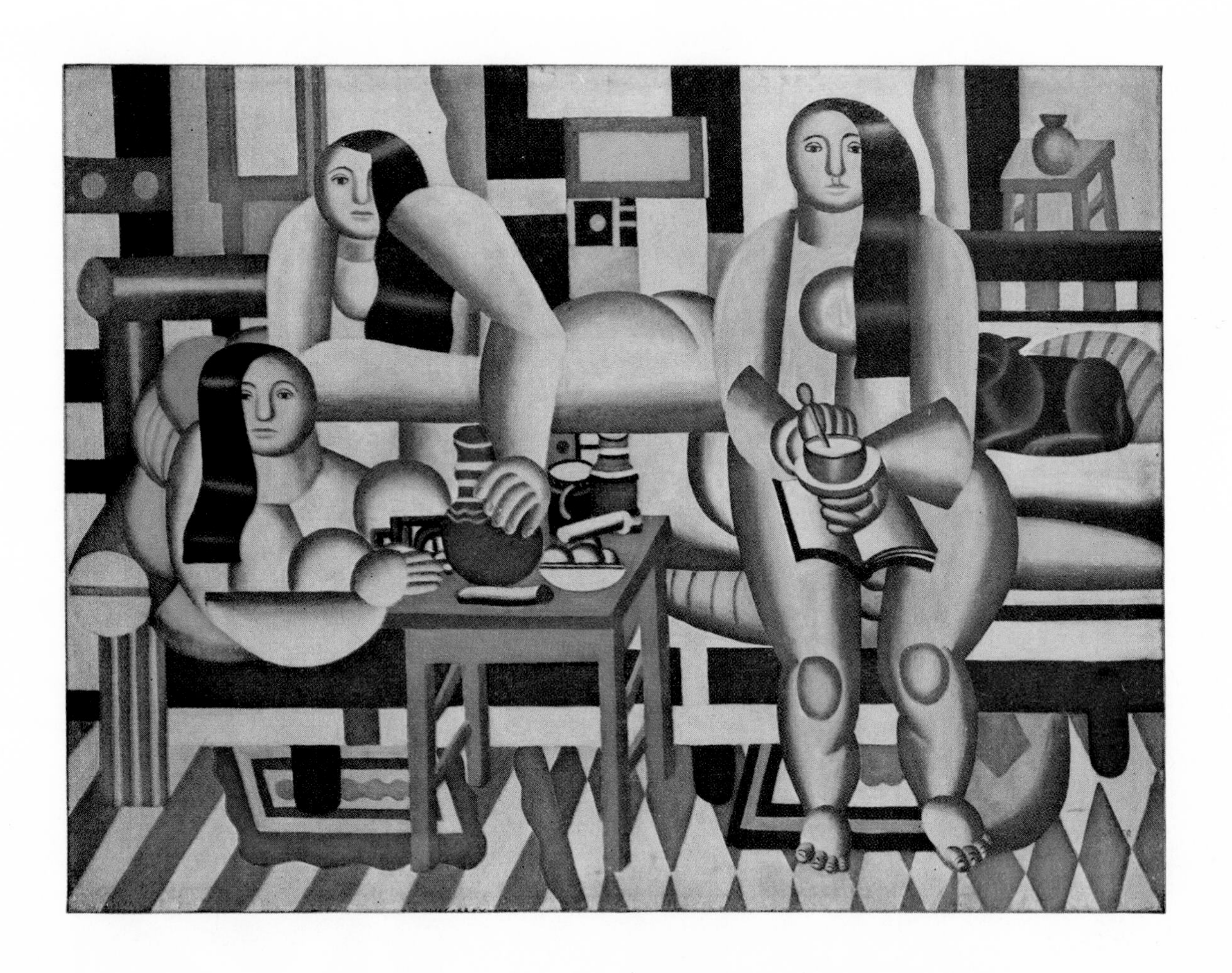

Fernand Léger (1881-1955), PETIT DEJEUNER, ca. 1921
Collection: Mr. and Mrs. Burton Tremaine, Meriden, Connecticut.

Plate 22

John Marin (1870-1954), NEW YORK AT NIGHT, NO. 3, 1950
Collection: Mr. and Mrs. Alan H. Rosenthal, New York

Stuart Davis (1894-   ), VISA, 1951 — *Plate 23*

The Museum of Modern Art, New York. Gift of Mrs. Gertrud A. Mellon.

Lyonel Feininger (1871-1956), THE STEAMER "ODIN," II
The Museum of Modern Art, New York. Acquired through the Lillie P. Bliss Bequest.

Plate 24

lends itself more than any of the others to explanations couched in terms of a mystique of personality. The point of these explanations is that the artist translates his perception of reality directly into the plastic elements of painting without the intervention of forms which already have many types of significance. The meaning of a picture resides only in the relationships set up on the canvas. It expresses the artist's experience and his personality as well.

In all three types of Abstract Expressionism the implied meanings of the third category are present, just as in all three the emphasis on the use of the elements of design is present. Each category, however, differs from the others in the relative emphasis placed on one of the following three characteristics: structure, action, symbol. It should be noted that there have been many combinations of these three main emphases, and that the categories are quite arbitrary and are useful only for

Adolf Gottlieb (1903–), EXCLAMATION, 1958
Courtesy of the artist.

Adolph Gottlieb (1903–), PREMONITION OF EVIL, 1946
Courtesy of the Artist.

The organization of flat areas in such patterns that we are haunted by some effort to communicate on a less than conscious level is Gottlieb's special art. He creates billboards, signs, and diagrams which are illegible to us—and yet we recognize them as eloquent. The compartmentation seen here is no longer characteristic of his work. Instead, he now magnifies a single symbol as a dramatic condensation of all that has gone before.

Bradley Walker Tomlin (1899–1953), No. 20, 1949
The Museum of Modern Art, New York. Gift of Philip C. Johnson.

Tomlin was at first influenced by Cubism, but in his late mature canvases he developed a pattern of pure relationships which has much of the formalism of Mondrian. Tomlin, however, was a sensitive colorist, and in his work the colors as well as the forms harmonize and relate to each other.

the purposes of discussion and analysis.

We can now provide a general definition of Abstract Expressionism, which we shall state in terms of subject matter, form and content. Abstract Expressionism is a type of painting with the following characteristics:

(a) It is "abstract," in the sense that it does not contain specific visual references. Thus it has no subject matter—unless we change the definition of subject matter given in Chapter 1, and suggest that the subject matter of the painting is the painting itself.

(b) The tangible marks of the creative process remain on the painting's surface, which has strong tactile qualities.

(c) The content consists of a non-specific but powerful expression of the painter's intuition of reality.

This definition cannot in itself give us a complete understanding of Abstract Expressionist painting. It does give us its primary characteristics, and it serves to help us distinguish it from other kinds of paintings. Thus, while many of the other schools of modern painting possess one or two of the three attributes listed above, none of them contains all three. Even such contemporary artists as Barnett Newman and Ad Rheinhardt, who exploit vast dimensions to achieve a striking emotional impact with color, area and line alone, are not Abstract Expressionists. For they are among those who followed Mondrian's later line of development, and their work does not have the obvious tactile effect of surface that Abstract Expressionism uses, nor the irregularity of "Image."

The impact of the style has been deep and almost universal. Although it has not been the only type of painting practiced in the past fifteen years, it has certainly been the dominant movement during this period. By 1950 it was firmly established with numerous participants including dealers, friendly critics, and museum directors, as well as the artists themselves. International in scope and appeal, it has adherents in all countries of the democratic world. Even behind the Iron Curtain some Abstract Expressionist canvases have been clandestinely painted, smuggled across borders and exhibited in Paris.

A vast apparatus in America has helped gain public attention for the Abstract Expressionists. New York City has two major museums dedicated to the fostering of modern art: the Museum of Modern Art and the Solomon R. Guggenheim Museum. The Whitney Museum of American Art has also done major work in sustaining the efforts of native-born or naturalized citizens. Editorial writers of national art magazines and the critics of major dailies are sensitive to the slightest change in the art situation. With all these forces operating together, Abstract Expressionism has come to be so well-established that, from 1955, those inimical to the movement have raised the cry that it is the new style of the Academies enshrined in College and University art departments, to the exclusion of every other approach to painting.

Apparently, too, some of the artists practicing the new style have become dissatisfied, perhaps because of the disregard for traditional subject references or because vast production on a world scale made the movement take on a quality of sameness or monotony. For whatever reason, one of the foremost of the structural Abstract Expressionists, Willem de Kooning, turned back to subject matter in such works as *Woman I*, 1952, (see Chapter 8) as contrasted to his *Open Road* of 1950. We have already seen Motherwell turn back to Cubism and Dada in his *Je t'aime* series 1955–57.

Another example of the current reaction to Abstract Expressionism might be the 1960 exhibition, "New Images of Man," presented by the Museum of Modern Art. The new images were conceived in terms of expressive deformation of the human figure and rigorously excluded the completely abstract type of painting. Another straw in the wind is the remarkable revival of the Dada movement, which led an ephemeral existence from 1916 to 1923. There is at present so much activity of the Dada type that a new term is becoming current: Neo-Dada. It is not particularly novel in approach but might be considered a refinement and extension of the "Beat" movement in literature.

Whatever the future holds, it is certain that Abstract Expressionism has already had a significant role and that America had the major lead in its formation. Critic Michel Seuphor made the observation that *"the contribution of the United States to abstract art is today as important as that of France. For several years Paris has been no longer the only capital of the avant-garde in art; it shares these high honors with New York."* [6] For a Frenchman, even one who has been in this country, to make a confession that the United States is on a par with metropolitan France is a sure indication of the remarkable pre-eminence of New York in the world of modern art. This it achieved through the development of Abstract Expressionism.

Willem de Kooning (1904–), OPEN ROAD, 1950
Courtesy Sidney Janis Gallery, New York.

1. Robert Motherwell, *The School of New York,* Frank Perls Gallery, Beverly Hills, 1951.
2. Hans Hofmann, "The Color Problem in Pure Painting —Creative Origin," *Arts and Architecture,* February 1956, pp. 14–15, 33–34.
3. H. Rosenberg, "The American Action Painters," *Art News,* December 1952.
4. Melvin Rader, *A Modern Book of Esthetics,* New York, 1952, pp. 112–113.
5. Michel Tapié de Céleyran, "Mathieu Paints a Picture," *Art News,* February 1955, p. 50 ff.
6. Michel Seuphor, *Dictionnaire de la peinture abstraite,* Paris, 1957, p. 76.

EIGHT

Creativity and Craftmanship

A CHILD COULD do it" or "My child could do better" are statements now less frequently heard than they used to be. Uttered with some heat, they suppose a lack of technical excellence in the work criticized, the absence of standards of performance. A misunderstanding of the artist's intentions often leads to such a slur, when in fact his performance should be judged in terms of these very intentions. Today, when every liberty is granted the artist, the critic can run more risk of criticism than the painter. He may hear that he is simply revealing the time lag in his own taste.

It is an inadequate answer, however, to tell the serious critic that he is out of fashion, for fashion will change again. Perhaps the critic whose "child could do it" is himself the child in Hans Andersen's story, "The Emperor's New Clothes," who is innocent enough to give the show away by proclaiming that the emperor is naked, that what is invisible (in art) does not exist. If anyone does not understand what a given work is about, there is a problem hidden, or more than one problem, which can perhaps be stated as a question or questions: What is the painter driving at? How well is he doing what he set out to do?

It is primarily the latter question that concerns us here. Stated more at length: Have new standards of excellence supplanted old standards? Do standards vary with each painter? Have standards (especially technical standards) simply ceased to apply?

Before we can even suggest answers, we must examine previous standards. We shall have to say whether previous standards are relatively stable, or whether they present a history of changes and upsets; and we may suddenly find that we have laid open the whole history of art.

A scientific grasp of perspective came in with the Renaissance, coincident with the great explorations and the discovery of America. It was a mathematical rather than an aesthetic discovery and as such was part of man's successful attack on his environment. This accurate placing of objects in space (instead of simply seeing the further objects higher up like people sitting in a theater) had an enormous impact on the artist. Later —we could almost say "lately"—we have reevaluated the Renaissance point of view, and we have judged art as emotional communication, rather than as the surveyor's conquest of territory. We have seen perspective do injury to the solid two-dimensional wall which is the very prop and support of a work of art, and we have seen it invite an illusionistic trickery which destroys the very possibility of great painting. The fact remains that the Renaissance artist suddenly believed that he had *learned how to draw,* and this very confidence encouraged superb performances. The survival of a Renaissance tradition down through Baroque art and into the romantic communications of the nineteenth century goes to prove the vitality of a point of view. There is life in this tradition still, and in all likelihood, contemporary art will make a compromise with it as the art of our time seeks its place in history.

Such an art had its standards, or rather, the Renaissance expected certain things of its artists. The Renaissance valued power, knowledge, and ability, and its artists chose the stability of the pyramid as a symbol of power: their compositions were symmetrical. The Renaissance liked clarity, spaciousness, and precision, and its artists were proud to show that they were in control of space and could draw accurately. The Renaissance required elegance of performance to prove that man was equal to his new powers, and it required the impression of omniscience to show that man was universal. It required too much; and the balance between solemnity and order on the one hand, exhilaration and expansion on the other, was to prove unstable.

The careful discipline behind the artist, grounded in impersonal humility, in long apprenticeship, in his membership in his guild, had equipped him with sacrosanct techniques: advance studies, underpainting, a methodical approach to images which could not escape him since their roles, too, were ordained. The artist's images were locked in their iconography, their set poses determined by precedent and the dictates of the church. These images did not belong to the artist,

Leonardo da Vinci (1452–1519)
TYPICAL PAGE OF NOTES FOR HIS TREATISE ON PAINTING
Reproduced by gracious permission of H. M. Queen Elizabeth

Leonardo was a scientist as well as an artist, and his work reflects the grip on a comprehended environment which he demanded of himself. Later, scientific reality and the subjectivity of the artist were to separate. But in Leonardo, nature and art fused: he was able to fulfill himself in terms of nature through his capacity to understand nature and to recreate her.

they belonged to society; and it was his part to realize them, not to create them. But with the Renaissance his role changed; he was soon looked to as an innovator, an improvisor of effects, a man who not only depicted miracles but performed them.

Men learned how to paint in oils, and the new technique filled a need for subtlety, brilliance, and the impression of newly-organized actuality, while more secular subject matter allowed more profane, less humble contact with the object. Oil painting brought in painting on canvas. In place of the wall decorated with fresco, the framed painting opened a window upon illusion, and the painting grew larger at the very moment that windows grew larger, as the castle became a palace.

Anonymity gave way to the concept of genius; personal skill was superimposed on technical knowledge, and this skill asserted itself in brushwork and handling. It became the very signature of such artists as Titian, Tintoretto, and later of Rubens, Velásquez, or Hals. With the new reliance on personality, a facile hand took the place of time-honored procedure.

In the Baroque period, the Renaissance (now become a century-old tradition) was inherited by the romantic hero, who required an art of motion, gesture, and bedazzlement. The emphasis of the times was more than ever on external living, and triumphal processions, pictorial or real, were a symbol of man's earthly reward. Artists pictured their princes triumphing over everything, even death, and Rubens himself lived the life of a prince.

The painters conveyed these circumstances in a theatrical art hanging on bold diagonals or describing swirling spirals, with figures and faces set off by violent lights and darks to compel conviction. Their world was split ideologically between Reformation and Counter Reformation, and their art served the purpose of propaganda, for doubt was the enemy of every man.

All this exuberance and special pleading was at the expense of thought. But man eventually calmed and sobered: he thought about mechanics and optics and discovered astronomy in the heavens; he realized how small he was and learned that he could only outgrow himself through knowl-

Giovanni Bellini (1430?–1516),
ST. FRANCIS IN ECSTASY
Copyright The Frick Collection, New York.

Bellini stands at the threshold of the Renaissance. He has the Venetian color and splendor, but he is not as facile as the great generations that followed. Painting is a difficult triumph for him and, as a result, his religious works, describing lives that were also difficult triumphs, are intensely moving and sincere.

edge, humility, and compassion. In Rembrandt, men who were less than princes and saints were found to people the earth; light descended like a benediction, and life became a pilgrimage.

From then on two currents, two ways of painting which reflected two temperaments, ran side by side: a reliance on order and procedure, with an emphasis on form; and a reliance on impulse, with an emphasis on movement and color. The French painter, Poussin, who found a home in seventeenth-century Rome, was perhaps the greatest of those whose paintings were coolly built. His work has given stamina to all the architectural builders and painters since his time, down through the classicist Ingres, to Cézanne, Seurat, and the Cubists. The second technical tradition, that of the painters who trust to impulse and color, relies on skill in brushwork. It traces from Rubens through Watteau and Fragonard, to Delacroix, Renoir, and on to the Fauves, Matisse, and the Abstract Expressionists of our own day.

It should not be forgotten that for all these centuries (until the middle of the last) the artist fed his need for symbolism on the omnipresent pagan and Christian themes, and that realism was for a purpose, to lend plausibility to events that were outside experience. This continued even when the dichotomy between pagan and Christian illustration was replaced by a new temperamental division, and the romantic and the classic in art and literature became the new cultural poles. Man was uneasy with his new responsibility after the French Revolution, and the artist of the first half of the nineteenth century looked backward—either romantically to themes of tumult related in mood to the Baroque, or more austerely to the "purity" of a Rome of which he knew little, or of a Greece of which he knew less. Only in the second half of the nineteenth century did the artist begin to look about him into a new, independent, complacent, and semi-educated humanity. He found a new subject matter, quite devoid of symbolic overtones, and in fact devoid of many spiritual necessities. But it was life, and he could describe it in the black and white forms which the newly-discovered camera persuaded him were actuality, or he could clothe this scene with the color which a new scientific awareness of nature was offering him.

In our time, as the artist ceased to feel that imitation gave him what he desired, the skills associated with imitation lost their value. The painter, and soon his audience, looked on unmoved by the floating in of atmosphere, the "lifelike" glitter of an eye, the recession managed with a delicate brush. On the other hand, the painted

Nicolas Poussin (1593–1665), THE TRIUMPH OF NEPTUNE AND AMPHITRITE, 1638–40
George W. Elkins Collection, Philadelphia Museum of Art.

Poussin, a French painter of the seventeenth century who lived in Rome, has influenced all French artists since his day. They admire the cerebral deliberateness, and a kind of intellectual sensuality, in this master of composition.

canvas took on a new significance as an artifact which incorporated the beauties or qualities which were supposed to reside elsewhere. As an artifact, painting offered some of the "real" aspects of sculpture, and a great increase in interest in texture resulted. This new concern for texture brought in technical effects which could not be obtained with a brush. By turns the surface was sandy or slick, or built inches deep. Paint was laid on with a knife. Colored areas were cut out of paper with scissors and applied to the surface. Newsprint was glued on.

If the late nineteenth century was intent on an account of man in terms of his environment, it is not surprising that it gave us an art that was detached and enamored of the evanescent and the momentary, a snapshot world, translated into literature as the "slice of life." Our own times have been more subjective; we have been more primitive, more intuitive. If we have been chaotic,

Peter Paul Rubens (1577–1640), THE TRIUMPH OF CHRIST OVER SIN AND DEATH
The Metropolitan Museum of Art, New York, Bequest of Ogden Mills, 1929.

The baroque period equated its men of genius with its princes, and its greatest and most successful genius was Peter Paul Rubens. He painted his time as a pageantry spread over the walls of palaces, a flamboyant medley of Christianity and mythology that captured the vitality of an epoch.

the chaos was man, and our art has at least possessed the monumentality of seeing man everywhere.

The modern artist deals with man's experience, and he paints what is invisible to us because it lies within us and can only be reached by symbols. The art of our century is realism, too, if it is considered self-portraiture in the widest sense, with man's composite nature its subject matter. It can be impulsive, childlike, overpassionate, overintense; or logical, cold, abstracted, and self-centered in its introspection.

Let us be more specific, and contrast and compare. The drawing in Rouault's *Three Judges* is not the clearly legible drawing of Ingres, nor is *Woman I* by de Kooning to be criticized by the same canon which pronounces *La Comtesse d'Haussonville* excellent. A new boldness, vio-

Rembrandt van Rijn (1606–1669), THE THREE CROSSES, 1653
Collection: Mr. and Mrs. Walter Maitland, Drake Colorado.

Rembrandt would have left us more etchings and fewer paintings if his eyes had not failed him. As an etcher, he created a world of light and shadow as mysterious as life itself; he combined the maximum of solemn feeling with the maximum of technical resource in the medium of his choice.

lence, and strength follow a gesture from the shoulder and not from the wrist. What *is* clearly legible in Rouault is the painter's moral indignation with the unjust judge. Rouault is a moralist: he is pressing an indictment with all the rugged eloquence he can muster.

We may reflect, however, that some judges are just and do not merit indignation; that the animosity must be deep in the artist's nature, or it could hardly have bitten into the style. In de Kooning's *Woman I* the violence is not directed against a particular woman, but seems aimed at womankind. We must admit that we are dealing with something highly personal: the painter is liberating his own driving force, or ferocity. Paint has relieved many an overcharged temperament

Georges-Pierre Seurat (1859–1891), FISHING FLEET AT PORT-EN-BESSIN, 1888
The Museum of Modern Art, New York. Lillie P. Bliss Collection.

Seurat believed that he was transforming Impressionism into a science. He studied laws of optics and reduced his technique to method. His sense of form, his sheer vitality, kept him from becoming stilted; in his hands Impressionism developed into a classical art.

from van Gogh to the present, and the impulse to violence can work itself out on a canvas and subside in the calm of the museum.

Let us assume that in Rouault there is no collapse of technique—his intention simply does not tolerate the detachment necessary for an Ingres' preoccupation with surface. Since Rouault carries out his intention and moves us with a powerful and dramatic statement, with the economy and intensity of great work, his painting must possess means equal to his ends, or his result simply could not have been achieved.

In the *Three Judges* * we are in a human situation, and Rouault's bold outlines make clear the limits of the individual—we are never left in doubt as to what is man and what is not. Man is incised, and all the rest is subsidiary. Yet environment is tonally related to man, much as in the painting of Rembrandt, an artist who was said to fill in his

* Plate 18.

Willem de Kooning (1904–), WOMAN I, 1952
The Museum of Modern Art, New York. Purchase.

backgrounds by cleaning his palette, thus setting man in a diffused essence of himself. Rouault's heavy outlines, however, are not only limits of personality, they are limitations: his men are somehow clumsy, truncated, dwarfed, by their huge heads. In Rouault, man is a toad with a jewel in his head; his body is too mean a house for a soul. For this latter-day Gothic artist, we are saints, sinners, and gargoyles all in one. But in Rouault, as in Rembrandt, we are not left with a Biblical reference which draws its solemnity from the text: we are faced with man's condition, and the statement is conveyed in the handling of the paint.

But if the handling of paint is to sweep all before it, we cannot stop with Rouault; we are led back to de Kooning's *Woman I*. Standards here are certainly involved with control of action: we should look at such a canvas as a producer or critic looks at a play, asking if there is any weak or dull area, or if the work is everywhere sustained. Do structure and fabric fuse, or are there stretches where there is only fabric? For there are no limits set, as in Rouault: an over-all effect seems intended, the artist's personality serving as content and diffused throughout the painting.

Pollock takes this process one step further—a step which is perhaps inescapable once we set out on the subjective path. He gives us the maximum of intensity, for which all else seems sacrificed. Painting now clearly takes on the quality of an art of performance: ideally Pollock should have been seen at work. The painting exists as the score of a composition or the recollection of a vital experience. We do not require Pollock to tell us of an outer world, although his painting relates to an age equipped to see the outer galaxies and to see matter dissolve in streams of electrons only to be known by their traces.

In living out his adventure on canvas, surrendering to his expansive impulse, Pollock was able to put himself in touch with a larger audience which has had a part in his tensions. If this is not conscious communication, Pollock is at least organizing a concomitant response: his painting brings a rational fulfillment in the sense that it is an experience shared.

We can put in a claim for craftsmanship for Pollock, quite as we did for Rouault, on the basis of purpose achieved. But perhaps we feel uneasy as we do so, when we see that so much has been gambled on impulse. So much depends on the happy accident in the name of spontaneity, that we wonder if we are accounting for craftsmanship simply because we feel that it ought to be present. The dominant impression is of a man who cannot pause for method. Wildcatting in the field of the subconscious, he has brought in a gusher.

When we try to assess his means, there are at least criteria which do *not* apply. The sense of order is either not present or is not valued. There seems to be little concern with the achievements of the conscious mind as it manifests itself in the grasp of relationships, of laws or principles, and by such means exerts a control over time and space beyond the individual's inner experience. Pollock, we feel, would resist such restraints. Instead, we sense a reversal of traditional values: we are witnessing the sort of conflict which is dramatized in Milton's *Paradise Lost,* the clash between the eternal order of Heaven and the destructive personalness of Satan. William Blake dramatized the same conflict in his *Marriage of Heaven and Hell.*

Intensity can present its own problem if the painter pays too high a price for it. Each of us differs from his fellow, and if we wish to be entirely ourselves we have no basis for communication. Conceivably a painting can be too close to the artist, have too much of *him,* and too little of *us.* But we must not assume this; nor should we lay the breakdown in communication to a breakdown in technique. It is the technique in Pollock which is the communicative thing, enabling us to "read" him, to recognize what we see and know what we may expect. It is his procedure which conveys the rhythms, the turmoil, the intensity he offers us.

We have been dealing with one development in modern painting, a trend toward an ever increasing intensity of expression. There is another trend, now equally familiar to us: the pursuit of form for its own sake. At the present date, we can see this formal trend as a long structural development, through Cubism, in which the object was transposed into geometric elements, to an art of pure relationships, with no object represented.

As the pioneers in this field explored their way, each new step was greeted as a further abandonment of standards, as though the artist were throwing off one obligation after another. Yet, in reality, as Picasso and Braque developed Cubism, their very detachment from representation forced upon them a technical concern with the surface. Their Cubism of 1910 to 1912, for instance, displayed subdued subtleties of controlled and precise brushwork and handling far more sensitive than the bold and impressive brushwork of their predecessors, the Fauves. Braque was perhaps the more surface-conscious of the two innovators. His father had been a house painter and decorator,

Jean Auguste Dominique Ingres (1780–1867), LA COMTESSE D'HAUSSONVILLE, 1845

and he served an apprenticeship which focused his attention on surface qualities. To Braque is due much of the variety of surface effect in modern painting: the sanded textures, the paper patterns affixed to the canvas. Collage was a relatively short-lived experiment in the nineteen-tens; but it added a new dimension, a new sense of reality to the surface, and recently the making of collages has returned to favor.

The innovations of the Cubists led directly, through the carrying of an idea to its conclusion, to the geometric paintings of Mondrian. Although Mondrian's lines have the accuracy of the ruler, and the colors are pure and flat, his paintings never suggest to anyone that a child could do them. Their subtle asymmetry, their machine-tool precision, their very technical proficiency, attest that the painter is dedicated to pure relationship, to a world of philosophic absolutes withdrawn altogether from the passage of time. There is no visible brushwork, no quality of signature in the handling. If Pollock condenses all into personality and the moment, Mondrian evokes eternity and effaces himself completely, quite as he smooths away the trace of the brush.

Yet the art of Mondrian is not a surface art simply because it requires precision. He has no wish to baffle us with appearances, as we find ourselves arrested by the craftsmanship of Ingres. *"The representation of matter crumbles of itself* [wrote Mondrian] *when we no longer take matter into account. We then come to representation of other things, such as the laws which govern the conservation of matter."* [1]

Mondrian has far more to offer than neatness and a compulsive cleanliness. He gives us mathematical miracles, positives made out of the multiplication of negations. We must remember that the inhibitions of the psychologist can be the triumphs of the saint.

There is still another phase of modern art, Surrealism, which leans heavily on the resources of technique in its effort to enforce plausibility. Here the means employed are quite traditional; traditional too is the demonic scene unfolded. The Surrealist has modernized the world of witchcraft and macabre fantasy rampant in the painting of Hieronymus Bosch and Pieter Breughel and has adapted it for the textbook of the psychiatrist. He has striven to create the effect of hallucination through the intensity of his implausible realism. He is close, also, to the sixteenth- and seventeenth-century artists who were striving to mock reality with their powers of deception. Dali forces conviction with all of the skill, but with none of the serenity, of Vermeer. Tanguy's *Slowly toward the North* * creates a three-dimensional deception with black shadows, his objects standing in the round like those of Caravaggio, who achieved an ominous sculptural effect by intensifying the lighting —a procedure which had an enormous effect on his century.

The unsettling purpose of the Surrealist relates certainly to the anxiety of our age. But Surrealism has the air of novelty, rather than the newness of creation, a way of astonishing by changing the subject. Technically, it is a putting of new wine in old bottles, with, of course, new labels. It is precisely the conservative technique of Surrealism which renders its contribution suspect.

A genius whose fantasy places him closer to the Surrealists is Paul Klee. But here there is technical invention, not opportunism. It would be hard to imagine more genius content with more evanescent effects. Such is his economy that the slightest scratch is a statement, either plastic (post-Cubist), or literary, or political, or philosophic, by turns. Klee seems embarrassed before the monumental or the pretentious.

We seem to find, then, a sudden broadening of technical effects in our time; and we must also admit that *something* suffers if an artist concentrates on a single effect. Technical standards may suffer if the artist includes them in the price of spontaneity, or of intensity, or of personality. This gives us pause, and we are not altogether reassured if we are told that control is present where impulse so obviously reigns. But we should not assume that standards have been annihilated simply because they have been loosened. If the artist is using more *basic* material, perhaps the critic too should concern himself with more basic standards, which are less subject to the changes in decades, or even in centuries.

To what standards can we turn in testing a work of art? A master work should have unity, should create the impression of a single statement, supported at all points. This characteristic seems so obvious that when the unity breaks down, when the artist seems willing to be diverted from his purpose, we instinctively withhold the epithet, "great." On the positive side, we feel that this unity introduces order. Even in the most emotional art, we should feel this need for order satisfied. The cohesive principle in Expressionist painting seems to be its appeal to the moral order. And in the most chaotic work, we should feel the power and the range in man's ability to transform. In this *ordering* there should be a sense of

* Plate 19.

revelation as well as of transformation: a sense of grasp of the nature of things which eliminates accident; a sense akin to the scientist's or the religionist's, that we can navigate, and are not adrift. There should be a sense of an endlessly new approach to something endlessly familiar; for since we only approach reality through metaphor, metaphor must be changed before its meaning or relevance wears off.

Unity and order should not be casual achievements. There should be a problem set appropriate to the goal. The unity in a Shakespearean tragedy or in Joyce's *Ulysses* draws together more elements than are dreamed of in an ode of Keats or in an Imagist stanza. In Picasso's *Girl before a Mirror* more disparate things are united than in Dali's *Persistence of Memory*, or even in Ernst's *Woman, Old Man and Flower*. It is here, perhaps, that the choice of the slight, of the minor key, in Klee sets a limit to accomplishment. And when we turn back to *La Comtesse d'Haussonville*, we are struck by perfection within a still narrower range; yet we do not blame the artist, since the constriction is within the society Ingres portrays.

The struggle to produce unity and order out of conflicting elements creates intensity; and often technique is conspicuous just where intensity is lacking, in other words, where technique has lost its purpose. Here the critic can be led to overindulge himself along with the artist, for it is a fact that many people do not like intensity, and prefer to be pleased rather than disturbed, because they do not have the stamina to participate in the work of art. The battle in a work of art is between intensity and control, and technical means are the weapons.

The artist has chosen means best adapted to his purpose and ability, and in proportion as he respects his own means, we should respect him. He will be wary of supporting his best means of expression with others not so native to him; he may offer us words but we should not ask for them.

In the last analysis, a painting is a technical performance: there is no miracle if the nonmaterial is not materialized, and for this there must be a structure, a vocabulary, a *way*. A painter, however otherworldly, raises his craft to a professional level, conveys a feeling that he can do what every man cannot do. He may grope, but eventually he has his way of going about his own business. We should feel this, and feel, too, that he has made his activity somehow our own.

These reflections are meant to offer no more than an approach to judgment. But at least we have left behind our references to dates and styles, our comparison of one century with another; and we have perhaps found a little firmer footing, so that we do not drown in the cross currents of taste. We can never have standards so firm that they replace the art of discrimination.

1. Michel Seuphor, *Piet Mondrian: Life and Work*, New York, Harry N. Abrams, Inc., 1956, p. 118.

NINE

The New Environment

IN OUR DISCUSSION of various kinds of twentieth-century painting we have suggested that each is a characteristic expression of our modern age. These works were produced in those decades of the twentieth century which have proved to be among the most revolutionary which man has ever experienced. The rapidly accelerated worlds of physics and psychology have created a "new" environment for the scientist, the philosopher, and the artist. Our concern in this chapter will be with the artist as he has been affected by various aspects of the new environmental forces, with the impact upon him of the ever-changing world of the twentieth century, and, in turn, with the artist's own impact on our time.

There are some, we should note, who claim that this approach has no meaning. For them, painting is something independent of time or place or its conditions of origin and development. Clive Bell, the English writer who coined the term "significant form" for the twentieth century, has argued persuasively that "*to appreciate a work of art we need bring with us nothing but a sense of form and color and a knowledge of three-dimensional space*," and that those who really understand art "*are concerned only with lines and colors, their relations and quantities and qualities, but from these they win an emotion more profound and far more sublime than any that can be given by the description of facts and ideas.*" [1]

This point of view has been a dominant one in the modern world. It has encouraged a new kind of detachment for the object: museums provide the works on display with an atmosphere of remoteness, divorced from the historical and social conditions and associations, and especially from the personality, that produced the painting. Photographs, reproductions, art galleries, and museums often minimize the environmental factors.

The opposite view is put by André Malraux: "*If every biography is encompassed by its times this is obviously so in the first place because the artist is at least submitted to certain capital values of these times. Even van Gogh's revolt belongs rather to the nineteenth century than to the seventeenth.*

"*'Locomotives have nothing to do with art,' said Ingres angrily. Perhaps not, but they have a great deal to do with the artist who, less than one hundred years after Ingres, is faced with a civilization in peril and who knows one hundredfold more pictures than did the master of the Villa Medici . . .*

"*But there is a more decisive reason still which links the artist at the outset to his own age—for he cannot belong to some age of his choice, nor to any other age than his own.*" [2]

We can find evidence for this "environmental" view in the changing themes which artists have dealt with in different periods. During the nineteenth century—from the early discovery of atmosphere by Constable to the monumental mountains of Cézanne—virtually every major painter dealt with the landscape as a basic subject. This was the culmination of man's discovery and exploration of his physical surroundings. The nineteenth-century painter worked out-of-doors, close to nature, in his attempts to capture fresh qualities of color, light, and form.

In the early years of the present century the painter returned to his studio for a more concentrated investigation of conceptual and imaginative problems. This shift in attitude and purpose from the nineteenth-century analysis of nature sometimes took the form of a withdrawal from the changing environment and a search for the expression of the "absolute," as we saw in Chapter 3. Sometimes, too, twentieth-century artists looked more intensely inward as they responded to intense emotion, probing the subconscious, as we have discussed in Chapters 5, 6 and 7.

But in other cases, artists have found new inspiration in the world of science and technology. Paul Klee has said, *"Is it not true that even the small step of a glimpse through the microscope reveals to us images which we should deem fantastic and overimaginative if we were to see them somewhere accidentally, and lacked the sense to understand them?"* [3] As suggested by Klee, man's imagination has been stimulated by a creative exploitation of new tools and instruments, and certainly there are many new visual environments now open to the painter. The shift in emphasis has been from the physical to the psycho-physical, from the natural to the man-made.

Our man-made modern world has produced wholly new surroundings: the city with its towers, slums, mansions, and complexes of transportation and production; the impressive maze of power stations, grain elevators, refineries, and factories. The painter was among the first to recognize and come to grips with the spectacle of mechanization and the new order of a scientific and industrial society. He extracted from the new physical and psychological setting patterns of pictorial relationships which were as revolutionary as the conditions of living.

As Mumford wrote: *"The new characteristics now touch almost every department of experience. Observe the derricks, the ropes, the stanchions and ladders of a modern steamship, close at hand in the night, when the hard shadows mingle obliquely with the hard white shapes. Here is a new fact of esthetic experience; and it must be transposed in the same hard way: to look for gradation and atmosphere here is to miss a fresh quality that has emerged through the use of mechanical forms and mechanical modes of lighting. Or stand on a deserted subway platform and contemplate the low cavity becoming a black disc into which, as the train rumbles toward the station, two green circles appear as pin-points widening into plates. Or follow the spidery repetition of boundary lines, defining unoccupied cubes, which make the skeleton of a modern skyscraper: an effect not given even in wood before machine-sawed beams were possible. Or pass along the waterfront in Hamburg, say, and review the line of gigantic steel birds with spread legs that preside over the filling and emptying of the vessels in the basin: that span of legs, that long neck, the play of movement in this vast mechanism, the peculiar pleasure derived from the apparent lightness combined with enormous strength in its working, never existed on this scale in any other environment: compared to these cranes the pyramids of Egypt belong to the order of mud-pies. Or put your eye at the eyepiece of a microscope, and focus the high-powered lens on a thread, a hair, a section of leaf, a drop of blood: here is a world with forms and colors as varied and mysterious as those one finds in the depths of the sea. Or stand in a warehouse and observe a row of bath tubs, a row of siphons, a row of bottles, each of identical size, shape, color, stretching away for a quarter of a mile: the special visual effect of a repeating pattern, exhibited once in great temples or massed armies, is now a commonplace of the mechanical environment. There is an esthetic of units and series, as well as an esthetic of the unique and the non-repeatable.*

"Absent from such experiences, for the most part, is the play of surfaces, the dance of subtle lights and shadows, the nuances of color, tones, atmosphere, the intricate harmonies that human bodies and specifically organic settings display—all the qualities that belong to the traditional levels of experience and to the unordered world of nature. But face to face with these new machines and instruments, with their hard surfaces, their rigid volumes, their stark shapes, a fresh kind of perception and pleasure emerges: to interpret this order becomes one of the new tasks of the arts." [4]

The paintings by the four artists selected for this discussion reveal, each in its own way, how these artists have provided a fresh interpretation of the man-made world. Fernand Léger in *Petit Déjeuner* * has taken a very direct approach. In his portrayal of a traditional theme of a group of women seated about a breakfast table, the human forms are descriptively geometrized along with the furniture and the architectural setting. His vision was consistently mechanical and structural, exploiting the sharp, hard metallic edges and polished surfaces as a means of giving his large canvas a sense of architectural grandeur. Léger found that beauty was not antithetical to those aspects of the modern world which were based upon new technologies. He perceived with great clarity some of the basic facts of a machine age

* Plate 21.

environment, and he brought out the richness, the dynamism latent in the technological revolution.

Unlike artists and critics of the nineteenth century—Ruskin, Morris, or Tolstoy—who wanted to retreat from the implications of the machine, Léger felt, as did other pioneering contemporaries such as Frank Lloyd Wright and Le Corbusier, that mechanization was one of the most exciting facts of modern man's life. Le Corbusier had even conceived of the house as a "machine for living." Léger was one of the many who were able to give new form and direction to the prophetic words of Wright, who spoke on this subject as early as 1930: "*Grasp and use the power of scientific automatons in this creative sense and their terrible forces are not antagonistic to any fine individualistic quality in man. He will find their collective mechanistic forces capable of bringing to the individual a more adequate life, and the outward expression of the inner man as seen in his environment will be genuine revelation of his inner life and higher purpose.*" [5]

If we shift from Léger's lathe-turned women to the *Classic Landscape* by Charles Sheeler, we find another response to an environment which had not been considered a "beautiful" subject for an artist. Here, however, the aesthetic discovered by

Charles Sheeler (1883–   ), CLASSIC LANDSCAPE, 1931
Collection: Mrs. Edsel B. Ford, Detroit.

Sheeler is revealed in the title itself. He found a classical quality in the majestic forms of the Ford plant at River Rouge. He perceived the whole complex of engineering inventiveness as one of the monuments of the modern world. Although Sheeler's art is less abstract or symbolic than Léger's, he has exercised great care in selecting, ordering, and simplifying to arrive at the significant.

One of the most important facts of modern existence has been the rapid concentration of population in the great cities of the world, and the urban scene in all its variety has assumed a great importance for the painter. In *New York at Night,** John Marin has expressed the quicker tempo, the noise, the thrill of New York. Alfred Barr commments: *"The roar of the El, the fifty story buildings scraping the sky—John Marin felt the excitement of the scene and painted it—not the scene so much as his excitement, breathlessly using great slashing zigzag strokes . . . for the angles of the buildings and even for the sky."* [6] This artist builds his architectonic subject on a

* Plate 22.

Charles Sheeler (1883–), COUNTERPOINT, 1949
Collection: Mr. Bernard Heineman, Jr., New York.

Impressed with American industry, Sheeler has recorded the factory scene, either contemporary Detroit (*Classic Landscape*) or the New England mill town of earlier days. As a photographer he has tended toward the factual, and when he reorganizes objects on a canvas, his arrangements of form suggest multiple images on a single photographic plate.

geometric scaffold of free angular shapes and lines. "*I see great forces at work*" (Marin wrote in 1913); "*great movements; the large buildings and the small buildings; the warring of the great and the small; influences of one mass on another greater or smaller mass. Feelings are aroused which give me the desire to express the reaction of these pull forces, those influences which play with one another; great masses pulling smaller masses, each subject in some degree to the other's power.*" [7] In contrast to the serenity and quiet mood of Sheeler, *New York at Night* is jangling, active, filled with motion and feeling.

The work by Stuart Davis enigmatically titled *Visa*,* like the painting by Marin, is part and product of the urban environment. The color has all the brilliance and brashness of a neon sign. He has used the most intense contrasts, screaming primaries—red, yellow, and blue—with black and white. It is a blatant, vivid statement growing out of the modern world. As the artist said, "*I very often use words in my pictures because they are part of urban subject matter.*" [8] Davis has capitalized upon the concepts of the Cubists in both the formal structure and the use of words as a basic part of the pictorial order.

Alfred Barr quotes the artist when he writes: "*In 'Visa' the word* CHAMPION, *'clearly the subject matter of the painting,' was derived from a matchbook cover. The word* ELSE *answered the artist's need for a short word without associations. The phrase,* THE AMAZING CONTINUITY, *besides 'animating the area at the extreme right,' refers to the experience of finding in paintings of very different subject matter and style the mysterious common factor, the 'amazing continuity,' which unites them as works of art. 'The content of this phrase is real,' Davis concludes, 'as real as any shape of a face or a tree'.*" [9]

Davis has extracted from a multitude of visual sensations qualities with which most of us are familiar, but which we may be reluctant to perceive as having an artistic significance. In 1945 the artist described his feelings about the environmental influences in this country. "*I have enjoyed the dynamic American scene for many years, and all my pictures . . . are referential to it. They all have their originating impulse in the impact of contemporary American environment. Some of the things that have made me want to paint, outside of other paintings, are: American wood and iron work of the past; Civil War and skyscraper architecture; the brilliant colors on gasoline stations, chain-store fronts, and taxicabs; the music of Bach; synthetic chemistry; the poetry of Rimbaud; fast travel by train, auto and aeroplane which has brought new and multiple perspectives; electric signs; the landscape and boats of Gloucester, Massachusetts; 5 & 10 cent store kitchen utensils; movies and radio; Earl Hines' hot piano and Negro jazz music in general, etc. In one way or another, the quality of these things plays a role in determining the character of my painting; not in the sense of describing them in graphic images, but by pre-determining an analogous dynamics in the design which becomes a new part of the American environment.*" [10] This particular work, *Visa*—dynamic, forceful, bright—is peculiarly a part of the twentieth century; and the cacophonic color and the animated linear shapes also spring from Davis' intense preoccupation with jazz music over the years.

* Plate 23.

Each of these works has been based upon significant aspects of the contemporary environment. Yet in every case it is clear that the artist has not merely reflected his environment passively. His role is still a creative one. He selects and designs as he chooses. Whistler, in his famous talks in the eighteen-eighties, was not referring to a man-made environment, but he made the same point: "*Nature contains the elements, in color and form, of all pictures, as the keyboard contains the notes of all music. But the artist is born to pick, and choose, and group with science, these elements . . . as the musician gathers his notes, and forms his chords, until he brings forth from chaos glorious harmony. To say to the painter, that Nature is to be taken as she is, is to say to the player, that he may sit on the piano. That Nature is always right, is an assertion, artistically as untrue, as it is one whose truth is universally taken for granted. Nature is very rarely right, to such an extent even, that it might almost be said that Nature is usually wrong.*" [11]

The artist, in other words, has not merely used his environment; on his canvas it is transformed. In turn, the works created add to the sum of the environment. There is a chain of impact and counter-impact. Once the work of art is completed, exhibited, and absorbed into the fabric of a time, the created object has a power and vitality for giving life to experience.

Take, for example, the wholly unexpected and revolutionary effect of Mondrian. Here was a painter who sought to transcend the immediate environment, the changing social milieu. Yet his work was to be a major influence upon the shape of the twentieth-century world. The influence of his thought and example was first felt by his colleagues in Holland. At Leyden in 1917 a group was established, consisting of painters, sculptors, architects, and poets who called their movement De Stijl or Style. To set forth their ideas, they brought out a magazine of the same name, which was published until 1932. Mondrian and Theo van Doesburg were the most forceful and creative of the new group, and they developed the abstract style now associated with Mondrian's name. The "Stijl" credo was direct and simple and had a very broad appeal. Its theories integrated all the visual and structural arts so they could function together through a common use of right angles, straight lines, primary colors, and asymmetrical, or occult, balance.

Theo van Doesburg was the most active advocate of the group's ideas, and it was he who made contact with the Bauhaus School of architecture and design in Germany and introduced the ideas of "Stijl" into the current of the "International Style" of architecture. Partially from the Bauhaus and partially from the "Stijl" activities in Holland, the straight lines, pure colors, and occult balance of the Dutch school spread throughout the Western World. The "Stijl" has had a colossal impact upon all levels of contemporary art, until —its origin forgotten—it has become practically synonymous with "modern" design.

Similarly the Cubist works of Braque, Picasso and Feininger may be seen as analagous to the

Ludwig Mies van der Rohe (1886–), PROJECT FOR A GLASS TOWER, 1920–1921
Courtesy of the Artist.

What is the new city environment to which the artist responds? Not merely the actual experience, the city which soars above him and roars about him and beneath his feet, but that environment which he can imagine, along with the architect, whose conceptions run ahead of practical opportunity.

structural design of architecture. By the time the painter had clarified his discoveries, he was able to help the architect and the industrial designer solve their problems.

As Henry-Russell Hitchcock has written, "*In relation to modern architecture, the central meaning and basic value of abstract art . . . is that it makes available the results of a kind of plastic research that can hardly be undertaken at full architectural scale . . . The processes of cross-fertilization by which creative influences are transmitted in the arts remain a mystery despite all that is written about them. Yet the study of important abstract paintings and sculpture of the last thirty years can help, at the very least, to suggest one of the ways modern architecture arrived at its characteristic visual forms.*" [12]

This "cross-fertilization" between painting and architecture is most aptly indicated in the architecture of Le Corbusier—the architectural *nom de plume* of the painter, Charles Edouard Jeanneret. Although such an intense duality of interest in one man is unusual, it symbolizes the kind of influence painting can exert on the art of building. As Hitchcock says, "*The delicate precision of pattern in his walls and their openings*

Le Corbusier (1887–), STILL LIFE, 1920
The Museum of Modern Art, New York, Van Gogh Purchase Fund.

Henri Matisse (1869–1954), PIANO LESSON, 1916–1917
The Museum of Modern Art, New York. Mrs. Simon Guggenheim Fund.

. . . is clearly related to the restrained elegance of form in his paintings. In theoretical writing Le Corbusier was stressing the analogies of the new architecture with the characteristic products of the machine . . .

"There are closer analogies as well. The smooth, flat rendered surfaces of his buildings had the immateriality of the colored shapes in post-cubist painting. And soon the darker colors of his pictures of the mid-twenties were introduced in addition to pastel tones in order to contrast certain wall surfaces more boldly with the off-white tone . . . Even the curves of the objects in the pictures were echoed in his plans in the freely bent shapes used for non-structural screens. Neither in plan nor elevation were his architectural compositions allowed to ramble; rather they are compactly ordered inside rectangles, as if within the frame of a painting." [13]

Another painter whose associations and interests reached out into other fields was the American-born Lyonel Feininger, who spent many years abroad. In his poetically abstract depiction of *The Steamer Odin II,** 1927, one may see qualities of both architecture and music, which were of great interest to him. Mary Rathbun has written of Feininger: *"His love of music and his continued fascination with the industrial and engineering activity he had seen as a child in New York were expressed in the broken lines and planes of his special forms of cubism . . . It was his ability to project such poetic moods with the most elementary devices of representation which impressed Feininger's architectural associates at the Bauhaus. For it suggested that the purified elements of the new architecture might likewise have their special poetry if they were handled with comparable refinement."* [14]

Feininger was the first painter to join the brilliant faculty of the Bauhaus School. Architecture was one of the most persistent thematic subjects for him: either the marine architecture of sailing vessels and steamships, or the patterned streets of the medieval or modern town. The sensitive cadence of his lightly-ruled pen lines, delicately modulated by the broken rhythm and the areas of water color which embellish the surface, are both musical and architectural.

We have also seen how Charles Sheeler, John Marin, and Stuart Davis have used the urban environment as the basis for their "architectural" painting in which an order, structure, or scaffolding for the subjects has direct implications for the architect. Most of these artists are direct descendants of the Cubist tradition and the systematic ordering of form as first developed by Picasso and Braque about 1910.

One of the important developments of modern times is this emergence of new relationships between the utilitarian and non-utilitarian arts. That which is creative and alive in one field may have significance for many other areas of expression.

This modern attitude has given the painter the power to influence the shape and scale and color of the city-scape in which we live and work. The painter was among the first to point to the tremendous potential for well-being in making color a significantly expressive and functional part of our lives. Van Gogh, Gauguin, the Fauve and Brücke groups, were all instrumental in making man perceive his surroundings with an emphatic vividness. As Whitehead said, *"The habit of art is the habit of enjoying vivid values."* [15] Matisse, Kandinsky, and others showed the importance of color as a vehicle of expression and emotion. We now know that planned color design for factories, offices, or hospitals has a positive effect upon the efficiency of the workers or on the health of the patients. The choice of color and shape and texture in our environment does make a difference.

Matisse was, throughout his long career, one of the great experimental colorists. You have seen how in *Red Studio* the dominance of a large field of red-orange makes the visual imagery of his studio come to life. Color may be broadly likened to sound. Dissonance, harmony, and unusual combinations are often the basis for a new aesthetic experience. *Piano Lesson* by Matisse is an example of using color and shape in a restrained architectural way. The broad planes have been treated flatly and simply, emphasizing the scale of the work which is of almost mural dimensions, seven by eight feet. The rich ground of gray is intersected by the subtly nuanced tones of blue, orange, violet and green. These grayed hues are stabilized in the lower part of the picture by the calligraphic tracery in black.

Out of such experiments we can see today how the color range and quality of hues used in *Piano Lesson* have been used for interiors and exteriors of houses and commercial structures. Often the choice of tone and hue by the painter affects the objects we use and live with daily. There has developed in the twentieth century a closer relationship between the non-utilitarian and the useful arts. One depends and draws upon the other.

Many new categories and purposes have appeared in which symbols and pictures play a vital part. Industry and commerce have rapidly found

* Plate 24.

Henri Matisse (1869–1954), THE BLUE WINDOW, 1911
The Museum of Modern Art, New York. Mrs. John D. Rockefeller, Jr., Purchase Fund.

a new usefulness for the artist; but the painter as often as not finds greater satisfaction in being free of the requirements for an advertising campaign or for illustrating a murder mystery in a popular magazine. It may seem surprising that the painter's non-utilitarian role of experimenting and exploring has had a profound effect upon the new range of utilitarian demands. Often the seemingly "useless" becomes the most "useful." The gap or "cultural lag" which has frequently been assigned between the "fine" arts and the "applied" or commercial arts is often bridged today because of the changed relationships among all the arts. The interactions among the many purposes to be served by creative men are flexible and no longer clearly defined. Ideas, forms, or technical devices developed by painters in the solitude of their studio for "pure" experimentation may have an almost instantaneous effect upon other avenues of graphic expression for commerce and industry.

Thus we can see that the relationship between the artist and his environment has been a significant one in the twentieth century. But the relationship is not necessarily one that the artist sets out to achieve, and his influence may have been the greatest when he was the least concerned with the world around him.

1. Melvin Rader, *A Modern Book of Aesthetics*, New York, Henry Holt and Co., Inc., 1952, p. 324.
2. André Malraux, "The Psychology of Creation," *Magazine of Art*, v. 42, April, 1945, p. 125.
3. Paul Klee, *Paul Klee on Modern Art*, London, Faber and Faber, Ltd., 1948, p. 47.
4. Lewis Mumford, *Technics and Civilization*, New York, Harcourt, Brace and Co., Inc., 1934, pp. 333–334.
5. Frank Lloyd Wright, *Modern Architecture*, Princeton, New Jersey, Princeton University Press, 1931, p. 23.
6. Alfred H. Barr, Jr., *What is Modern Painting?*, New York, The Museum of Modern Art, 1943, p. 19.
7. Frederick S. Wight, *John Marin*, Los Angeles, Art Galleries, University of California, 1955, verso front cover.
8. Alfred H. Barr, Jr., Editor, *Masters of Modern Art*, New York, The Museum of Modern Art, 1954, p. 117.
9. *Ibid.*
10. James Johnson Sweeney, *Stuart Davis*, New York, The Museum of Modern Art, 1945, p. 34.
11. James McNeill Whistler, *The Gentle Art of Making Enemies*, New York, Charles Scribner's Sons, 1911, pp. 142–143.
12. Henry-Russell Hitchcock, *Painting Toward Architecture*, New York, Duell, Sloan and Pearce, 1948, p. 54.
13. *Ibid.*, pp. 26–28.
14. *Ibid.*, p. 70.
15. Alfred North Whitehead, *Science and the Modern World*, Pelican Mentor Edition, New York, New American Library, p. 200.

TEN

Freedom and Responsibility

IN THE LAST chapter we explored some of the relationships between the artist and society. We have not, however, considered adequately the question of what kinds of responsibilities a society should expect the artist to undertake, and what degree of freedom it ought to leave him.

This has not always been a crucial issue in art. In other times the artist was very much a part of his society, and his role was clear and highly regarded. For example, it was the painter who enunciated the ideals and ambitions of Renaissance man. The painter appeared long before the printer; and the picture reached a far larger audience than the word. Painting was both popular and aristocratic, public and private, religious and secular. The new humanistic impulses opened up an unprecedented opportunity for the artist to satisfy the demands of society, and painting responded to the vitality and expansiveness of the era.

The painter was commissioned to paint portraits, religious works of many sizes (from the monumental to the cabinet), historical scenes, mythological themes, and later, landscapes and still-lifes. By the seventeenth century each of the major categories of subject matter had its specialists, and the painter was one of the personalities most prized by the Court and the Church.

But in the course of time there was an erosion of the social function of the painter. In the first place, royal and noble patronage dwindled, destroying a stable source of income. The artist's audience became an amorphous one, less specific in its demands than the patron. Creative work had to be developed independently of traditional means of patronage and established social institutions.

Secondly, the invention of the camera in 1839 quickly deprived the artist of his work as a portrait-painter. Virtually every major painter from the fifteenth century to the nineteenth had exploited his role as the limner, and often the creator, of the idealized image of the nobleman. The genius of Van Dyck had, as Henri Focillon playfully suggests, created an image of the English gentleman that the British have been struggling to emulate ever since. But by the nineteenth century, royalty had neither the political nor economic power to keep the tradition alive. With the camera everyone could have a portrait; why bother, then, with the expense and the tedious sitting when in a few moments one could be typed on paper? And this was simply the first step in the successive stages of man's ability to create new modes of visual representation. The motion picture and now television have both assumed many of the social purposes previously filled by the painter, and they have also opened new and competitive possibilities for creative expression. The painter is no longer needed as a reporter of the contemporary scene or as an interpreter of the past.

So, by the eighteen-nineties the artist was free of many traditional influences and functions. He was also free to starve. The neglect and deprivation suffered by many of the major talents—Daumier, Millet, van Gogh, Pissarro—are well known. Understanding of their work often came after or shortly before their deaths. If there was a response during their lifetimes it was frequently in the form of a furious uproar among critics and public. Today it is difficult for us to see why there should have been such an outcry against the shimmering landscapes of the Impressionists or the grand, often monumental, works of Cézanne. But it was typical of the successive misunderstandings between artist and audience throughout the nineteenth and twentieth centuries as painters have explored fresh areas of experience and concentrated on problems of formal organization and pictorial structure.

Faced with a seemingly hostile society, and with a harsh industrialism whose rapid, unplanned growth seemed to leave little room for the creative personality, the artist tended to turn inward. Ever since the seventeenth century, inventive and original minds—El Greco, Rembrandt, Chardin, Goya, Delacroix—had been painting first of all for themselves and their fellow artists. But these men anticipated what was to become virtually true for creative men in all fields by the late nineteenth century. By then the process of the alienation of the artist was far advanced, and many painters sought refuge in exile: van Gogh in southern France and the asylum; Gauguin in the South Seas; Cézanne in Provence; while in America, Eakins, Homer and Ryder built their own private worlds and worked in solitude.

All the emphasis in this situation would be on the freedom of the artist, and this emphasis has been accentuated in the twentieth century. The painter's freedom is seen as a necessary condition of artistic achievement, and it has been related to the political concept of democracy. President Roosevelt in a speech in 1939, given on the occasion of the opening of the new building for the Museum of Modern Art, said, "*The arts cannot thrive except where men are free to be themselves and to be in charge of the discipline of their own energies and ardors. The conditions for democracy and for the arts are one and the same. What we call liberty in politics results in freedom in the arts. . . . A world turned into a stereotype, a society turned into a regiment, a life translated into a routine make it difficult for either arts or artists to survive. Crush individuality in society and you crush art as well. Nourish the conditions of the free life and you nourish the arts too.*" [1]

The universal validity of this broad "romantic" assumption by politicians and writers may be questioned. If we look to the past it is clear that most art was produced under conditions which we would call "authoritarian" today, and many of the great developments in the arts were the result of strict discipline.

When we look, however, at both artistic and political developments since the eighteenth century, there are new factors to consider: the rapid ascendancy of democratic principles and the importance of individual rights; technological developments based upon radically new and dynamic scientific principles; a changed relationship between patron and artist and between the audience and the work of art. From these changes it seems reasonable to draw the implications suggested by the philosopher Horace Kallen: "*The freedom of taste is joined to the liberty of the artist even as the liberty of the consumer is joined to free trade among producers. Art, equally with industry and science, comes to abundance and achieves general use only as it provides manifold alternatives for its lovers, generous variety for its consumers to choose from. Abundance of choice and the act of choosing which is the exercise of taste, are alike grounded upon the artist's liberty to create, the critic's spontaneity to prefer. Now, this liberty and this spontaneity are also intrinsic to the happening of beauty.*" [2]

Yet this does not dispose of the issue of this chapter. If it be accepted that the artist must have freedom, that no one shall dictate to him what he shall or shall not paint; there is still the question of how he will use that freedom. Does freedom not carry with it the concept of responsibility? What might this responsibility consist of in the twentieth century?

It could take the form of visual interpretation of the new industrial and mechanical forces of our age, such as we found in the previous chapter in the works of Léger and Sheeler. It might comprise social and moral commentary, like the works of Rouault, or Max Beckmann's allegory of agony and survival, *The Departure*. We shall take two other examples here of this approach to the problem of responsibility: Picasso's *Guernica* and Lebrun's *Crucifixion*. Both of these men intermittently throughout their careers have attempted poignant, often painful, interpretations of political, social or religious themes, and have drawn attention to the evil and destruction present in the contemporary world.

Picasso's monumental conception of the bombing of Guernica was based upon an actual historic catastrophe. One of the most authoritative commentators on Picasso, Alfred Barr, has written, "*On April 28, 1937, the ancient and hallowed Spanish town of Guernica was destroyed by German planes flying for General Franco. The Luftwaffe was said to have been very pleased with the night's work: about a thousand people—one out of eight—were killed. It was the first 'total' air raid.*

Paul Gauguin (1848–1903), THE MOON AND THE EARTH (HINA TE FATU), 1893
The Museum of Modern Art, New York. Lillie P. Bliss Collection.

Of all the painters who were once Impressionists, Gauguin went furthest in developing a style of his own. He gave up prismatic depth in favor of color in bold decorative areas. So used, Gauguin's color became arbitrary and symbolic; reds, greens, and golden tans are spread hypnotically before the eye. Appropriately his forms became full generalizations, little concerned with precise articulations of anatomy.

Albert Pinkham Ryder (1847–1917), MOONLIGHT MARINE
The Metropolitan Museum of Art, New York. Samuel D. Lee Fund, 1934.

A belated and benighted Transcendentalist out of New England, Ryder was a poet in paint with a superb feeling for space and form. His limitations were technical; he lived like a hermit and he despised craftsmanship as he despised wealth.

"Two days later the Spaniard, Picasso, took an artist's revenge; he began work on his Guernica, a huge mural canvas nearly twenty-six feet long, commissioned by the Republican Government for the Spanish building at the Paris World's Fair.

"The artist has given no exact explanation of Guernica, but the general meaning of his allegory is clear. At the right a woman, her clothes on fire, falls shrieking from a burning house, while another rushes in toward the center of the picture, her arms flung wide in despair. At the left is a mother with a dead child in her arms, and on the ground are the fragments of a sculptured warrior, one hand clutching a broken sword. In the center a dying horse sinks to his knees, his screaming head flung back, his back pierced by a spear dropped from above like a bomb. To his left a bull stands triumphantly surveying the scene. Over all shines a radiant eye with an electric bulb for a pupil, symbolizing night. Beneath it to the right a figure leaning from a window bears witness to the carnage, the lamp of truth in her hand . . . He has made full use of the special weapons of modern art which during the previous thirty years he himself had helped to sharpen: the free distortions of expressionist drawing, the angular design and overlapping transparent planes of cubism, surrealist freedom in the use of shocking or astonishing subject matter. Picasso employed these modern techniques not merely to express his mastery of form or some personal and private emotion but to proclaim publicly through his horror and fury over the barbarous catastrophe which had destroyed his fellow countrymen." [3]

In this large-scale mural of carnage and destruction Picasso has used only blacks, whites, and grays. Here the absence of color is symbolic; tones of sadness and mourning are deliberately funereal. Picasso, too, may have been reminded consciously or subconsciously of Goya's graphic outbursts in his series of bitterly etched plates, *The Disasters of War*, and the enigmatic group called *The Dreams*. Both these great Spaniards employed the most inventive and "modern" formal means of their times to illuminate the subject matter.

For the past several years Rico Lebrun has been seriously concerned with one of the most dramatic spiritual themes of the Western World: the passion of Christ, and the suffering and salvation to be found in this great sacrifice for mankind. In 1951 he completed the monumental triptych symbolizing the Crucifixion, the climax of hundreds of drawings and paintings. Like Picasso's *Guernica*, it is almost panoramic in scale, and although it was painted in a relatively short time (about six weeks) it is the result of years of study, a sum-

Pablo Picasso (1881–), GUERNICA, 1937
Owned by the Artist. Courtesy Museum of Modern Art, New York.

mation of a lifetime. Lebrun relies on symbol, metaphor, and allegory, but it is impossible to miss the intense mood of tragedy and suffering. He is reminding the world of the need for finding its sanity before chaos and catastrophe engulf us all —as they have come so close to doing in our times. It is also a reminder that the Christian world has a tradition based upon love as the positive force for the renewal of man's constructive energies.

Picasso, Lebrun, Rouault, Beckmann have perceived, perhaps more clearly than diplomats and scientists, the horror and anguish which our world has experienced. They have expressed their perceptions with a strong sense of moral responsibility. Yet few of their works were the result of direct commission. They sprang from the artists' need to re-state, visually and symbolically, thought and ideals which had an urgent significance for the painters. For their purposes they chose the tools and techniques of the free and independent twentieth-century experimentalists. They did not seek to re-create a representational version of an event, but to interpret in new and individual ways. They were expressing a sense of moral responsibility, but their works were still products of the artist's freedom.

What are we to say then of the many kinds of twentieth-century painting which do not have this kind of purpose? Picasso in his earlier Cubist paintings, Mondrian, the Abstract Expressionists, were not making explicit moral judgments on social tragedies. They did not necessarily go as far in the opposite direction as Dadaism, described by Marcel Duchamp as "*a sort of nihilism . . . a way to get out of a state of mind—to avoid being influenced by one's immediate environment, or by the past; to get away from clichés—to get free.*" [4] Still, the desire to "get free" has characterized many of the painters of our era, including Pollock, Kline, Gottlieb and de Kooning.

Are we to say of these men that they are irresponsible? It is, in fact, alleged by a number of critics that the Abstract painters lack any sense of purpose. The apparent disdain for long-established techniques; the absence of recognizable social or human content—these have been interpreted as indicating a withdrawal by the painter from his function and an alienation from his world.

Against this case, two main points of view should be cited. The first is that the painter's primary responsibility is not to make social comment, but to paint. It is what he puts on the canvas that counts, and this should be considered strictly in its own terms. Judged in this way, many contemporary works which contain no recognizable references may still be enormously significant to the individual viewer.

Le Corbusier has written: "*Modern painting has left on one side wall decoration, tapestry, and the ornamental urn and has sequestered itself in a frame—flourishing, full of matter, far removed from a distracting realism; it lends itself to meditation. Art is no longer anecdotal, it is a source of meditation; after the day's work it is good to meditate.*" It is for this reason, says Le Corbusier, that "*today painting has outsped the other arts. It is the first to have attained attunement with the epoch.*" [5] Can we say, then, that the artist has failed in his responsibility if he provides us with "a source of meditation," or of excitement, or, simply, of delight?

Secondly, it can be argued that the artist's exclusion of social comment from his work is in itself a strong statement of a position. The artist in the nineteenth century did not become merely an exile, a displaced person. Freed of his traditional external responsibilities, he anticipated and helped establish the importance of the individual. He expressed a new and daring attitude toward what may well be the basis of creative activity, the awareness of the power within man himself, the primacy of the person. Perhaps there is no more important social function for the artist to fulfill than to demonstrate the vitality of the individual creative act. As Alfred Barr suggests: "*Freedom of expression, freedom from want and fear, these are desirable for the artist. But why would the artist's freedom particularly concern the rest of us? Because the artist gives us pleasure or tells us the truth? Yes, but more than this: His freedom as we find it expressed in his work of art is a symbol, an embodiment of the freedom which we all want but which we can never really find in everyday life with its schedules, regulations and compromises. Of course we can ourselves take up painting or some other art as amateurs and so increase our sense of personal freedom; but even in a nation of amateur artists there would still be a need for the artist who makes freedom of expression his profession. For art cannot be done well with the left hand: it is the hardest kind of work, consuming all of man's strength, partly for the very reason that it is done in greater freedom than other kinds of work.*

"*The possibilities open to the painter as he faces his blank canvas, or to the composer before his untouched keyboard are so complex, so nearly infinite, that perfection in art may seem almost as unattainable as it is in life. Mondrian perhaps comes in sight of perfection by limiting his prob-*

lem to the subtle adjustment of rectangles. An 'abstract' painter who passed beyond Mondrian into geometry would indeed find perfection, but he would leave art behind him just as . . . the painters in counterfeiting reality are expert craftsmen but scarcely artists. For complete perfection in art would probably be as boring as a perfect circle, a perfect Apollo, or the popular, harp-and-cloud idea of Heaven.

"Yet the artist, free of outer compulsion and practical purpose, driven by his own inner passion for excellence and acting as his own judge, produces in his work of art a symbol of that striving for perfection which in ordinary life we cannot satisfy, just as we cannot enjoy complete freedom to tell the entire truth." [6]

It is true that modern painters, in their various expressions of the "inner passion for excellence" have produced such a range of styles in such rapid succession that some have found it bewildering and irresponsible. Yet the artist, after all, is simply reflecting the pace of innovation, the mobility and the freedom of choice which is available to all of us in so many areas of life. Creative experience has always been basically experimental and unexpected. Whatever the art of the future may bring, we know that there will be individuals who are dedicated to a form of expression which seems strange, remote, difficult. These revolutionaries take time and patience to understand. It also takes time to winnow the true from the false, the merely fashionable from that which will be lasting. In a world inundated by novelty, with armies of organizations strenuously devoted to change for the sake of change, the task of judgment is indeed a difficult one.

To help us with this we have a relatively new but influential factor: art criticism. Some describe the critic as a necessary evil; others feel that he is

Rico Lebrun (1900–   ), CRUCIFIXION, 1950
Courtesy of the Artist.

a pontifical parasite making judgments without being a practitioner of the art he is judging. If we take a dispassionate view, we must first admit the presence of the art critic. Many metropolitan newspapers, periodicals, art and scholarly journals publish the writings of the critic. We enjoy reading about art and artists. It can be argued that in the complex pattern of art activity all over the world, the critic, the expert is indispensable. For example, in New York a critic for an art magazine or newspaper will have to study and review twenty to thirty exhibits a week. At times it is impossible for one person to attend all the events related to the arts.

The critic's position as a combination of judge and expert is a demanding one. He has a great responsibility to evaluate many different types and categories of painting. He must weigh the objective facts with his subjective, intuitive responses. The critic is doing in a more professional and refined way what we all do constantly. We must today continuously make judgments and decisions. Some of our tests are more sharply defined than others. Many women are truly expert in their knowledge of fabrics, textiles, or tailoring. Often they take for granted such knowledge, based upon years of training and experience, and expect to be equally expert in appraising works of art where most of us have had only a limited amount of first-hand knowledge. The true critic is perceptive, sensitive and tolerant. He does not ignore standards, and he employs standards of performance like a variable slide rule, depending upon the intention and range of the work under consideration. He realizes that his freedom to pass judgment carries with it a dual sense of responsibility: on the one hand to the artist and on the other to the public for whom he is writing.

Irwin Edman, a wise critic, poet, and philosopher, has written: "*criticism . . . is simply the application of standards to perception, like those the artist, the scientist, and the practical man use for estimating the effectiveness of their techniques. Criticism does for our discrimination what it does for our control. It is simply perception become exact and enlightened.*

"*It is not legislation, it is not vague appreciation. It is, through a training in exactness of perception, in historical sympathy, in intellectual understanding, the education of taste to purity, clarity, and intensity. Criticism is, in the arts as in life, simple experience become conscious, precise, and disciplined.*

"*It is the imagination both nourished and nurtured. Ultimately what criticism tries to elicit in the fine arts, the discrimination of values intrinsically justified, is a clue to the business of all philosophy, the criticism of criticism, the ultimate attempt to define and discriminate value.*" [7]

We have talked in this final chapter of the responsibility of the artist. Whatever his stated intentions, he will have fulfilled his responsibility if he expands our response to our total environment, and enables us to examine freshly the nature of the physical world, or to clarify the depths of our psychological ambient, or to enliven the realm of man's social problems. We have suggested, too, that the professional critic can help us in finding the standards by which to evaluate the vast and varied field of contemporary painting.

But it is not enough to talk about the responsibilities of artists and professional critics. We, too, must undertake to develop and refine our own judgment. This is a demanding process, calling for a great deal of comparative study of modern painting with those works of the past which have been sources of inspiration for the present. The rewards of this effort will be high. For the informed, sensitive viewer participates in the fresh experience of seeing a new world along with the artist and takes part with him in the experience of creation.

1. *New York Times*, May 11, 1939, p. 29.
2. Horace Meyer Kallen, *Art and Freedom*, Vol. 1, New York, Duell, Sloan and Pearce, 1942, p. 984.
3. Alfred H. Barr, Jr., *What Is Modern Painting?*, New York, The Museum of Modern Art, 1943, pp. 36–37.
4. Katherine S. Dreier, James Johnson Sweeney, Naum Gabo, *Three Lectures on Modern Art*, New York, Philosophical Library, 1949, p. 45.
5. Le Corbusier, *Towards a New Architecture*, London, The Architectural Press, 1946, p. 23.
6. Barr, *op. cit.*, p. 39.
7. Irwin Edman, *Arts and the Man*, New York, W. W. Norton and Co., Inc., 1939, pp. 149–150.

Biographies of the Artists

MAX BECKMANN Born in Leipzig in 1884, Beckmann is one of the major Expressionist figures, although he opposed such organized movements as *Der Blaue Reiter.* He first studied in Weimar, around 1900, then in Florence and Paris. At the close of World War I, he had developed his bold, vigorous style, congested, sensuous, and often sadistic. A decade later he was represented in the Exposition of Contemporary German Painters and Illustrators by *Le Pont, Plage,* and *Femme Couchée.* He was able to project those drives deep in the nature of man which only symbolism can express. His art at once reflected and pilloried the Nazi temperament, and it was a foregone conclusion that he would be persecuted. Between 1932 and 1935 he painted *The Departure,* which he called *Scenes from Shakespeare's "Tempest"* to mislead the Nazis. He was denounced in 1936 and left Germany the following year.

Arriving in the United States, he developed a wide following while teaching at the University of Indiana and at Mills College, California. Many triptychs followed *The Departure* in a series that were sermons on the moral and immoral nature of man. His reputation was already firmly established in this country when he died in New York in 1953.

CONSTANTIN BRANCUSI Born in Craiova, Rumania, in 1876, Brancusi attended a local art school and was trained as a cabinetmaker. Until 1902 he studied at the Bucharest Academy. He then moved to Paris where he resided until his death in 1957. He studied under Mercier at the École des Beaux-Arts until 1906, when the sculptor Rodin advised him to leave the school. At first under the influence of Rodin, he became aware of primitive art early in the century and he developed a style at once new and permanent. He created symbolic, often highly sensuous forms that were quite abstract. Unlike the Cubists, and Cézanne before them, Brancusi's forms appear to be founded on a curvilinear geometry. From 1910 on his style continued to perfect itself, although it remained inherently unchanged. Brancusi created very few new forms over a long lifetime, but he created them at an early date, and he must be seen as one of the most important figures of twentieth-century sculpture, neither encompassed by nor a part of any artistic movement.

Brancusi was one of the first sculptors of this century to be strongly influenced by the inherent nature of his materials. Wood reveals itself as such, displaying the patterns of the grain and often maintaining a rough primitive surface. His work in metal frees its surface by the use of a high, light-reflecting polish. Simplification and refinement to a point of unbreakable unity characterize Brancusi's imagery, whatever his media. The mood of his work ranges from the humor of the wooden head with rusty crown entitled *King,* to the lofty idea-image of *Bird in Space.* Another principal of Brancusi's symbolism is his *Endless Column* sending its repeating pattern out into space, implying an infinite extension of man, of his art, and his accomplishments. The column ends, as all things must, but Brancusi leaves us with a beautifully subtle statement of the interrelationship between actual termination and conceptualized infinity.

GEORGES BRAQUE Born in Argenteuil in 1882, of a family of house-painters and amateur artists, Braque learned his father's trade and acquired skills of imitating wood and marble surfaces, etc. After completing his military service in 1902, he studied art in Paris. He abandoned his early Impressionistic style by 1906, and he became one of the Fauves. Then, strongly influenced by Cézanne's architectonic work, during a stay in L'Estaque in 1908, he reduced his brilliant palette to somber grays and earth colors, and became, with Picasso whom he met the following year, one of the originators of Cubism. Here his early training in producing varied surfaces stood him in good stead, and the introduction of *collage* may probably be credited to him.

During World War I he was wounded and received two citations. After the war he produced ballet sets for the impresario, Diaghilev, and painted in a variety of styles: Cubism, Neo-classicism, and a fluid, tasteful and decorative manner which became his most personal expression. *Yellow Tablecloth,* 1928, received first prize in the Carnegie Exhibition. He repeated his triumph at the Golden Gate Exhibition in 1938. His *Billiard Table,* 1946, won first prize at the Venice Biennial Exhibition in 1949. Braque's importance as an innovator and his position as a leader in the modern movement have been underscored by numerous retrospective shows in Europe and the U.S.

ALEXANDER CALDER Born in Philadephia in 1898 of a family of artists, Calder was first drawn to engineering, but he turned to painting in 1921 and held his first exhibition five years later. He went to Paris in 1927, where he began executing wire sculptures, including his famous miniature circus of animated toys. Here he formed friendships with Miró and Mondrian, who urged him toward the use of color and more abstract composition. His interest in animation was reactivated by an exhibition of eighteenth-century mechanical birds, and he produced the first manual and motor mobiles in 1930–31 and wind mobiles in the following year. In 1934 he returned to the United States and constructed outdoor sculpture.

A period of experimentation in materials culminated in his Mercury fountain for the Spanish pavilion at the 1937 Paris Exposition, his water ballet fountain display for the New York World's Fair two years later, and his first exhibition of jewelry in 1940. The wit and lightness of his work, his technical ability, his successful use of color, and his incorporation of motion, combine to make Calder a notable and original figure in mid-twentieth century art. He is one of the few Americans to have influenced European artists.

PAUL CÉZANNE Born in Aix-en-Provence in southern France, in 1839, Cézanne was to spend most of his life in this part of the country painting its people and its landscape. His banker father insisted that he attend law school but at last allowed him to go to Paris to paint. Here (in 1861) he met his childhood friend, the future novelist, Émile Zola. In Paris Cézanne was at first influenced by the work of Courbet which he saw in the Salon des Refusés of 1863. Then Pissarro drew him toward the new methods of the Impressionists, and in 1875 he exhibited with them at their first Salon. *The House of the Hanged Man* shown at this time reflects the Impressionist influence, but already demonstrates Cézanne's concern with a solid formal content rather than with the dissolution of form into light. Impressionism was an outgrowth of the misty northern atmosphere, and Cézanne's paintings related to the rocky mountainous landscape of the south, with its clear forms and flat blue sky. Already in his work a series of planes guided the eye carefully through space. In 1877 he showed seventeen canvases to the still hostile public at the Third Impressionist Exhibition. Then he retreated to the south, working by himself for the next fifteen years. Monet, Renoir, Monticelli, and Zola occasionally visited him, but his painting lost all traces of the Impressionist influence.

His father's death left Cézanne financially independent. He moved to Fontainebleau in 1892, and lived there for six years painting the famous series of *Baigneuses*, *Montagne Sainte-Victoire*, and the *Card Players*. The dealer Ambroise Vollard gave him his first one-man show in 1895, where his work was again denied by the critics, spurned by the public, and acclaimed by the artists. From this time on his fame steadily increased. In 1904 the newly-organized Salon d'Automne devoted an entire room to his work. The next year he finished the *Grandes Baigneuses*, on which he had been working for seven years. He died in 1906 in Aix-en-Provence.

A large retrospective show, in 1907, demonstrated the great indebtedness the new movements felt toward him. This indebtedness was to increase. Fauvism was attracted by the way in which he modeled in color, using yellows for forward movement, blues for recession. The Cubists were more concerned with his breaking up of space into carefully analyzed plastic volumes. Cézanne desired to control and stabilize his environment, and he used pure color relationships to establish a permanent structure, rather than to record momentary effects. Taking his given subject—the human figure, landscape, or still life—as a point of departure, he freely distorted his subject elements to serve formal ends. His attention to total formal effect has led both objective and non-objective painters of the last fifty years back to the mastery of Cézanne.

MARC CHAGALL Born in Witebsk, Russia, in 1887, of a poor Jewish family, Chagall first studied art at the Imperial School of St. Petersburg, producing genre scenes of a childlike, Expressionist character. Living in Paris from 1910 till the advent of World War I, he met the critics and poets Max Jacob and Apollinaire, the painter Modigliani, and others, and abandoned the somber tone of his earlier painting for strong bright colors. He became acquainted with the work of the Cubists, adapting their use of geometric abstraction to his own personal blend of fantasy and nostalgia (*I and My Village*). The playful irrationality of his painting in Paris had an important influence, later, in the Surrealist movement. After the Revolution he was appointed Director of the Academic Jewish Theatre in Moscow, but he returned to Paris in 1922. He remained there until 1941 and then came to the U.S. Five years later, he designed the decor for Stravinsky's *Firebird* ballet, and was given a retrospective exhibition by The Museum of Modern Art. Despite his affiliation with the French Surrealist movement, his work closely parallels that of the *Blaue Reiter*, and his pictorial folklore has made him one of the most popular contemporary painters.

GIORGIO de CHIRICO Born in Volvo, Greece, in 1888, son of an Italian construction engineer, de Chirico first studied painting in Athens. His father died during de Chirico's childhood, a circumstance often related to the morbid backward-looking quality in his art. He moved, with his mother, to Florence; then he studied in Munich, and was much influenced by the late nineteenth-century mystic painter, Böcklin. He went to Paris in 1911 and produced, during the following decade, a series of important works that were to be significant for the development of Surrealism and the Neo-romantic movement. These paintings, employing dramatic, deep space, fell into two categories: those dealing with a brooding evocation (*Recollections of Italy: The Joys and Enigmas of a Strange Hour*, 1913), and those of a more psychically troubling aspect (*The Disquieting Muses*, 1917).

Upon his return to Fascist Italy, his painting lost its arresting intensity, and his style gradually changed from that of the so-called Metaphysical School to a less powerful, more naturalistic manner. As he lost his static intensity, de Chirico undoubtedly felt that he was becoming liberated, and he presents the curious spectacle of a painter recovering from his morbid ability as though it were an illness.

SALVADOR DALI Born in the Spanish province of Catalonia in 1904, Dali received his academic training at the School of Fine Arts in Madrid. He first exhibited in Barcelona in 1925 and then moved to Paris, where he demonstrated an instinctive theatricality, both in his art and in his life. He was strongly influenced by the theories of Freud and the work of the Cubists, Futurists, and Italian Metaphysicists. Although he did not join the Surrealist movement until 1929, his painting brilliantly dramatized the Surrealist flair for the bizarre, and did not conceal its literary weakness and its leaning toward illustration.

Dali described his art as "paranoiac painting." Such works as *The Persistence of Memory* (1931) and *The Enigma of William Tell* (1934) are extraordinary *pastiches*, combining the technique of Vermeer and the invention of the sixteenth-century mannerists. His amazing, realistic draftsmanship fuses the disparate elements that make up his work: illogical dream-like images, set against the barren landscape of Spain, and calculated, ambiguous effects that function as a visual pun. Besides his double-image paintings and the so-called "Surrealist objects" which he has made, he has to his credit fantastic jewelry and two early Surrealist films: *Le Chien Andalou* and *L'Age d'Or*. An international figure, he lives much of the time in America; and he has achieved a spectacular if controversial popularity and renown.

HONORÉ DAUMIER Born in Marseilles in 1808, Daumier from early childhood experienced the struggles of the lower classes he was so graphically to portray. He drew continually and in secret, while his father, a mediocre poet, tried to acquaint him with the business world, first in the law courts and then as a bookseller. His first lithograph was published when he was twenty, and for the next decade he served as a cartoonist for *La Caricature,* a newspaper that satirized the Royalist regime. Daumier's sharp comment reached its climax in the lithograph *Gargantua,* a caricature of the King himself, and he was sent to prison for six months. From then on his satire was social rather than political, and he lampooned the pretensions of the new middle class. With occasional interruptions Daumier produced two lithographic plates a week for the better part of a lifetime, making a total of over 4,000 prints.

Late in life he gave up lithography and turned to painting. His canvases were somber and dramatic, describing the world he had always shown, the rich and vital if sordid life recorded in the writings of Balzac. Although these paintings are among the finest of the century, Daumier could have starved but for his friend, the landscape painter, Corot. Poverty-stricken, and almost blind, he had his first exhibition in 1878, and died the following year.

Daumier achieved far more than social and political satire. His Parisian types, the beggar, man of justice, Bohemian, and railway passenger, possess a kind of monumentality through the expression of the form itself. His figures, at once simple and grandiose, have a sculptural quality. Daumier made bronze or clay models for many of his lithographs, and he may well be considered as a sculptor in his own right. As a result, his graphic work has volume as well as contour. His *Third Class Carriage* is a fine example of summary form: the massive effect of bulk and the concentration of interest in a conglomerate, the class itself, rather than in individuality or detail.

The modern movement is indebted to this man who was able to work plastically in space, to use subdued but expressive color, and to introduce a new kind of subject matter made moving and monumental through its form rather than through its content.

STUART DAVIS Born in Philadelphia in 1894, Davis grew up in the atmosphere of a newspaper's city desk. His father was in charge of illustration for the *Philadelphia Press* and close to a group of Philadelphia artists and illustrators, including Robert Henri. This group gradually migrated to New York and Davis' father moved to East Orange, New Jersey. Davis left school at 16 to study with Henri in New York, and three years later was producing covers and drawings for *The Masses* and working as a cartoonist for *Harper's Weekly.* He was represented in the Armory Show of 1913 by five water colors, and he held his first one-man show four years later, while working at map-making for the Army Intelligence Department. His trip to Paris in 1938 consolidated his experiments and turned him in the direction of a geometric decoration (the *Eggbeater* series), under the influence of Gauguin's and van Gogh's color innovations and the structural emphasis of Cézanne, Léger, and Picasso—he had profited by the experience of Cubism. He began teaching at the Art Students League in 1931, and the next year participated in The Museum of Modern Art's mural exhibition and produced a mural for Radio City Music Hall. He took part in the WPA Federal Art Project in 1932, and from 1934–39 he was active in the Artists' Congress, from which he resigned in 1940 when he began to teach at the New School for Social Research.

His work has grown increasingly abstract, brilliant, even deliberately jarring in color, reflecting at once his lifelong interest in jazz music and his awareness of the sharp color patterns and the strident pace of American life. His paintings have the quality of a poster that describes and advertises the American temperament. One of our most significant painters, he was honored in 1945 by a retrospective showing at The Museum of Modern Art and was given a second retrospective by the Walker Art Center, Minneapolis, in 1957.

WILLEM de KOONING Born in Rotterdam in 1904, Willem de Kooning left school at the age of 12 to work as an apprentice in a painting and decorating firm. The next year, studying evenings at the Rotterdam Academy of Fine Arts, he was introduced by one of his instructors to the abstract art movement, *De Stijl.* Graduating in 1924, he left two years later for America, where his first job was painting houses in New Jersey. He moved to New York and worked as a stage designer, commercial artist, and decorator. During the period of his association with the WPA Federal Art Project (1935–36), he began to develop his Abstract Expressionist style. He executed a mural for the New York World's Fair in 1939, and almost a decade later (1948), held his first one-man show in New York. He taught at the Yale School of Fine Arts in 1952–53, and exhibited at this time his famous series of pictures of *Woman.*

This bare account omits his purpose and power, and a drive which has led de Kooning into abstraction and out of it again.

ANDRÉ DERAIN Born in Chatou, France, in 1880, Derain was painting at the age of 15, and by 1898–99, he was studying art at the Académie Carrière where he met Matisse. At the van Gogh Exhibition in 1901, he introduced Matisse to Vlaminck. That year he shared a studio with the latter, doing his first book illustrations for Vlaminck's novel. Later he studied at the Académie Julian and after his military service in 1905, joined Matisse in the south of France. As one of the early Fauves, he produced his most brilliant and distinguished painting in such canvases as *Blackfriars Bridge, London.* Later his style became semi-Cubist, under the influence of Cézanne and of Picasso whom he met in Spain in 1910. *The Last Supper,* which marks the end of Cubist influence in his work, was painted in 1914, when he was again called for military service. After the war he was commissioned to do the sets for the ballet, *La Boutique Fantasque.* His subsequent painting, of an eclectic nature, continued to show a great concern for plastic composition, yet it seemed to lack direction, and to lose in sensibility. From 1935 until his death in 1954, he seldom exhibited.

MARCEL DUCHAMP Born in Normandy in 1887, Duchamp is one of the most paradoxical artists living today; and although he has long since ceased to paint, he is one of the most influential. In 1912, extending the Cubist idea of simultaneity to include a sense of motion in the subject as well as in the observer, he produced a "blueprint of movement": the famous *Nude Descending a Staircase* which was the major sensation of the Armory Show of 1913, and which gave great impetus to the ideas of the Italian Futurists. He was anarchic and ironic in his attitudes, and his mobiles, "ready-mades" (*The Fountain,* 1917), and such gestures as the addition of a beard and moustache to a print of the Mona Lisa (1919) indicate his Dada affinities. Always more attracted to mechanism than to brush and canvas, by 1925 he had given up painting entirely. However, his creative activity did not cease. He invented his "rotary demisphere," produced an extraordinary film, *Anemic Cinema,* and devised his rotoreliefs of the nineteen-thirties which, when placed on a turntable, act as phonograph records for the eye. Since his arrival in the U.S. in 1941, he has remained an enigmatic figure ostensibly devoted only to chess.

MAX ERNST Born in Brühl near Cologne, Germany, in 1891, Max Ernst was a student of philosophy at Bonn University and an artillery officer in the First World War. He caught public attention at the Dada exhibition at Cologne shortly after the war. He practiced the creation of "ready-mades" along with Picabia and Duchamp and showed some of his more important paintings at Düsseldorf in 1922: *La Belle Jardinière, Children Frightened by a Nightingale,* and *The Virgin Mary Punishing the Christ Child in the Presence of Three Witnesses.* Soon afterward he left for Paris and joined the group which was to form the nucleus of the Surrealist movement. He published his first book of *collages,* utilizing nineteenth-century illustrations to create fantastic picture stories. Always inventive, three years later he developed a special process of rubbing to create the drawings published in the volume, *Histoire Naturelle.* In subsequent years he followed this process in painting, particularly during the summer of 1934 in Carcassonne, with a series of pictures such as *The Moon and the Forest.* With the outbreak of the war in 1939 he came to the U.S. and later settled in Arizona where the desert landscape greatly influenced his work. Following a large retrospective show at Brühl (1951) he returned to live in Paris the following year.

LYONEL FEININGER Born in New York in 1871, Feininger grew up in a world of music. His father was a violinist and composer, his mother accompanied his father and taught singing, and young Feininger was playing the violin in concerts at the age of 12. At 16 he followed his family to Germany to study music, but instead he studied art for the next five years in Berlin. From 1893 he was active as a cartoonist and illustrator in Berlin and then in Paris, and about 1907 he gave up cartooning and returned to Berlin to paint. He was aware of the work of the Cubists, and in 1911 he was again in Paris where he knew Delaunay and other contemporary painters. He insisted, however, that the major influence upon his highly structural work came from Bach and the other formal German composers of the eighteenth century.

Franz Marc invited him to exhibit with the *Blaue Reiter* group in 1913, and in 1919 Feininger (who had been in Berlin all through the war) became the first member of the Bauhaus staff. Here he taught for a decade, along with Kandinsky and Klee.

While he was at the Bauhaus, he produced many woodcuts (in the early 'twenties) and his brittle and congested style became more spatial, architectural, and serene in mood. His work was considered degenerate by the Nazis in 1933, and he returned to the United States in 1936. He executed murals for the New York World's Fair of 1939, and he continued to produce outstanding canvases and water colors for another two decades, with little change in his highly disciplined and deliberate art. Greatly admired in Germany, he was given over 20 one-man shows in the United States, and he died in New York in 1956.

NAUM GABO Born in Bryansk, Russia, in 1890, Naum Gabo, brother of Antoine Pevsner, studied mathematics, physics, and engineering at the University of Munich in 1909. He and Pevsner spent three years in Oslo, Norway, where Gabo made his first "construction" in 1916. After the Russian Revolution the two brothers returned to Russia and published the *Realistic Manifesto of Constructivism* in conjunction with the first Constructivist exhibition in 1920. Gabo and Pevsner left Russia soon after, for their artistic expression did not serve the propaganda needs of a rising dictatorial government. In 1927 they collaborated on the stage design of the ballet, *La Chatte.* Later Gabo's constructions were exhibited in Berlin, Paris, and New York. He now lives in Woodbury, Connecticut, continuing to work in metal and plastics with an ever-present optimism concerning the future development of Constructivism. Recently he has worked on an extremely large sculpture, erected in front of a department store in Amsterdam designed by the modern architect, Marcel Breuer.

The unique aim of the Constructivists was the use of space as a sculptural element. Gabo tried to abandon the concept of volume and mass, insisting upon depth alone as the proper measure of space. The use of transparencies, plastics, or wire mesh allows space or air to become an integral part of the sculpture itself. Gabo's purely non-objective forms rest in complete balance and equilibrium, both space and time being held in their pervasive tranquillity. They are meant to reveal an idealized universal state, an environment at once related to, and created by, man himself.

PAUL GAUGUIN Born in 1848 in Paris, Gauguin spent his early childhood in Peru where he had connections on his mother's side. As a young man he entered the merchant marine and made trips to Brazil. He settled down in Paris, achieving success as a stock broker, and had a family with five children. Then he began to take an interest in art, became a Sunday painter, and finally gave up his business. He lived in poverty in Paris and Rouen, separated from his family, and withdrew to Pont-Aven in Brittany where he painted *Vision after the Sermon* in 1886. A trip to Panama and Martinique added illness to poverty. In Brittany again in 1889–90, his *Yellow Christ* shows his synthesis of the many influences (Japanese prints, the paintings of the Impressionists and Cézanne) which he had absorbed. Still harassed by poverty and resentful of civilized life, he held a sale of all his paintings to raise funds to go to Tahiti. This first trip to the Pacific produced such paintings as *The Spirit of the Dead Watches* (1893), canvases glowing with tropic color.

When he returned to Europe, a small legacy temporarily helped his purse but not his fortunes. He went back to Tahiti in 1895 and continued with his resplendent canvases of the South Seas, culminating in his large, philosophic *Whence Do We Come? What Are We? Where Do We Go?* (1898). His desperate circumstances led to a suicide attempt, and trouble with the local authorities caused him to move to the Marquesas Islands where he died in 1903.

As a Post-Impressionist, Gauguin threw off the Impressionists' commitment to representation. He introduced generalized forms and rich symbolic color. With Gauguin, painting ceased to be receptive and became a conscious act of creative will.

JEAN LÉON GÉRÔME Born at Vesoul, France, in 1824, Gérôme displayed an early talent for drawing. He studied in Paris with Delaroche, a painter of anecdotal illustration, and accompanied him to Italy in 1845. Later Gérôme visited Turkey and Egypt, acquainting himself with the exotic Middle Eastern subject matter currently popular. In the Salon of 1855 he exhibited the *Age of Augustus and the Birth of Christ* which may well stand as the epitome of the sterile academicism prevalent in the mid-eighteen-hundreds. It was immediately purchased by the state.

Gérôme felt that the first duty of the artist was the correct representation of phenomena. As a bitter critic of every avant-garde painter of the last half of the nineteenth century, Gérôme condemned Delacroix, Courbet, Manet, and the Impressionists, proclaiming that the work—the very existence—of each artist represented a further decline in the moral tenor of the state. He continued his official persecution of the Impressionist group until his death in 1904.

VINCENT van GOGH Born in Groot-Zundert in southern Holland in 1853, van Gogh was the son of a minister of a country parish and the grandson of a famous preacher. Three of his uncles were art dealers, a profession which his devoted brother Theo was to follow. Van Gogh first intended to be an art dealer himself, but he was also drawn to the religious life—the other family dedication. He failed as a dealer, was frustrated in love, and determined to become a missionary; in this he also failed dismally before he decided to take up painting. His style during the first years of solitary experiment in Holland was dark and gloomy (*The Potato-Eaters*, 1885), paralleling his somber and difficult private life.

In 1887 he went to Paris to his brother Theo, with whom he had been in continuous correspondence. Living with Theo for a year, he came under the influence of Japanese art and his contemporaries Toulouse-Lautrec, Pissarro, Degas, Seurat, and Gauguin. He adopted the Impressionists' palette and began the colorful painting for which he is known. At first he used the vibrant brushwork characteristic of the Impressionists (*Père Tanguy*, 1887), but this was only a transition to something much more powerful, plastic, and expressive. After one more crisis in human relationships, he left his brother, who continued to support him, and went to Arles in February, 1888. Here he worked furiously in the blaze of the southern sun. His color gained in brilliance, his work grew stronger, and the inner tension built up once more. A three-month visit from Gauguin led to a tragic conclusion: the men fought; van Gogh's violence turned back on himself, and he mutilated his own ear. The two painters had, however, influenced each other. Van Gogh gained something from Gauguin, as such a masterpiece as *L'Arlésienne* testifies. He was hospitalized early in 1889 and spent the better part of the time that remained to him in an asylum at nearby St. Rémy. He was allowed to paint, and the great canvases from this period were tumultuous and harrowing, their composition characterized by a swirling vortex (*The Starry Night*, 1889).

Late in the spring of 1889 he again joined his brother. Paris was too much of a strain, but Theo had provided shelter for him in the countryside at Auvers. Here he was under the protection and care of an eccentric physician and art patron, Dr. Gachet. He continued to paint furiously and even sold a painting—the first sale of a lifetime. He was still mentally disturbed, and he shot himself in July, 1890.

ADOLPH GOTTLIEB Gottlieb was born in New York City in 1903. At the age of seventeen he studied briefly with John Sloan and Robert Henri at the Art Students League, New York. In 1921–22 he worked independently in Paris, Berlin and Munich. Upon returning to the United States he continued to develop along advanced lines and 1935 marked the founding of "The Ten Group" which was committed to avant-garde principles. Gottlieb and Mark Rothko were among the founding members. In 1937 he travelled to Arizona and Yerrington, Nevada, where he spent two years completing a post office mural for the U.S. Treasury Department's Section of Fine Arts. By 1939 he was back in New York where he created arc curtains for the synagogue of Congregation B'nai Israel, Milburn, New Jersey, and for Temple Beth El, Springfield, Massachusetts. In 1955 he completed a stained glass façade for Park Avenue Synagogue Community Center. Since World War II his paintings have received wide acclaim. His early work looked to the symbolic, totemic imagery of primitive art, combining simplified cuniform signs with subtle color and modulated texture. His more recent painting tends toward total abstraction and functions close to the frontal plane. Gottlieb currently lives in New York and has been teaching at the Pratt Institute, Brooklyn, since 1955.

MORRIS GRAVES Born in Oregon in 1910 (although his family came from Seattle), by the age of twenty Graves had made three trips to the Orient as a seaman. Settling in Seattle in 1935, he worked for the Federal Art Project the following two years, producing the *Red Calf* and *Message* series. In the decade from 1938 on he lived primarily in the Puget Sound area, with trips to Puerto Rico and Honolulu and a year in the Army interspersed. Living primarily in wilderness areas, he developed his intuitive style in gouaches and water color and ink on paper (*Little Known Bird of the Inner Eye* and the *Pine* series). He was strongly influenced by Oriental philosophy and art, and in the late nineteen-thirties he adapted Mark Tobey's "white writing" calligraphy to his own style. He travelled to Europe in 1948–49, spending most of his time in Chartres, where he painted a series of the cathedral which he later destroyed. After returning to the U.S. he journeyed to Japan and then settled in County Cork, Ireland, where he lived for two years. In 1956 he returned to his home in Seattle.

Graves is a symbolist, a creator of images of mystical import; and bird, fish, and tree are sufficiently transformed, in low-keyed evanescent gouache, to stand for spiritual, or human, qualities. At his rare best, he has created master works of American art.

JUAN GRIS Born in Madrid in 1887, Gris entered the Escuela de Artes y Manufacturas at the age of 15. Here his training in engineering prepared him to become the classicist of the Cubist movement. He was in Paris by 1906, living in the same building with Picasso and his friends; at this time he was drawing for periodicals and it was not until 1910 that he seriously began to paint. Two years later he emerged as one of the most prominent of the Cubists, and for the next decade his paintings in their tan and slate tonalities are distinguished and austere.

After an illness in 1920, Gris's architectural style gave way to his "poetic" painting. The next year he began his series of *Open Windows* and in 1923 he commenced his association with Diaghilev, designing the decor for two operas and a ballet. It was during this period that he experimented in sheet iron sculpture and published *Notes on My Painting*. In 1925 he published *Chez les Cubistes* and held a one-man show. His health began to fail (he was diabetic) and he died two years later in 1927.

HANS HOFMANN Born in the Bavarian community of Weissenburg on March 21, 1880, Hofmann showed an early aptitude for science and mathematics. Before he was eighteen he had invented an electromagnetic comptometer that brought him a thousand marks, which was invested as tuition in the first of several Munich art schools. His teachers were mostly traditional and he learned well, especially from his last master, Willie Schwarz, who introduced him to Paris and Impressionism.

He settled in Paris in 1904 under the patronage of Phillip Freudenburg, Berlin department store owner. At this time he knew Matisse, Braque, Delaunay, Picasso and Juan Gris. He witnessed the birth of the Fauve and Cubist movements and experimented in both areas, with Matisse functioning as his earliest and strongest influence. None of his works from that period are still in existence.

In 1915, after returning to Munich, he opened an art school which set his lifetime pattern of teaching. With the advent of National Socialism, he left Germany for the United States and became a citizen in 1941. Since that time he has concentrated on painting, though teaching, too, seems necessary to his well being.

Still vital in his eighties, Hofmann's vibrant sense of color, his fleeting image, and his "push-pull" spatial tensions mark him as unique.

EDWARD HOPPER Born in Nyack, New York, in 1882, Hopper first studied under Robert Henri, the founder of the so-called Ash Can School, a movement which preferred the street scenes and back alleys of the new industrial America to the then-current idealistic studio painting. Hopper went to Paris and painted for a year out-of-doors, fascinated with light and its reflection. He returned to America and exhibited with Henri's other pupils, Coleman, Golz, Friedman, and Bellows, in their first independent show in 1908. While such men as Rockwell Kent and Bellows were gaining recognition, Hopper remained unnoticed. He sold one painting, *The Sailboat*, at the Armory Show of 1913. After this Hopper began to paint in water color, learned the etching process, and tried to earn a living at commercial work. In 1923 the Brooklyn Museum bought one of his water colors, the second painting he had sold in twenty-three years. This was followed by a one-man exhibition of water colors at Frank Rehn's gallery. From that point on Hopper was able to stop doing commercial work and to return to oil painting. In 1933 The Museum of Modern Art gave him a one-man exhibition. Other shows followed at Frank Rehn's, the Carnegie Institute, and finally the large Whitney Museum Retrospective of 1950.

Hopper's ascendancy has been slow and steady, befitting his quiet, deliberate temperament. He is well represented in private collections and in major museums throughout the country. He lives in New York in the same apartment he has had for over forty years, painting approximately two pictures a year and forever watching and looking at the country which surrounds him.

Hopper's subject matter deals entirely with the American scene: gas stations, Victorian houses, hotel lobbies, side streets, and cafés are seen with a sober passion. His landscape or architecture is lonely and stark, and his figures as well as his buildings seem generalized, immutable, locked in a terrible desolate silence. His use of light is particularly his own. A hard glare carves out the objects on which he focuses and organizes the purely formal qualities of the painting.

JEAN AUGUSTE DOMINIQUE INGRES Born in Montauban in 1780, the son of a painter, sculptor, architect, and musician, Ingres was precocious and from the beginning exhibited a mature perfection of draftsmanship. He studied at Toulouse, then at the École des Beaux-Arts in Paris under David, the man who re-established the values of classicism in French art. David looked to Republican Rome for prototypes for the art of the French Revolution. Ingres quarreled with his master and, although he in his turn was to champion classicism, he based himself on Raphael and the Renaissance.

He won the Prix de Rome in 1806, and left for Italy where he remained for eighteen years. In the Paris Salon of 1824 he exhibited the *Vow of Louis XIII*, a painting filled with Italian 15th century devices. This painting was hailed by those who wished to set up a classical figurehead to overshadow the romantic and popular art of Delacroix and Géricault. David died in 1825, and Ingres took his place as the dictator of the art of France. Five years later he was again in Rome, this time as the Director of the French Academy.

When he returned to Paris in 1840 he was given every manner of official and royal recognition. Before his death in 1867 he had a large-scale retrospective exhibition and was awarded the Grand Croix of the French Legion of Honor. While the new realists, Courbet and Manet, were struggling for public acceptance, Ingres reigned supreme. He rose far above his political and academic position, and continued to thwart the hopes of his lifelong rival, Delacroix.

Ingres' high regard for the Renaissance and Raphael disciplined his superb draftsmanship. His flowing, sinuous line added sensuality to his nudes and odalisques, and his portrait sketches done in fine pencil remain a paragon of naturalistic rendering. He would freely distort the limbs or features of his subject in order that they might fit more perfectly into an abstract formal pattern. The organization of the arms and upper torso as well as the countenance of *La Comtesse d'Haussonville* is a fine example of this abstraction within a controlled outline. His dictum, "drawing is the probity of art," describes his power, integrity and weakness. He was the enemy of colorists, of free brushwork, and the art of impulse.

CHARLES ÉDOUARD JEANNERET (Le Corbusier) Born in Switzerland in 1887, Charles Édouard Jeanneret was apprenticed at the age of thirteen at a local trade school. His interest in architecture was immediate. In 1910 he worked in Paris with Perret, one of the first men to build with reinforced concrete. He also worked in Berlin with Behrens, the architect who trained Walter Gropius. He returned to Paris, but there was no work for a young architect during the war years, and he began to paint. With Amédée Ozenfant he founded the art movement, Purism, in 1918. Their aesthetic undertook to purify Cubism, and elaborated the clear, precise form found in the products of the new machine age.

While he was still painting, Corbusier found work in an architectural partnership with his cousin, Pierre Jeanneret. The two disciples were in no way disparate. Purism sought to transform what it called the purely decorative art of Cubism into an architectonic art; the architectural beauty Corbusier sought was based on the functional perfection of classic and simple geometric form.

Corbusier (he preserved the successful nom de plume) has been a city-planner as well as architect, and the grandiose exaggeration of his early plans, far beyond the sphere of the practical, made him famous at the same time that it defeated him as a builder. As a result, he wrote and published even more than he constructed. He is responsible for the vast vertical apartment building in the form of a cross, set in open green space. He offered this conception full blown in the early nineteen-twenties, only to have lesser men adapt it to the cities of a score of countries. He made plans to transform Paris, Algiers, Antwerp, Moscow, and Buenos Aires, while he had to content himself with modest commissions.

In the late 'twenties he won a competition for the League of Nations building, only to be tricked out of it. This injustice embittered him, yet in 1932 he was able to build a house, the Savoye Villa, outside Paris, with no expense spared. Here he set his clinically white building on stilts—another Corbusier specialty—and designed terrace and windbreaks that resembled the superstructure of a passenger liner. The architecture he created has taken on the name International Style, and one of its characteristics is its freedom from any local adaptation. It stands aloof from its environment, in contrast to the intricate association with site developed by Frank Lloyd Wright. Corbusier's Swiss Pavilion in the Cité Universitaire built at the same date, 1932, rose dramatically on similar stilts.

He was largely responsible for the Ministry of Education in Rio de Janeiro, and he was able, after the last war, to carry out his plan for a gigantic apartment building in Marseilles. The block encloses 350 apartments and complete community services as one large unit. Typically, it stands on piers, has no basement, and is entirely above ground.

The United Nations building is essentially a Corbusier plan, at least in appearance, although he was only one of an international panel of architects. At long last Corbusier has been able to carry out a city plan, this time in Chandigarh, India. And his recent church in Ronchamp, Notre Dame-du-Haut, is a fantasy by a genius, although whether it is architecture or pure sculpture, it would be hard to say.

No one architect can claim to be responsible for the new look of all our buildings and cities, but Corbusier has contributed more than any now living to the changed appearance of the twentieth-century world.

WASSILY KANDINSKY Kandinsky was born in 1886 in Moscow, and after studying economics and law he was offered a university teaching position. He decided, however, to study painting in Munich. He was familiar with the Fauve and Cubist developments in Paris and, together with Franz Marc, Paul Klee, and others, was responsible for the *Blaue Reiter* movement. He wrote his influential book, *Concerning the Spiritual in Art*, in 1910.

Utilizing color, form, and line unrelated to recognizable imagery, for their emotional impact, he became the pioneer modern painter of "non-objectivity" in his "compositions" and "improvisations." Returning to Russia with the outbreak of World War I he held various official positions after the Revolution in the fields of art education, until he was disillusioned by the political concentration on propaganda art. He returned to Germany in 1922 and joined the staff of the Bauhaus, where with Klee, Feininger, and Jawlensky he formed the Blue Four. He taught at the Bauhaus until the dissolution of that school by the Nazis in 1933. From that year on he lived and painted in Paris until his death in 1944.

His art in the nineteen-tens was a loose-knit tumult of color and form, akin to Abstract Expressionism in our own time. Under the influence of the Bauhaus he turned to architectural forms, and his geometric constructions were crystallizations of his earlier work. His third phase in Paris was a condensation of the two earlier periods. Kandinsky possessed one of the great plastic imaginations of this century.

ERNST LUDWIG KIRCHNER Born at Aschaffenberg, Germany, in 1880, Kirchner began to paint in his spare time while studying architecture at the Technical Institute at Dresden. His early work employed the pointillist style he found in the Neo-impressionist exhibit at Munich in 1904. He was familiar with the theories of Helmholz and Goethe, and his interest in light and color theory persisted throughout his lifetime. But these interests gave way to his great Expressionist passion, released early in his career by the work of van Gogh, Gauguin, and Munch. Kirchner's tortured sense of spiritual values now came into violent conflict with what he felt to be the superficialities, indignities, and brutalities of external reality. He perceived and expressed an environment filled with anguish, often taking subject matter common to the new psychology and to the naturalistic writers of his day. By 1905 Kirchner had received a degree in architecture, but he turned to painting.

Seeing a direction similar to his own in the painting of Heckel and Schmidt-Rottluff, he founded *Die Brücke*, and assumed the leadership of the group. He exhibited with this group throughout Germany until its dissolution in 1913. When the war broke out, Kirchner was found physically and mentally unfit for military service. He was tubercular, his physical condition depressed his mind, and he was confined to a sanatorium between 1915 and 1918. During the following fifteen years he worked as a designer of carpets while continuing to paint. He lived in Switzerland for his health, and the landscape was well suited to the exaggerated verticality of his style. He employed intense and arbitrary color; yet perhaps his greatest accomplishment is not in painting, but in his bold, powerful woodcuts. His thin splintered Gothic forms exploit a bitter perception of a damned humanity. Disease and severe depression over the political developments in Nazi Germany led Kirchner to suicide in 1938.

PAUL KLEE Born near Bern, Switzerland, in 1879, Klee studied art at the Munich Academy in 1898–1900. He returned to Bern for four years where he expanded his interest in reading, music, and art, studying the work of Beardsley, Blake, Goya, and da Vinci. Moving again to Munich after his marriage to a pianist, he absorbed the influences of Ensor, van Gogh, Cézanne, and Matisse. 1911 marked the first major exhibition of his work in Munich, and the next year he participated in the second *Blaue Reiter* show. Visits to Tunis and Kairouan (1914) and his awareness of Cubism contributed to his colorful, abstract style. After two years in the German army, he began a period of intensive experiment in Switzerland. He was appointed to the staff of the Bauhaus in Weimar where he taught with Kandinsky and Feininger, and he continued his sensitive and whimsical explorations. He published his *Pedagogical Sketchbook* in 1925. Travels to Italy, Brittany, and Egypt followed.

In 1931 he joined the faculty of the Düsseldorf Academy from which he was dismissed the following year, and his work was confiscated and included by the Nazis in their exhibition of "Degenerate Art" in 1935. Honored by visits from Picasso, Braque, and Kirchner and exhibits in New York, Paris, and Zurich, he died in Bern in 1940.

He was the most personal of modern artists, establishing a delicate balance between the whimsical, the eerie, and elements of architectural structure only remotely related to Cubism. No painter of our century, not even Picasso, has had a more fertile fancy.

FRANZ KLINE Born in Wilkes-Barre, Pennsylvania in 1910, Kline grew up in Philadelphia. His art education began in 1931 when he attended the School of Fine and Applied Arts, Boston University. 1937 found him in London where he studied at Heatherly's Art School. The next year he returned to New York City where he has lived ever since. He first exhibited at the National Academy of Design in 1942. In the summer of 1952 he taught at Black Mountain College, North Carolina; the Pratt Institute in Brooklyn, 1953–54; and the Philadelphia Museum School of Art in 1954.

His painting grew from an academic tradition into monumental statements in black, white and gray where angular, jagged bars of black tone tear their way across the surface, toward the viewer and back into the space implied by the monochromatic background. Kline's painting is the result of an attitude which seems most aptly put in the following statement:

"Half the world wants to be like Thoreau at Walden worrying about the noise of traffic on the way to Boston; the other half use up their lives being part of that noise. I like the second half. Right?"

OSKAR KOKOSCHKA Born in Poechlarn, Austria, in 1886, he had an Austrian mother and Czechoslovakian father, a man of sober, puritanical turn of mind, to whom Kokoschka owes his political idealism. Kokoschka studied in Vienna, and was producing paintings, poems, and plays by 1907, a tumultuous outpouring which caused violent criticism and set him off on the first of a series of journeys, to Switzerland and then to Berlin. Here he became affiliated with the *Sturm* movement in 1910 and held his first one-man show which established him as a revolutionary Expressionist painter.

Back in Vienna he had a meteoric success in spite of continuing criticism and produced such paintings as the *Portrait of the Painter Pointing to His Breast* (1913) and *Tempest* (1914). When war broke, he enlisted as a hussar and was soon invalided out with a serious head wound. His painting grew more intense and disturbed during the war years, and eventually he sought the help of a brain specialist in Stockholm, where he painted *The Harbor* (1917), one of the first of his panoramic city-scapes.

After the war he moved to Dresden and became a professor in the Academy of Art, a position he was forced to resign in 1924. At this time he was painting in a heavy, turgid manner, reminiscent of the heaviest brushwork of Cézanne.

Traveling widely in the next decade, he painted his great series of cities: London, Paris, Marseilles, Constantinople, Jerusalem, etc. A Czech patriot and liberal, he was early a refugee from the Nazi regime, leaving Austria for Prague and Prague for London at the last moment, in 1934. The Nazis confiscated 417 of his works and showed 16 in their famous exhibition of "Degenerate Art."

Kokoschka began as a painter of Expressionist portraits of great psychological intensity. In the 'twenties his panoramic landscapes, loose and colorful, suggest a wanderer remote from his subject. His painting suffered during the war years in England, but when he returned to the Continent, he regained some of the lost richness; but he never returned to his earliest Expressionist vision. He has been twice in the United States and now teaches summers in Salzburg and winters in London.

RICO LEBRUN Born in Naples in 1900, Lebrun was trained as a banker although he had begun to paint at an early age. After fighting with the Italian army in World War I, he attended the Naples Academy of Fine Art and privately studied fresco painting. He came to the United States in 1924 as a designer of stained glass. During the nineteen-thirties he worked for the WPA Federal Art Project and won two Guggenheim fellowships. Lebrun has taught at the Art Students League, the Chouinard Art Institute, and Tulane University, and he was the Director of the Jepson Art Institute in Los Angeles in 1951 and 1952. He spent several years in Mexico, returning to Los Angeles in 1955. He has since taught at U.C.L.A. and at Yale University.

His draftsmanship won him recognition in The Museum of Modern Art show "Americans 1942." The following year the Metropolitan Museum purchased *Bull Ring*. At about this time he began to break through his Renaissance training. He relied on traditionally universal subject matter, which he reinforced with psychological content and dramatic gesture. These qualities are immediately recognizable in his series on the Crucifixion. Begun in 1947, the impressive cycle culminating in the large controversial *Deposition* was completed in 1950, and displayed in New York and Los Angeles.

Lebrun has confidence in man's communication, and his use of monochromatic color with its contrast almost entirely in terms of light and dark reflects his interest in the art of the motion picture and his belief in the power of a black and white reproduction. His tonality as well as his construction shows the influence of Italian Baroque painting and of Picasso, as well as the modern Mexican muralists. Lebrun, however, uses his somber Synthetic Cubism, which always deals with an easily recognizable human figure, as a kind of stagecraft to imply the dignity of man in the face of his eternally tragic setting: brutality and war.

FERNAND LÉGER Born in Normandy in 1881, Léger was apprenticed to an architect at the age of 16. Three years later he was earning his living in Paris as an architectural draftsman. On the completion of his military service in the engineer corps he continued his studies, but lack of funds kept him at work as a draftsman and photo retoucher. In his paintings he had an instinct for powerful, simple forms, *Corsican Village: Sunset* (1905). His meeting with the primitive, Henri Rousseau, and his association with the Cubist movement helped him to develop the formal style of his *Nudes in the Forest* (1910), and *Woman in Blue* (1912).

During the war, in which he was gassed, he served as a stretcher-bearer and designed breechblocks for guns. This latter activity increased his interest in the machine-made aspect of modern life.

The concept of the machine reacting upon its maker became dominant in his composition, and not only man's environment but man himself appeared as a man-made production in Léger's decorative and forceful art. *The City* (1919) states his thesis, of which *Le Grand Déjeuner* (1921) is the master work. His *Ballet Mécanique* (1923–24) is another aspect of the same conception.

He lived in the United States during the Second World War and his subject matter was now primarily athletic. *Les Grands Plongeurs* (1942–43) is typical of his somewhat muscle-bound and metallic later style. He returned to France in 1946 where he designed mosaics and stained glass windows for the modern churches of Assy and Audincourt. He died in 1955.

JOHN MARIN Born in Rutherford, New Jersey, in 1870 of a family of Revolutionary stock, Marin was to become the most important American painter of this century. He attended Stevens Institute, Hoboken, worked four years in an architect's office, then studied for two years at the Pennsylvania Academy of Fine Arts and briefly at the Art Students League. These activities were broken by casual sketching trips, and he was thought something of a failure at thirty-five when he went to Paris to paint. He spent six years abroad (1905–1911), and it was his good fortune to meet Edward Steichen who showed his early water colors to Alfred Stieglitz, the impresario of modern American art. Stieglitz showed these water colors in his gallery "291" in New York, and Marin returned to America to see the show. Rediscovering America, he broke finally from his Whistlerian style and began the brittle, condensed water colors that made him famous.

He spent most of his winters in Cliffside, New Jersey, and his summers in Maine, painting his finest and richest water colors in the nineteen-twenties. Gradually his interest shifted to oils which became his major form of expression from 1940 on; and although his staccato technique was perhaps best suited to the water color medium, he gained in power and originality down to the last years of his life.

Eventually Marin knew great success: he had a one-man show at The Musuem of Modern Art, was exhibited widely throughout America and Europe, and was one of the few American artists with a reputation abroad. He died at Cape Split, Maine, in 1953.

GEORGES MATHIEU Born at Boulogne-sur-Mer in 1921, Mathieu became a student of philosophy and law, though he finally took a degree in English literature. He did not begin to paint until he was twenty-one. Then, finding art to be his main aim in life, he moved to Paris in 1947. Here, along with Bryen and others, he was instrumental in the presentation of several abstract exhibitions which claimed to be "lyric," "psychic," and "in a spirit of reaction against abstract formalism" which dominated the Paris art scene at that time. His basic ideas are in close accord with those of the American Abstract Expressionists who were developing during this same period. In recent years there has been creative interplay between these two groups, but they were independent in origin.

At present, Mathieu is living in Paris. His work is characterized by loose, active, calligraphic strokes and smears which are raised against a carefully applied background of a single hue. He physically attacks the canvas, allowing accidents and intended movements alike to grow into a sensitive, unified whole. As a rule his titles are drawn from literary accounts of actual battles, and though they do not apply to the appearance of the painting they give some hint of the activity expressed. Much has been made of Mathieu's performances in costume which, though colorful, should not be confused with the works themselves.

HENRI MATISSE Born in St. Quentin, France, in 1869, Matisse became one of the most influential and creative artists of the twentieth century. He began conservatively as a student at the École des Beaux-Arts in Paris. Here, under Gustave Moreau, he developed a sound academic foundation and met Rouault, Marquet, and others who were to take part with him in the Fauve movement. His palette grew brighter under the influence of Impressionism, then post-Impressionism, and Japanese and Persian art. By 1904 he was painting in the broad flat areas of vivid color that occasioned such adverse criticism in the first Fauve exhibition of 1905.

His *Joie de Vivre* (1905), *La Musique*, and *La Danse* (1910) established his decorative, two-dimensional style. Two trips to Morocco and a tangential interest in Cubism resulted in canvases of powerful simplicity: *Blue Window* and *Piano Lesson* (1915–16). By the end of the war his style was less austere, and he painted many relatively realistic nudes in Oriental settings as *Odalisques*. During the nineteen-thirties he revised some of his Fauvist tendencies, notably in the murals in the Barnes Foundation (1931). Retiring at the end of the decade to Vence, his career as a great decorative artist reached its climax in the Dominican chapel which he designed and decorated.

Matisse was an innovator within the Mediterranean tradition. He was a master colorist, a manipulator of forms, a hedonist little touched by human values. He was influenced admittedly by Cézanne, and as a Fauve, doubtless by Gauguin. He celebrated existence and left it more beautiful than it was before. He died in Vence in 1954.

JOAN MIRÓ Born near Barcelona, Spain, in 1893, Miró entered the Barcelona School of Fine Arts at the age of 16. Three years later family circumstances forced him to give up painting. In 1913, however, he resumed his studies at the Academy Gali, Barcelona, and left there two years later to pursue his career independently. He settled in Paris in 1920. His work was still quite realistic in intention (*The Farm*, 1922) until 1925, when he exhibited with the Surrealists in their first group show. A trip to the Netherlands in 1928 coincided with a series of abstract works developed out of a painting by Jan Steen, the *Dutch Interiors*. This series was followed by other whimsical fantasies derived from realistic models. He executed a mural for the Paris Exposition in 1937 and a decade later, during his first visit to the United States, he painted a mural for the Terrace Plaza Hotel in Cincinnati. In 1951 he completed his murals for the Harvard Graduate School in Cambridge, Massachusetts—a building designed by Walter Gropius and his associates.

Miró's numerous easel paintings are his major achievement. In these he sets a balance between the whimsical and the structural, between brilliant color and ingenious form; and in this he resembles Paul Klee. He stands out among the Surrealists for his freedom from literary effects, and many critics consider him the greatest painter in the generation after Picasso.

LÁSZLÓ MOHOLY-NAGY Moholy-Nagy was born in Hungary in 1895. He spent four years in the army during World War I and found release from his revulsion at his surroundings through sketching. After the war he completed work for a degree in law at the University of Budapest, although his interest was fast turning toward painting. On graduating, he left for Berlin, and came under the influence of Russian Suprematism and Constructivism, both extreme forms of geometrical non-objective art. At this time, he also met Kurt Schwitters who was to be famous for his *collage*, and a new interest in accidental pattern led to his development of photomontage.

Walter Gropius appointed him to the staff of the Bauhaus along with Kandinsky, in 1923. During his years at the Bauhaus he taught metal shop, introduced photography and the photogram, and invented a new system of typography. He began making his own constructions, which revealed, like his painting, a concern with the interpenetration of transparencies and solids. Moholy rejected all symbolic representation for what he termed visual fundamentals: color, shape, and form relations. Light was used as a formal element in this supreme effort at clarification. It was seen as reflection, and also as an element of penetration through pierced solids or through transparencies. He invented a "Light Modulator" with which he experimented with the play of light and shadow over moving shapes of metal and plastic. While at the bauhaus he served as editor of the school's numerous publications. His own book, *The New Vision*, was first published at this time.

In 1937 he came to America and founded the New Bauhaus in Chicago, now known as the Institute of Design. Here, as an inspiring and brilliant teacher, he introduced into America design techniques which are now used almost universally in American schools of applied art. In his lifetime he was able to make significant contributions as painter, sculptor, photographer, and typographer, and as theorist, writer, and most particularly as a teacher. He died in Chicago, in 1946.

PIET MONDRIAN Born in Amersfoort, the Netherlands, in 1872, Mondrian received his first art lessons at the age of 14 from his uncle, a professional painter, and he went to Amsterdam in 1891 to study "scientific drawing." Through Toorop and Sluyters, he became acquainted with the major developments of late nineteenth-century painting. His attempts to penetrate surface appearance to structure turned him towards abstraction. When he arrived in Paris at the age of 38, he was strongly influenced by the Cubists. He felt that they had found "the right path" but had not accepted the consequences of their discoveries. Throughout the next decade, he collaborated with van Doesburg in the establishment of the *Stijl* group; and he now evolved, by the continuous reduction of means, his mature and influential "pure plastic" style, based upon horizontal-vertical intersection, and black, white and the three primary colors applied in flat areas. Returning to Paris after the war, he published in 1920 the first of many essays.

Twenty years later he arrived in the U.S. where he admired the "ripe mentality of the Americans." New York and jazz music had their effect upon his style, and he responded to his new environment with such paintings as *Broadway Boogie Woogie*. At this time, he was experimenting anew, and speeded up his method by composing with colored strips of Scotch tape, a species of experimental *collage*. At the age of 70, he held his first one-man show, and he died in 1944.

CLAUDE MONET Born in Paris in 1840, Monet spent his childhood in Le Havre and met Pissarro upon his return to Paris in 1859. After his military service, he entered the studio of Gleyre in 1862, where he met Renoir, Sisley, and Bazille, with whom he painted at Fontainebleau and at Honfleur on the Channel coast. 1866 marked his great success at the Salon with the portrait of his wife, *Camille*, and his meeting with Manet; but subsequent poverty and rejection led, a few years later, to a suicide attempt.

Settling in Argenteuil in 1872, he frequently painted from his boat on the Seine, developing a high-keyed, broken-color technique, perhaps related to the broken reflections of river water. This technique was adapted and jointly developed by many of the painters he had come to know, and the title of one of his landscapes furnished the designation "Impressionists" to the members of the 1874 group exhibition. The Impressionists continued to exhibit from time to time, although not all of them were to be found in all of these showings. In 1880, Monet finally had a painting accepted by the Salon, and he never entered a painting for the Salon again. Two years later he ceased to contribute to the Impressionist exhibitions, although he continued to develop his style. In his late works, the *Haystack* and *Water Lilies* series, he strove for what he termed "instantaneity," and he had achieved great popularity and success by 1890.

Although his work was criticized as reducing the Impressionist method to absurdity, he was largely responsible for a way of seeing and a technique which bound together some of the greatest painters of the nineteenth century.

ROBERT MOTHERWELL Robert Motherwell was born in Aberdeen, Washington in 1915. After high school he attended Stanford University where he received a B.A. in 1937. The following year he did graduate work in philosophy at Harvard and in 1940–41 he studied in the School of Architecture at Columbia University. His interest in painting developed late. He is primarily self-taught though he learned the art of printmaking from the Surrealist artist Kurt Seligmann and from S. W. Hayter. He first exhibited with the International Surrealist Exhibition, New York, in 1942.

After travelling in Europe he settled in New York City where he, along with Rothko, Newman and Baziotes, organized a group known as "The Club" which espoused the cause of avant-garde art. Motherwell became the philosopher-spokesman of this group as well as being one of its major painting members. His current work is best described as ambiguous in that it draws from both the intellectual and emotional sides of his personality. The works usually consist of a number of shapes and lines held together in a loosely geometric framework. These shapes set up push-pull tensions in an open space created by the consistent background. His is a battle of the conscious and the unconscious, projecting undefinable objects into objective space. He, like Miró and Matta, extends the Surrealist horizon.

Motherwell lives in New York where, since 1951, he has been teaching at Hunter College.

EDVARD MUNCH Born in Engelhaug, Norway, in 1863, Munch lost his mother when he was five and an older sister a few years later, both dying of tuberculosis. His father in great depression turned to religion with a fanatical fervor. A preoccupation with death, and the fear that love was punished by death, provided much of the subject matter for Munch's morbid, intense, powerful art. At seventeen he entered the State School of Art and Handicraft and studied under Krohg, Norwegian exponent of realism. The influence of Ibsen and the Bohemian ferment in Oslo at the time intoxicated Munch. He concerned himself with psychological relationships between people, and the interpretation of sexual problems.

In 1889 he had a one-man show and won a grant to study in Paris. During his five years abroad he came to know the work of van Gogh and Gauguin, was particularly interested in the latter's woodcuts, and began the experiments which made him into a greater print-maker than painter. He determined that his paintings should form a cycle, which he called the *Frieze of Life*—an essentially Wagnerian conception.

In 1892 Munch was invited to exhibit in Berlin. Bold color, sensuous themes, and a disturbed mood aroused the public to praise and condemn, and the show closed after a week. Munch came to Berlin at this time, and remained in Germany for the next fifteen years, enjoying a great if controversial success. He produced his finest paintings and prints in the eighteen-nineties: *The Scream* (1892), *By the Deathbed* (1895), *The Dance of Life* (1900), *Girls on a Bridge* (1901). Realistic detail gave way to generalizations, in large loose form and arbitrary color; and his figures became disembodied gestures, realizations which a later psychology called archetypes.

In 1908 Munch suffered a nervous collapse. If he had died at this time, his life would have paralleled van Gogh's, but he recovered, under the care of a psychiatrist. He spent the last thirty years of his life more quietly, living in the country in Norway. His paintings grew larger, more diffuse, and less compelling as he escaped from his intense personal expression and turned to more social themes. Thus he veered away from the main trend of German Expressionism, the movement which he had liberated at the beginning of the century. He died in Oslo in 1944 while the country was still occupied by the Nazis, acclaimed by all the world save the country which had first recognized his genius.

PABLO PICASSO Born in Málaga, Spain, in 1881, the son of an art teacher, Picasso studied with his father. His family moved to Barcelona where Picasso entered the School of Fine Arts in 1885. He then studied in Madrid where he came to know the work of Goya and Velásquez. He moved to Paris in 1901, encountering there the work of van Gogh and Toulouse-Lautrec, and he developed a romantic, nostalgic art (his Blue and Rose periods) quite unrelated to the interests of the painters around him.

His interest in African Negro sculpture largely determined the style of an important painting, *Les Demoiselles d'Avignon* (1906–07), and he saw here a method of breaking down the object into its structural components. Cézanne had already resolved objects into geometrical elements, and Picasso carried this process to its conclusion. The result was Analytical Cubism which he developed, along with Braque, from about 1908 or 1909 until the beginning of the war. Synthetic Cubism, which followed, reconstructed the object, but it was now a conceptual object, more adaptable to the artist's purpose than a representational image.

After 1920 Picasso changed again. His new images were heavily charged with symbolic, subconscious, and sensuous content as though the Cubist days were only a structural discipline for working with this new imagery. These symbols took many forms: some drawn from the bullfight, some distorted to suggest movement or violence, some suggesting a Darwinian depth of evolution from more rudimentary life.

Picasso had taken part in the first Surrealist exhibition in 1925, although he did not consider himself a Surrealist. The mural scale of *Guernica* (1937), not his greatest painting, demonstrates the sophisticated resources that he had developed by the mid-nineteen-thirties. His repertory of imagery has provided a new language for half the painters of our day; many have used it and all have been under its influence in some degree.

Active and imaginative in every field, Picasso was interested at one time in designing for the ballet, and he has been etcher, lithographer, sculptor, and lately ceramist.

JACKSON POLLOCK Born in Cody, Wyoming, in 1912, Pollock spent his youth in the West (primarily Arizona and California), finishing his schooling in 1925–29 at Manual Arts High School, Los Angeles, where he also began studying art. Upon graduation he moved to New York where for two years he worked at the Art Students League, mostly under the tutelage of Thomas Benton. During the next four years he made a series of return trips to the West, and in 1938–42 was affiliated with the WPA Federal Art Project where he worked for a time with Hans Hofmann, who greatly influenced his style. He had his first one-man show in 1943, and his *She-Wolf* was purchased the following year by The Museum of Modern Art.

He has to his credit the technique of dripping paint in linear patterns onto a canvas laid flat on the floor—a procedure which created a new intensity and brilliance, inviting the freedom of accident and impulse, and the rhythms of physical performance.

He lived, in recent years, at Easthampton, Long Island, and was killed in an automobile accident in 1956. A retrospective exhibition at The Museum of Modern Art was then in preparation, and was held in 1957.

ODILON REDON Born in Bordeaux in 1840, Odilon Redon failed as a student at the Beaux-Arts after attempts at architecture, sculpture, and painting. He made many studies of insects and butterflies under the influence of the botanist Clavaud. In 1863 he studied etching with Bresdin, and these early prints already show him transforming reality into fantasy. Later he turned to lithography under the direction of Fantin-Latour.

He published his first series of prints, *Dans le Rêve*, in 1879, and began to illustrate such writers as Flaubert and Poe. In his symbolic language he combined the minute description of insects and flowers with a dreamlike face pervaded by a kind of strangeness drawn from his own temperament.

Although Redon was of the same age as the Impressionists, and exhibited in their first group exhibition in 1884, he never shared in their experiment. His friends were among the poets, Gide, Valéry, and most particularly Mallarmé, rather than the painters. He equated thought or poetic feeling with drawing and painting, and he combined something of the nineteenth-century interest in science with a world of symbol and magic.

After his long apprenticeship as a draftsman, Redon began to work in oil, water color, and pastel. Arbitrary color added to an effect which foreshadowed Surrealism. Durand-Ruel, the dealer, gave him a show, "Hommage à Odilon Redon," in 1899. After this he went into retirement, meditating and painting as a recluse. He died in 1916.

The space around one of Redon's alternately lovely or shocking images, is as ambiguous as the image itself. Beneath a gently sensual surface lie disquieting, mystical depths. The Surrealists hailed him as the spiritual father of their movement.

GEORGES ROUAULT Born in Paris in 1871, Rouault's introduction to the social realism of Daumier via his collector grandfather, and his early apprenticeship to a stained glass maker, provided two major components of his fine art. From 1891–95 he studied with Gustave Moreau at the École des Beaux-Arts, where he met Matisse. Along with Matisse, he was to occupy an important place among the Fauves. Moreau (whose favorite pupil he was) provided him with a sinecure for life; he bequeathed his paintings and home to the city of Paris, and Rouault was appointed curator of the Gustave Moreau Museum.

During the Fauve years, Rouault's painting was brittle and explosive, and he dealt with social themes: judges and tribunals, prostitutes and the down-trodden, with all the indignation of a Daumier. By 1910 his work had taken on a pattern of black outline surrounding luminous pools of color, which recalls the effects of the stained glass over which he worked as an adolescent. His themes now were religious and symbolic: the life of Christ, the king oppressed that he must rule, and man as the tragic clown. The nineteen-twenties were devoted almost exclusively to book illustration, after which he resumed work on a number of unfinished canvases. He ceased to date his works after 1932, and he burned 315 of his works in 1948, the same year that he executed his great stained glass windows for the village church of Assy. He died in 1958.

GEORGES SEURAT Born in Paris in 1859, Seurat entered the Municipal School of Design at 16 and spent two years painting in museums, copying Raphael, Holbein, Poussin, and Ingres. He entered the École des Beaux-Arts in 1878 and became acquainted with the color theories of Chevreuil. On return from military service in 1880 he continued studying the theories of optical mixture and complementary colors which led him to develop a divisionist system, Pointillism, which formalized the broken color of the Impressionists.

His first large canvas in the new method, *Une Baignade à Asnières*, was rejected by the Salon but exhibited in 1884 at the first Salon des Indépendants, which he had helped to organize. He formed a friendship with the painter, Signac, who shared his experiments and introduced him to Pissarro. The eldest of the Impressionists, Pissarro not only encouraged Seurat, but became a convert to his new method.

In 1885, Seurat commenced 38 painted studies and 23 drawings which were synthesized into his great *Sunday Afternoon on the Island of La Grande Jatte*. Repudiated by a number of the Impressionists and excoriated by the public, he nevertheless became the spokesman for Neo-impressionism; and he followed *La Grande Jatte* with a series of major canvases in his newly-invented manner: *Parade*, *Les Poseuses*, *Le Chahut*. The last, *Le Cirque*, remained unfinished at his premature death at the age of 32 in 1891.

CHARLES SHEELER Born in Philadelphia in 1893, Sheeler studied applied design at the School of Industrial Art, Philadelphia. He followed this with three years under William N. Chase at the Pennsylvania Academy of Fine Arts. With Chase's class he went to London in 1904, Spain in 1905, and in 1909 to Italy, Paris, and London. In Paris he came in contact with Cubism, and on his return he began conscious experiments with precise form, totally at variance with the school of free presentation in which he had been trained.

He lived in Philadelphia and spent weekends in Bucks County in the decade of the nineteen-tens and took up architectural photography as a means of earning a living. He exhibited in the Armory Show in 1913 and held his first one-man show of photographs three years later. He moved to New York in 1920 and collaborated with Paul Strand on the film *Mannahatta*. An assignment in 1929 to photograph the Ford Plant at River Rouge was an important event in his life and led to a decade of highly simplified paintings dealing with American industry, set patterns of which did no basic violence to representation. A number of these works were reproduced in *Fortune* magazine. Industry alternated with architectural aspects of the past in such canvases as *Kitchen*, *Williamsburg*, or *Of Domestic Utility*. In the nineteen-forties and 'fifties this austere transcript of reality was handled with much greater freedom. Sheeler abandoned literal images for paintings descriptive of industrial complexity. What he has given us, however, is still related to photography, having a certain appearance of double exposure on a single surface. He was given a nationwide retrospective exhibition, organized by the University of California, Los Angeles, in 1954.

YVES TANGUY Born in Paris in 1900, Tanguy was sent to sea at the age of 18, sailing to Africa and South America with the merchant marine. Drafted two years later, he met Jacques Prevert with whom he went to Paris following their discharge from service. There Vlaminck called the attention of the critic Fels to Tanguy's sketches although it was not until 1923 that, attracted by the work of de Chirico, Tanguy began to paint. Provided with both studio and materials by a friend, he began producing "ready-made" objects; and the next year, with his meeting with the poet and critic André Breton, he became firmly allied with the Surrealist movement. His work grew increasingly subjective, moving from anecdote to automatism. *Composition No. 11* of 1928 displays his typical silver gray color and his deft forms which are at once familiar and strange. Over a decade later he met Kay Sage, in Paris, and upon his reunion with her in the U.S. after the war, they married. He died in 1955.

MARK TOBEY Mark Tobey, the most influential of the Northwest painters, was born in Wisconsin in 1890. Self-taught, he first earned his living as an illustrator for mail-order catalogues. Then he moved to New York in 1911 and for a while painted society portraits. Renouncing both these drudgeries, he took a trip to the West in 1922, and he settled the following year in Seattle, teaching at the Cornish School two years. He traveled in Europe and the Near East, in 1925–26, returning to Seattle and spending the next year between New York, Chicago, and the Northwest. He was resident artist at Dartington Hall in South Devon, England, from 1931 to 1938. He journeyed during this period to Mexico, again to the Near East and Europe, and to the Orient. In the Far East he studied with the Chinese calligrapher, Teng Kwei, and returned in 1939 to stay in Seattle.

The importance of Oriental art as an influence over Tobey has been frequently remarked. Adapting the dynamics of calligraphy to his own more structural uses, he developed his "white writing" in such works as *Drift of Summer* and *Threading Light*. His paintings alternate between recognizable images, and patterns as non-objective as Pollock's, and back toward representation again. His work has always possessed elegance, refinement, and an air of rightness in composition, together with a feeling for organized complexity—all characteristic of Oriental art.

BRADLEY WALKER TOMLIN Born in New York in 1899, Tomlin graduated from Syracuse University in 1922 with a bachelor's degree in painting and was soon awarded a fellowship for European study. He held his first one-man show within the next two years and spent most of the following four years abroad in independent study in England, France, and Italy. Soon after his return to the United States he joined the faculty of Sarah Lawrence College (1928) and resigned nine years later to devote more time to his new experiments in painting. Tomlin was an illustrator early in his career, and his naturalistic work grew gradually more formal and acquired a decorative elegance. In the nineteen-thirties his paintings were essentially Cubist still lifes in sensitive minor-key tonalities. There was a break-through in the next decade, and his late style emerged as flat patterns of broad strokes set at right angles in grays, tans, blacks, and whites, subtly combined; or his "petal" paintings of pink spots based on green. His experiments had a great influence on the Abstract Expressionist movement.

His first show in his final, mature style was held in 1950, three years before his death.

MAURICE VLAMINCK Born in Paris in 1876, Vlaminck's parents were musicians, and his diffuse talent turned him at first toward music and writing; he did not begin his art studies until he was 19, married, and a father. He broke off his early Impressionist studies for his military service in 1896, and after his discharge earned his living as a musician. He met Derain, established a studio with him in 1901, and began to paint in earnest. He was influenced by the van Gogh exhibition of 1901, and it was at this exhibition that he met Matisse. During this early period, he wrote three novels, the first illustrated by Derain. In 1905 he met the painters van Dongen and Picasso, and the critics and poets Max Jacob and Apollinaire, and participated in the first Fauve exhibition. The following year the dealer, Ambroise Vollard, purchased all the paintings in his studio. Increasingly influenced by the work of Cézanne after 1907, he abandoned his brilliant pure colors for a more somber palette.

He moved to Ruel-la-Gadelière in 1925, making it his permanent home. His paintings since then have tended to repeat earlier patterns and triumphs, notably in his scenes of farmhouses, set in a snowy countryside under a slate sky—subjects which he has produced with monotonous regularity. He was a Fauve painter who played an important part in the youth of the movement but missed the maturity of a Matisse or a Rouault. He died in 1958.

Schools of Painting

ABSTRACT EXPRESSIONISM The Abstract Expressionist movement was born during the last years of World War II. It is often thought of as a purely American affair, but it should be remembered that Bryen, Mathieu and others were coming, independently, to similar conclusions in France. It results as a reaction against the, then, over-emphasized abstract formalism of Mondrian and the American regionalism of Grant Wood and Thomas Benton which had been supported by the WPA government art project.

Visually, Abstract Expressionism relies on automatic calligraphy, exploitation of the accident and strong color or value patterns. In this appearance it owes much to the older Surrealist and Fauve movements as well as the more recently emphasized awareness of Zen philosophy, which direct one toward contemplation of "self" through intuition.

Though Abstract Expressionism is currently considered an organized movement, the major proponents, Hofmann, Pollock, de Kooning, Kline, Still, Rothko and others, deny any group affiliation and prefer to think in terms of independent action. In fact, since the "attack" upon the often large scale canvas depends upon a denial of preconceived ideas and intellectual adjustment each work should be evaluated independently. Its validity is determined by its ability to carry the weight of the expressed personality.

CUBISM The Cubist movement, perhaps the major development of early twentieth-century art, was developed out of experiments by Picasso and Braque, who were influenced by the abstract planes of African Negro sculpture and the architectonic painting of Paul Cézanne. By 1909 "Analytical Cubism" had crystallized, based upon a limited palette, shifting points of observation, disintegration, and geometric reconstruction of the subject (usually still life). By 1912 Metzinger, Gleizes, Léger, Gris, Duchamp, and others had joined the movement; and Braque and Picasso were developing the pasted-paper technique of *collage*. The later phase, "Synthetic Cubism," is characterized by more solid forms, conceptual rather than observed, richer in color and texture.

DADAISM Primarily literary in its inception, Dadaism was launched in Zurich in 1916 by a group of writers and painters, including Tzara, Arp, and Hugo Ball. Dada spread to Berlin in 1917, where the group was headed by George Grosz, and the next year to Cologne, with Max Ernst and Arp as leaders. The Dadaists utilized shock techniques, created monuments made of corsets, cuckoo clocks, and other "non-artistic" objects, and in the work of Kurt Schwitters, adapted the *collage* technique of Cubism, emphasizing the irrational relationship rather than the formal pattern. The movement originated as a protest against accepted canons of morals and taste, and the anarchic post-war spirit of Dada can be seen in the works of Duchamp, Picasso, Picabia, and others.

DER BLAUE REITER In 1912 in Munich, Kandinsky, Jawlensky, Franz Marc, and Mäcke formed a group known as *Der Blaue Reiter* (the Blue Rider). The first two, under the influence of the Fauves and the German *Die Brücke* (a group organized in Dresden in 1905), were already using brilliant and expressive color, and by 1911 Kandinsky was painting non-objective canvases, conveying mood solely through plastic elements. Although the group, which later included Paul Klee and Max Ernst, was somewhat influenced by Cubism, its primary intention was emotional and expressive. Kandinsky, Jawlensky, and Klee later formed, with Lyonel Feininger, the "Blue Four" at the Bauhaus in Dessau.

DE STIJL *De Stijl* (The Style) is one of the many movements deriving from Cubism. It was initiated by Piet Mondrian, Theo van Doesburg, Vantongerloo, and the architect, J. J. P. Oud, in 1917 in Leyden, Holland. The major purpose of this group was the extension to all arts of the principles of abstract geometrical design, namely the rectangular forms and the primary hues. Based upon the writings of Mondrian and van Doesburg in the periodical, *De Stijl*, as well as upon their austere, non-objective work, the movement was primarily influential in the field of architecture, spreading in the early nineteen-twenties, via van Doesburg, to the Bauhaus School in Germany.

EXPRESSIONISM The broad term Expressionism describes an emotional art, often crudely executed, and making free use of distortion and arbitrary color. Expressionist painters rarely consider painting an end in itself but are intent on commenting on man's life and nature. Often they speak with a strong moral bias, expressing love and hate, pity or condemnation; or an inner subjective quality may reveal itself through shocking, non-natural color, violent posture, and exaggerated facial expression.

When the term "Expressionism" is used more specifically, it refers to a group of German painters who took the title, *Die Brücke* (The Bridge), in 1905. Kirchner, Heckel, Schmidt-Rottluff, Nolde, and Pechstein strove to embody subjective content in powerful, symbolic imagery, which was often socially critical. This group found its immediate ancestry in the work of Munch, Gauguin, and van Gogh. Van Gogh's tormented vision, Gauguin's beauty of design and symbolic color, and Munch's blatantly emotive form, were all qualities the Expressionists sought. The *Brücke* artists used the medium of the woodcut as another dramatic form of expression, related not only to the prints of Gauguin but also to the German graphic tradition that reaches back to Cranach and Grünewald. Primitive art, with its brutal force and distorted forms, was another source of strength to them. The Belgian painter, Ensor, whose satiric images and masked figures portrayed the inner drives and concealed impulses which were to emerge later in Surrealism, provided still another inspiration.

German Expressionism had its sculptors, notably Lehmbruck and Barlach, and its later exponents, Beckmann and the Austrian, Kokoschka. Soutine, with his flair for violent color, was the greatest Expressionist among the Russian painters. Expressionism has been rare among the rational and constructive French, but Rouault, follower of the nineteenth-century Daumier, is a powerful exception.

Since World War II there have been two new and strong movements in Expressionist art. In Europe the *Art Brute* of Dubuffet and Appel stresses bald, rough, unsophisticated or child-like imagery, using far greater textural emphasis than is found in earlier Expressionism. More important has been the Abstract Expressionism spearheaded by the work in New York of Pollock, de Kooning, Motherwell, and Hofmann. This movement relates closely to the early painting of Kandinsky and represents the union of non-objective imagery with Expressionistic techniques.

FAUVISM The Fauve movement, though lasting a scant three years, was one of the most influential developments in twentieth-century painting. Under the impact of the van Gogh exhibition of 1901, the Salon d'Automne's showings of Gauguin and Cézanne (1903 and 1904), and the bold color and patterns of the 1903 Mohammedan Exhibition, the group emerged in the Salon d'Automne of 1905. Derisively termed *les Fauves* (the wild beasts) by a critic, the group at one time included Matisse, the acknowledged leader, Vlaminck, Derain, Dufy, Marquet, Rouault, Braque, Friesz, and van Dongen, all of whom began to go their separate ways after 1908.

FUTURISM One of the many groups to evolve from Cubism, the Italian Futurist movement was inaugurated by a manifesto by the poet Marinetti in 1909. Utilizing the shifting planes and points of observation of the Cubists, such artists as Balla, Russolo, Boccioni, Carra, and Severini celebrated speed, motion, and the machine. This glorification of mechanics, typified by Severini's *Armored Train,* lent itself to the martial spirit developing in Italy. It is interesting to note in this connection that Marinetti later became a Fascist senator. Duchamp's famous *Nude Descending a Staircase* is, in its diagramming movement, allied to the Futurist style.

IMPRESSIONISM Although the first Impressionist exhibition was not held until 1874, the group had begun to form a decade earlier when Monet, Renoir, Sisley, and Bazille met as students at the Académie Gleyre. Painting outdoors, they utilized theories of optical mixture and the divided brushstroke to capture the effects of light. Around 1866 they began to meet regularly at the Café Guerbois with Édouard Manet, who is often termed the father of the movement. Receiving their name from one of Monet's works, the Impressionists were from the first a target of much adverse criticism. The group, which included Pissarro, Berthe Morisot, Lautrec, Degas, etc., held its last exhibition in 1882. By the end of the century, the movement had won its battle, and its way of seeing and painting laid the foundation of the new academicism of the twentieth century.

POST-IMPRESSIONISM The last fifteen years of the nineteenth century saw a complicated reaction to Impressionism. From the casual subject matter of that movement, Toulouse-Lautrec turned towards a more expressive linear stylization of his subjects. Gauguin carried this stylization a step further, using bold outlines that enclosed symbolic or decorative color. By 1890 van Gogh's emotionally-charged works and life added an intense subjective content which gave a new meaning to color and distorted form. The reaction against the formlessness of Impressionism is still better demonstrated by Seurat's monumental systematization of the Impressionist method and Cézanne's careful synthesis between depth and picture plane, between motif and structure, which so influenced both Fauvism and Cubism.

SURREALISM Surrealism, like Dadaism to which it is allied, was originally a literary movement, officially inaugurated in 1924, with the Paris publication of its first manifesto by the poet-painter, André Breton. Some of its features, such as "automatic writing," had been prevalent as early as 1919; and such painters as de Chirico and Chagall produced work that has much in common with the romantic, emotional character of Surrealism and that was influential in its development. Based upon the dream, the irrational, and the fantastic, Surrealism's major adherents were Tanguy, Ernst, Joan Miró, and Salvador Dali. Miró and Dali are typical of two distinct aspects of the movement: the former emphasizes plastic patterns which rely on symbolism and have moved progressively further away from the recognizable object; the latter has clung to clear and detailed imagery and relies on a shock to be found, not in terms of paint and composition, but in the literary illogicality of the things represented. The movement also claimed Picasso, who had taken part in its first exhibition.

Glossary of Terms

Plastic
The term as used in traditional criticism or art history refers to the illusion of three-dimensionality, or roundness, by modeling sculpturally. In contemporary criticism the term refers to the total organization of the canvas; all the elements (line, color, texture, plane, space) are related to each other in such a way as to eliminate the illusion of infinite space while connecting the various shallow depths of the picture to its surface, or picture plane.

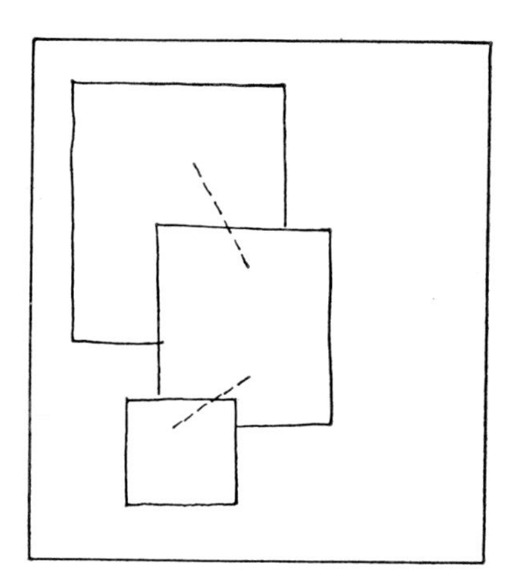

Overlapping Planes
A series of surfaces placed partially in front of one another, creating a movement back into the depth of the picture. The recession into depth is not dependent, as in scientific perspective, upon planes which diminish in size and converge toward a vanishing point.

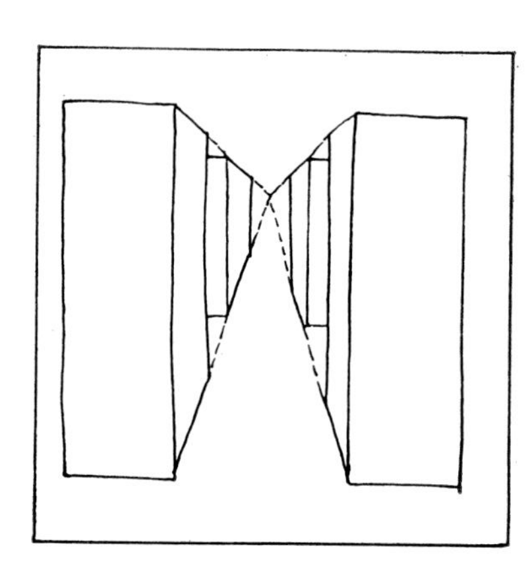

Perspective
The overlapping planes recede toward a vanishing point at the horizon. The illusion of depth is created by the diminishing of the size of the planes and their convergence.

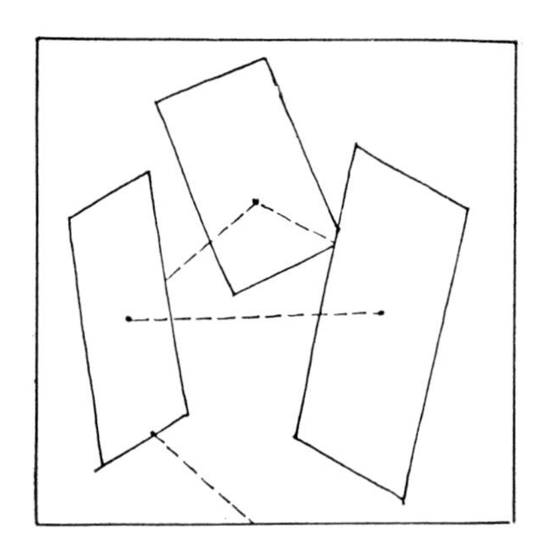

Tension between Planes
Tension, in general, means *pull*. Tension between planes is the *pull* between planes created by their movement toward and away from each other.

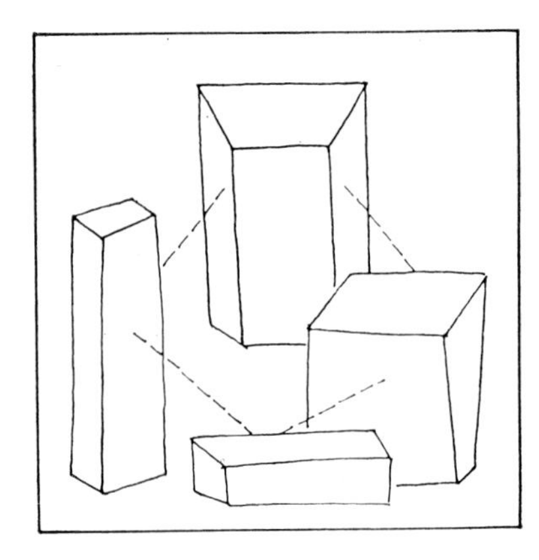

Negative Space
Negative space, as illustrated here, is the space between volumes.

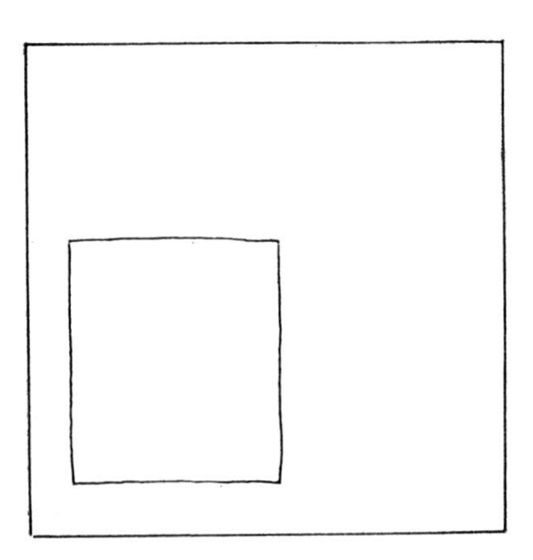

Picture Plane
The picture plane is the flat surface of the canvas or paper upon which the picture is to be projected.

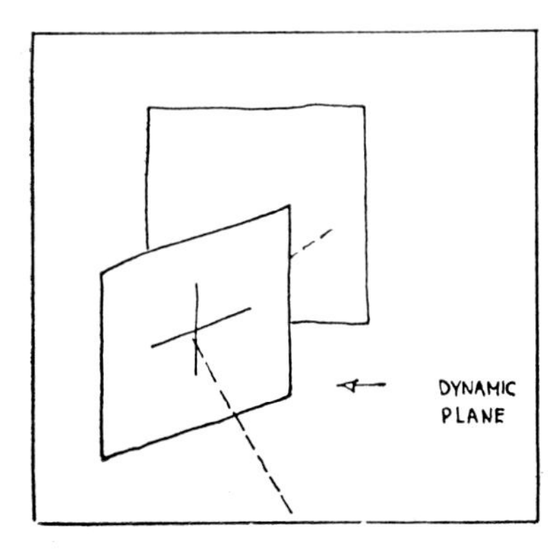

Static Plane
A plane which is parallel to the picture plane.

Dynamic Plane
A dynamic plane is a plane which rotates or moves at an angle to the picture plane.

The Analysis of Form

I. Mondrian—BROADWAY BOOGIE WOOGIE

It is suggested that the short analysis which follows be understood as an example of how one might go about looking for areas which balance each other. This can be an enjoyable, and in a way, endless pursuit, and one dictated by one's own personal responses to the painting. Also, areas coming forward and receding are in a state of flux since the eye does not always take in the same area when returning to places already viewed. When observing the different lengths of rectangles making up the strips themselves the rhythm varies according to where one looks; isolation of these strips—to study the rhythm—tends to partialize and limit the rhythmic experience of the painting as a whole.

The canvas is divided vertically, asymmetrically. The off-center vertical strips of squares divide the canvas into two unequal areas, the larger on the left. (*Side A*)
The *upper left complex area* (*Side A*) seems to provide the necessary weight to equalize the *large white space* in the lower right (*Side B*). The bulk of the *large red, blue, and yellow rectangles* in the upper right (*Side B*) is balanced by the white space to the left (*Side A*) and the *large white space* below. (*Side B*)

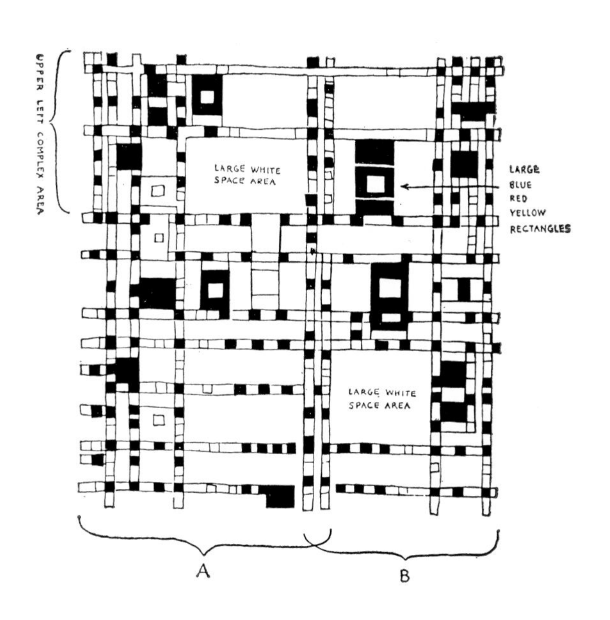

134)

There are three main *horizontal divisions,* the middle division having the greater density and activity of color. This area could be seen as one of the strong horizontal pulls against the tension created by the twin off-center vertical strips.
The dark blue rectangle in the furthest right-hand corner recedes in relation to the larger red square below it. However, the other large blue squares throughout the painting come forward.
Some areas within the strips themselves are longer than others; the eye takes longer to see or pass over them than over the shorter areas. This creates a time element or rhythm in the picture.

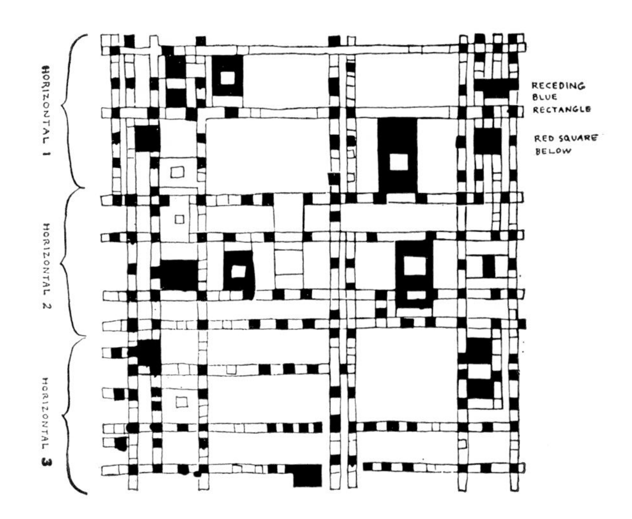

The eye has a tendency to move continuously over the surface of the canvas, drawn by the larger color masses. The smaller squares create an illusion of blinking or staccato rhythm.
The larger colored rectangles in the upper two-thirds of the canvas are pulled down by the *small red rectangle* in the lower right area. (*Side* A)

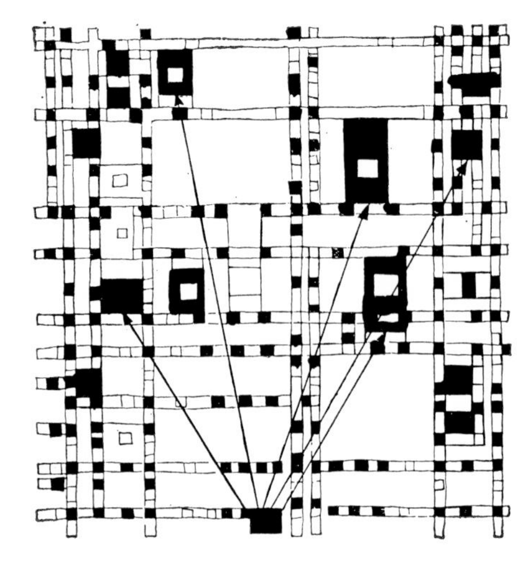

II. Picasso—GIRL BEFORE A MIRROR

The following may serve as an example of how to go about looking at *Girl Before a Mirror* from the standpoint of *form:*

1. One can extract *two large areas moving in opposition to each other* in this painting; *one created by the figures, the other by the background.* The area created by the figures includes the four large, circular shapes (two heads, right and left side of picture; two lower parts of the bodies, right and left sides of picture), which create a loosely defined square static plane, parallel to the picture plane, with the lower right-hand area carried to a straight edge defined by the post of the mirror. Behind this loosely defined square is the criss-crossed yellow background moving in opposition to it toward the left.

2. There is a strong vertical division down the center of the canvas.

3. *Reading from right to left:* The orange on the mirror frame which defines a strong oval (right) is balanced (left) by a repetition of circular and oval forms, the strongest of which is behind the head (left, white with pale green diagonal stripes).

4. *Reading from left to right:* The arm reaching across the canvas and treated in a light color remains on the same plane as the figure on the left, thereby bringing that part of the right-hand side up to the same picture plane as the areas on the left.

This is also accomplished by the lighter areas on the bottom right; the white plane at the bottom of the picture (right) also comes forward on to the same plane as the figure on the left. The arm reaching across helps tie together the two sides of the picture.

5. The use of more brilliant and lighter color on the left (figure) helps to bring this plane (figure) forward, counter-balancing the weightiness of the darker forms on the right (receding plane).

6. The upper left triangular red plane behind the head also serves to force this lighter plane (figure below) forward.

7. The criss-cross Byzantine effect in the background seems to serve the purpose of flattening the entire picture into two-dimensional space.

8. The warm yellow criss-cross behind the left figure comes forward, whereas the cooler yellow criss-cross with green (behind figure on right) moves back.

9. The use of black flowing shapes from right to left, crossing both figures, is emphasized by occasional use of red stripes throughout the area and helps to bind the split created by the center vertical division.

10. The eye flits back and forth between circular breast forms and other circular shapes. This, too, tends to unify the right side with the left.

11. The use of curvilinear forms and lines invites the eye to a smooth, rocking motion from right to left and back again.

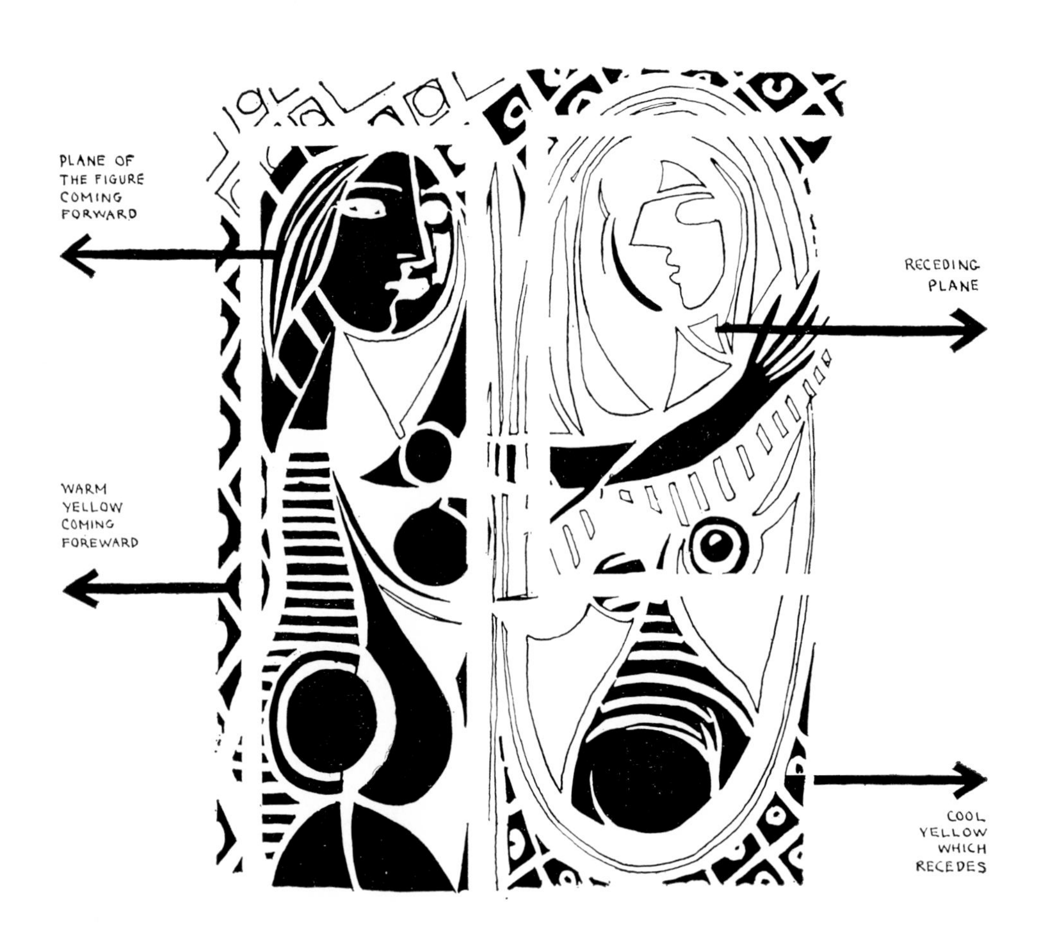

Selected Readings

The following list of books and periodicals is supplementary to the bibliographical notes related to the text and is planned to complement these other readings. This list is highly selective and is not intended to be at all definitive. Literature and criticism on many aspects of modern painting have grown enormously during the past several decades. The suggested titles are of varying degrees of importance and are listed for different reasons. Some may be helpful for the ideas or the philosophy which they express, others for a presentation of the historical record in greater detail.

The serious student may want to explore in the library some of the many publications sponsored by The Museum of Modern Art in New York and the Documents of Modern Art Series edited by Robert Motherwell, published by Wittenborn, Schultz, Inc., New York. It should also be borne in mind that during the past several years important works have been reprinted in many of the paperback series. The art publishing field has been greatly expanded by many of the distinguished series and volumes produced by such firms as Skira, Harry Abrams, Inc., and others.

Apollinaire, Guillaume—*The Cubist Painters; Aesthetic Meditations, 1913*, Documents of Modern Art, Vol. 1, New York, Wittenborn, Schultz, Inc., 1944.

Barr, Alfred H. Jr.—*What is Modern Painting?*, New York, The Museum of Modern Art, 1943.

Brion, Marcel (and others)—*Art Since 1945*, New York, Harry N. Abrams, 1958.

Canaday, John Edwin—*Mainstreams of Modern Art*, New York, Simon and Schuster, 1959.

Cheney, Sheldon—*The Story of Modern Art*, New York, The Viking Press, Inc., 1941.

Edman, Irwin—*Arts and the Man*, New York, W. W. Norton & Company, Inc., 1939.

Goldwater, Robert, and Treves, Marco, Eds.,—*Artists on Art*, New York, Pantheon Books, Inc., 1945.

Grosser, Maurice—*Painting in Public*, New York, Alfred A. Knopf, Inc., 1956.

Grosser, Maurice—*The Painter's Eye*, New York, Mentor Books, 1956.

Hess, Thomas B.—*Abstract Painting: Background and American Phase*, New York, The Viking Press, Inc., 1951.

Hunter, Sam—*Modern French Painting*, New York, Dell Publishing Co., 1956.

Kahnweiler, Daniel-Henry—*The Rise of Cubism*, Documents of Modern Art, Vol. 9, New York, Wittenborn, Schultz, Inc., 1949.

Kepeš, Gyorgy—*The Language of Vision*, Chicago, Paul Theobald, 1944.

Moholy-Nagy, Laszlo—*The New Vision 1928*, Documents of Modern Art, Vol. 3, New York, Wittenborn, Schultz, Inc., 1949.

Mondrian, Piet—*Plastic Art and Pure Plastic Art*, Documents of Modern Art, Vol. 2, New York, Wittenborn, Schultz, Inc., 1951.

Mumford, Lewis—*Art and Technics*, New York, Columbia University Press, 1952.

Myers, Bernard—*Modern Art in the Making*, The McGraw-Hill Book Company, Inc., 1950.

Myers, Bernard—*The German Expressionists: A Generation in Revolt*, New York, Praeger, 1957.

Read, Herbert—*The Grass Roots of Art*, New York, Wittenborn, Schultz, Inc., 1955.

Read, Herbert—*The Philosophy of Modern Art*, New York, The Noonday Press, 1955.

Rewald, John—*The History of Impressionism*, New York, The Museum of Modern Art, 1946.

Rewald, John—*Post-Impressionism,* New York, The Museum of Modern Art, 1956.

Robb, David M.—*The Harper History of Painting,* New York, Harper and Bros., 1951.

Selz, Peter—*German Expressionist Painting,* Berkeley, University of California Press, 1957.

Soby, James Thrall—*Contemporary Painters,* New York, The Museum of Modern Art, 1948.

Venturi, Lionello—*Painting and Painters: How to Look at a Picture,* New York, Charles Scribner's Sons, 1946.

Periodicals:
Arts and Architecture
Art News
The Arts (formerly *The Art Digest*)
New York Times (Sunday Art Section)
New York Herald Tribune (Sunday Art Section)

Index